A LIFE WORTH LIVING

A LIFE
WORTH LIVING

Michael Smurfit

·OAK·TREE·PRESS·

Published by
OAK TREE PRESS, 19 Rutland Street, Cork, Ireland
www.oaktreepress.com

A catalogue record of this book is available from the British Library.

ISBN 978 1 78119 012 8 (Hardback)
ISBN 978 1 78119 013 5 (ePub)
ISBN 978 1 78119 014 2 (Kindle)

Cover design: Kieran O'Connor Design.
Cover image: Justin Mac Innes. Where known, sources of images are
shown; omissions will be rectified in future editions.

Print management by SprintPrint, Dublin.

CONTENTS

ACKNOWLEDGEMENTS

The two most important people that I would like to thank for their invaluable support in the compiling and writing of this book are Valerie Cordell, for the years she painstakingly interviewed both myself and nearly everybody else mentioned in the book, and Stafford Hildred, for his diligent work on my behalf. They ensured that I got as many facts right as possible; there may be some errors in dates but the stories associated with the dates are as best I can remember.

There are quite a number of people and incidents that are not recorded in this book, due to space considerations. In fact, the material for the book was gathered over a four-year period and amounted to more than 20 times what has been published. I humbly apologise to everyone I did not or could not mention.

I would like to thank especially Howard Kilroy, Maurice Buckley, Mary Finan, Mark Kenny, Norma Smurfit and all the members of my family for their support to me during the years of endeavour, as well as my six children and 13 grandchildren.

I would like to acknowledge the great help given to me by the late David Austin, a Smurfit Group Director, a great colleague and a true friend over many decades. Many of the things I achieved would never have been possible without the tremendous support I received over more than three decades from my long-time secretary, Kate Kelly, who still helps me in an advisory capacity since my retirement. A very perceptive person, like Howard Kilroy, she watched my back and saved me on many an occasion. I also had great help and support over the years from Helen O'Brien, who managed hundreds of Smurfit Group events. And to my loyal driver for so many years, Pat Dempsey, many thanks for keeping me safe and secure.

Finally, but not least, I would like to acknowledge the many successful businessmen in all walks of life who were trained on a Smurfit Graduate Programme that I instituted and then went on to achieve great things for Ireland. They know who they are and I wish them ongoing success and achievement.

FOREWORD

I never look over my shoulder and ask "What if?".
Michael Smurfit

I first met Michael Smurfit in the early 1980s when I worked in the Irish Management Institute. Michael served on the Institute's Council. He invited me to dinner in the Russell Hotel on Stephen's Green, long since gone. He arrived in a great black square Mercedes, designed I believe for heads of state. Two things I remember about the dinner: first was Michael's boundless energy and curiosity and second that the Russell gave you little wooden mushrooms to plunge into the champagne to get rid of the bubbles. That could have upset the monk in Épernay who discovered champagne and announced to his startled brethren that he was drinking stars.

When, on 12 January 1987, I spoke with Michael for the first book in a series on Irish leaders, he had tears in his eyes when he remembered his father. Michael started on his own in England, partly because he did not want to work in Dublin in his father's back-yard. However, his love for his father, rather than lessening, increased his relentless competitiveness.

"One thing I do know", he said, "If you don't go on the field determined to win, you're not going to win. A guy who starts off believing he's going to fail is going to fail. There are no rewards for second place".

In 2005, Michael featured again in the final book in the series. In that year, there were clouds no bigger than a man's hand in the clear blue sky. The book began with a piece from the American poet, Langston Hughes:

We have tomorrow
Bright before us
Like a flame.
Yesterday
A night-gone thing
A sun-down name
And dawn today.

How time-bound our judgements are. Now, the sky is dark and there is fear of the future. We look for a rainmaker – we get no rain.

How did the 80 leaders in the series fare? For some, *to all things there is an end and an extremity and as soon as they reach their culminating point, they topple over, as they cannot remain long in that state* (Rabelais, 1532). Others imploded, having totally lost focus.

Focus is the key. Many Irish leaders built enduring organisations. That is the touchstone. They had in common the ability to focus exclusively and unremittingly on an ultimate objective. Denis Brosnan, founder of the Kerry Group, said, "You must be absolutely focused". Dermot Desmond, a serial entrepreneur, said, "When I believe in something, I give myself totally to it. When I commit, I have nothing left in the reservoir". Brendan O'Regan, who established in Shannon the first duty-free airport in the world, said, "If you're involved in developing an important idea, you have to let it possess you".

These are qualities that Michael Smurfit epitomises. But more than that, he combines the sometimes lonely entrepreneur with the ability to select, build and lead a multicultural team. He was no lofty CEO, concerning himself only with 'strategy'. He had an intimate understanding of the ebb and flow of international markets, combined with a sound understanding of the workings of a paper mill. He also had, as he would say himself, a nose for a deal. His greatest legacy is that, in building the first Irish multinational company, he inspired a generation to take risk.

Ivor Kenny

PREFACE

As the crow flies, it is 815 miles from my birthplace in St Helens, Lancashire to my present main home in Monaco, but the journey of my life over an energetic three-quarters of a century has taken me on a much more interesting route over many millions of miles all around the world. As I look back, I feel as if I have been forever on the move, beginning when I was a young boy with a sudden move across the Irish Sea to Dublin, Ireland, where my father's business took his growing family during the dark days of World War II. My Dad was always a large and dominant figure in my life and, even today, many years after his death, he is never too far from my thoughts.

A number of reasons prompted me to write this book. Before my father passed away, he put down on paper his memories of his extraordinary life. These insights into the early history of the Smurfit business revealed something of the astonishing drive and energy of the man himself. I wanted my family and others to share some of those memories and I also wanted to record my own recollections of building the great company that we became.

Smurfit was Ireland's first multinational company and the first Irish company to become the world leader in any major industry. Eventually, we came to have companies in Ireland, the United Kingdom, North and South America, in many countries of Europe, as well as in Nigeria, Australia, China and Indonesia.

Here was a little Irish company that, in the lifetime of one man, became the biggest packaging company in the world. How could that happen? Because of risk-taking, because of measured steps, and because we knew the business better than the people we were taking over from.

I hope this book inspires young Irish people to see what can be achieved from humble beginnings. I firmly believe that, if my family could do it, other families also can succeed. The accomplishments of

Denis O'Brien, Dermot Desmond and others show clearly that entrepreneurship in Ireland is alive and well.

Last, but by no means least, I wrote this book to let Irish people know that there *is* a future for this country. The current storm, no matter how harsh it is, will eventually pass. So far as I am concerned, the bottle is always half-full, not half-empty. I am reminded of this poem:

> *When things go wrong, as they sometimes will,*
> *When the road you're trudging seems all uphill,*
> *When the funds are low and the debts are high,*
> *And you want to smile, but you have to sigh,*
> *When care is pressing you down a bit,*
> *Rest if you must, but don't quit.*
>
> *Success is failure turned inside out,*
> *The silver tint of the clouds of doubt,*
> *And you never can tell how close you are,*
> *It may be near when it seems afar;*
> *So stick to the fight when you're hardest hit,*
> *It's when things seem worst that you mustn't quit.*

Michael Smurfit
Monaco
February 2014

I
FOUNDATIONS

CHAPTER 1
JOHN JEFFERSON SMURFIT:
A HARD ACT TO FOLLOW

Opportunities come to pass, not to pause.

The summer of 1936 was both a time of enormous achievement and of looming change in the world. Jesse Owens won four gold medals at the Berlin Olympics; Fred Perry completed a hat trick of Wimbledon victories; and the BBC broadcast the first talking pictures on television. But, in the workplaces of Britain, the ailing economy was in serious trouble as the Jarrow marchers prepared to take their appeal for jobs to London while, in Europe, much greater dangers were growing as Adolf Hitler ruthlessly planned for world domination.

For my father, John Jefferson Smurfit, who at 26 was suddenly jobless and struggling to recover by establishing a new business in St Helens, Lancashire, I like to believe that all those remarkable developments were overshadowed by two much more important events: the success of his beloved home town football club Sunderland in winning the English First Division championship for the sixth time and the birth of his first child, Michael.

I was born on 7 August 1936, less than two months after Dad had proudly set himself up as a tailor, against an unhappy background of family rows and a bitter career disappointment. Money was very tight but Dad had recruited a sign-writer to inscribe 'Jeff Smurfit Limited' and the bold message 'Creator of Good Clothes' on the window of the first floor room he had rented from an accountant in Harchurch Street. The name Smurfit might now be recognised all over the world but it first went up as a business name in St Helens in the summer of 1936.

DAD'S EARLY DAYS

Dad had been born in the family home in Wood Street, Roker in Sunderland, where his father worked as a riveter in the shipyards. The family suffered some hard times when the work dried up in the days of the Depression, but gradually things improved. My grandfather evidently was a very skilled worker, as he became 'boss riveter' for a section of around six men, which brought an increase in pay and responsibility and a move to a better house in nearby Hylton Street. According to my father, while my grandfather did not drink or smoke, he was very keen on backing horses, which was an enthusiasm my father inherited along with a lifelong affection for Sunderland Football Club. As a boy, my Dad loved to be carried on his father's shoulders down the Chester Road to Roker Park. They would go every Saturday in the season, watching the first team one week and the reserves the next.

In time, Dad was delighted to have two sisters added to the family. With his father in regular work at last, things seemed to be looking up until a cruel accident changed everything. One day, there was a 'terrible flurry' in our household and his father was brought home by ambulance. A splinter from the riveting machine had gone into his eye. He had been taken to hospital where the metal had been removed but he had lost permanently the sight in one eye and was off work for several months. That was bad enough in the days before proper compensation for injuries, but soon afterwards my grandfather came home from work feeling off-colour and went to see the local medic, Dr Hayes. He came back as white as a sheet and said to my grandmother, "I have just received the death sentence. Dr Hayes says I have sugar diabetes".

Dad was just 10 years old when my grandfather was given this shattering news. In those days, there were no regular doses of insulin to manage this condition. My grandfather was devastated and spent the final six months of his life indulging his passion for betting on horses, even fulfilling his ambition actually to go to race meetings, which he had never done before. Dad made a long walk every day to the charity clinic for a special kind of brown bread that was supposed to be better for diabetics. Nonetheless, he had to watch his father go into a terrible terminal decline. My grandfather's body developed painful abscesses, which my grandmother tried valiantly to tend. His last days were spent in agony and he died aged just 32, leaving my grandmother with three children to care for and the rent to pay. After she had collected the insurance on my grandfather, the sum total of her wealth was £90.

MY GRANDMOTHER'S SURVIVAL PLAN

Over the years, the Smurfit family has done many things to build up its reputation for enterprise and hard work. But all those years ago, still wracked by her bereavement, my grandmother came up with a survival plan that even today impresses me. She used her precious £90, and the family's standing in the community and name for honesty, to establish an early credit business. She approached certain local shops and persuaded them to agree to accept her tickets and to supply customers with goods to be charged to her. She charged her hard-up patrons a shilling in the pound for the privilege of using her service. And, remarkably, it was left to my then-schoolboy Dad to provide the all-important collection service. Aged just 11, he was hardly the traditional 'heavy' and, at first, he struggled with the job.

Dad explained years later that, initially, he was palmed off by dodgy debtors, who paid just a small fraction of what they owed. It was only when he saw his mother in tears that he knew things had to change. She had bills from the shops to pay and she did not have the money to pay them. Dad realised he had to get his act together. He vowed, as he put it in typically colourful language, that "I was going to become the greatest bastard that God ever created". He refused to accept a penny less than what his mother was owed and simply said he would stay on the doorstep until he got his money. There was great shame in those days among the working people of northern England in not paying your way. Everyone in that community took great pride in always settling their debts, whenever possible. Dad said he knew that simply standing on the doorstep and repeatedly demanding the money that his mother was rightly owed would improve the family cash flow dramatically. He was delighted to find his scheme worked; it was an early business lesson that my father never forgot.

My grandmother's money-lending activities kept the family afloat for years, thanks to her shrewdness and integrity. It was still very much a hand-to-mouth existence but my grandmother's skill at feeding a family well from a limited budget was one of her other great gifts. This was just as well, as my Dad noted as he grew up that there was little or no help from any members of my grandfather's large family. Dad was angry that they "practically ignored my mother" in her hour of need.

FOOTBALL & DAD'S FIRST JOB

Dad was a keen footballer as a boy and was proud to land a place in the school team in his last year. In closely contested games, he often came up against a young Raich Carter, who showed as a schoolboy all the skills that later made him such a star of the game. Dad had no such escape route from working for a living and left school on his 14th birthday with experience and world-weariness way beyond his years. He often said, "Looking back, I was a little old man at 14 years of age. Life had done that to me".

There was little or no careers advice. After my Dad's last day at school, my grandmother pointed out an advert in the local paper for boys wanted by Laidler Robson's department store. Remarkably, out of more than 100 hopeful lads who turned up, Dad got the job. That Saturday, after he scored a hat trick in his farewell match for the school team, my grandmother took him into town to buy his first pair of long trousers. They were navy blue and Dad used to say, "I was terribly proud of them". The job was apprentice salesman and the wages were seven shillings per week, but another surprise was in store.

His old headmaster called round with the news that Dad had been selected to play for Sunderland Boys at football. This was the dream of all young sportsmen in the area because, in those days, it meant an automatic contract with Sunderland Football Club at an impressive £8 per week. Dad must have had a very old head on his young shoulders because, although he was delighted to be selected, he thought only for a moment or two before turning to his headmaster and insisting he would not be taking up the football offer. He had a precious job and, although it paid much less money, it offered more security than a career as a footballer. All these years later, it seems a hard decision for a young man to have to make. But Dad did not regret it.

One of the many important things I learned from him in later years was the importance of swiftly making the right decision and then sticking firmly to it.

Now he was the working man of the family, Dad handed over his seven shillings to my grandmother every week, and she would give him a shilling back. This was not enough for the daily tram fare to and from work – so he walked.

His job in Laidler Robson's broadened his horizons. For the first time in his life, he encountered rich people. They came into the store daily and he saw them spend sums that made his eyes water. Dad felt real envy at the gulf between his humble lifestyle and those of the shop's most affluent customers. Watching the well-dressed customers purchasing expensive goods, he decided that, one day, he too would be rich. He was needled by his comparative poverty and developed an obsession to amass great wealth. At home at night, he used to tell his mother and his sisters that, one day, he would become a millionaire. They laughed at his wild dreams but the laughter never dimmed an ambition that was to stay with him for the rest of his days.

He realised that he needed to be better educated to make the most of his life. He had hardly excelled at school, where most of his efforts were directed towards sports, but now he began to read widely and with great enthusiasm. He set about learning all he could about the department store and continued his general education by reading every book he could get hold of. He began with *The Three Musketeers* by Alexandre Dumas and went through other classic adventure stories and onto Shakespeare and many other authors.

My grandmother's family came from the St Helens area of Lancashire and appeared to be mainly well-off. Her oldest sister was Mary, who always took a great interest in my Dad. It was Aunt Mary who was responsible for my Dad's distinctive name. Her first husband had been called Jefferson and she asked my grandmother to name Dad in his memory. Aunt Mary promised that, in return, she would look out for Dad's best interests as long as she lived.

A TAILOR-MADE OFFER

Aunt Mary was then married to a man called Jim Parr, who had a profitable tailor's business in St Helens. She visited my Dad's home in Sunderland several times a year. On one visit, after my Dad had spent almost three years with Laidler Robson, she presented him with a tempting job offer.

Aunt Mary suggested Dad joined his 'uncle' in the tailoring business and, as they had no children of their own to leave it to, the business would one day be his. Dad was all for it. Aunt Mary and her husband seemed very prosperous – they even had their own car; in contrast, prospects at Laidler Robson were limited. So he decided this was his chance to really make something of his life.

Placed among the clothes displayed in Jim Parr's shop window were cards printed with aphorisms, which were regularly changed. One of these caught Dad's eye and became one of his lifelong mottos. In time, it became the motto of the Smurfit business: "Opportunities come to pass, not to pause".

Dad embraced the tailoring trade with enormous enthusiasm and said many times later that, even at the age of 17, he realised for real success you needed to be the best around. Dad worked very hard at learning everything he could about tailoring but, however hard he tried, he could never please Jim Parr.

Jim was a poor tailor himself and was infuriated by the way his wife put this newcomer first at all times. He constantly took his resentment out on Dad. It hardly made for the happiest working environment, although Jim did satisfy Dad's determination to learn the trade by providing him with plenty of tailoring books.

Dad set his mind to making the most of every opportunity that came along. He learned everything about tailoring and read every book that he could find on the subject. He learned about buying fabric, cutting it, making good suits and selling them at a profit. He learned quickly and he worked quickly, preparing six suits in an hour. Being naturally ingenious, he also devised a method of recording details from each fitting onto cardboard to further speed the process.

After a while, he knew he had a real aptitude for tailoring. He even began developing a range of ladies' clothes that he had designed himself. Soon, customers began to ask for him by name and he became in much more demand from customers than Jim Parr, the proprietor. Although his wages were nudged higher, his 'uncle' never seemed to take to him and they did not get on well together.

LOVE & MARRIAGE

Women had never played much of a part in Dad's life until he met a special Irish girl called Ann Magee, who was to become my mother. Dad and his friend Alan Yates went on holiday to the Isle of Man with some other young lads. Half a dozen of them had booked into Westlake's Hotel in Douglas for a week and their holiday was brightened when they met four Irish girls from Belfast who were staying in the same hotel. My Dad fell in love with Ann and, happily, his friend Alan fell for her sister, Kathleen.

But there was a major cloud over these two budding relationships. Not for the last time in the Smurfit family, religious divides presented problems. Ann and Kathleen came from a devout Catholic family and, as my Dad put it, "Neither Alan nor myself had any religion whatsoever". It was made very clear to both Dad and Alan that, unless they became Catholics, the relationships could not continue. They both agreed and took instruction at Holy Cross Church in St Helens.

After three years, both couples got engaged and, with Alan as best man, Dad and my mother married a year later, on 10 June 1934 at St Malachy's Church in Belfast, with the reception at the Grand Central

Hotel. My mother's father did not attend. In spite of their conversion, Dad and Alan were angrily written off as "a couple of King Henry's bastards".

Appropriately enough, Dad and my mother chose to honeymoon in the Isle of Man.

In spite of his father-in-law's disapproval, this was a happy time for Dad and my mother. His mother-in-law showed her support by offering to buy them a house on the understanding that Dad would provide the furniture. He threw himself into supervising the construction and getting together all the furniture.

Throughout the engagement, Dad proudly claimed that he never spent any money on beer. The only ale he consumed while he was saving for marriage was with his pal Alan, who worked as a clerk in Greenall Whitley's brewery where some free beer was available.

Aunt Mary prodded and pushed Jim Parr into giving the newlywed a much-needed wage increase to £5 a week. In those days, that sort of income was more than enough to live very well. And so, Mr and Mrs John Jefferson Smurfit moved into a lovely home with a quarter of an acre of garden and could even afford to employ a maid.

FALLING OUT

Unfortunately, everything was not quite as rosy as it seemed. My Dad's employers, his Aunt Mary and 'Uncle' Jim Parr, took a profound dislike to his new wife Ann. They resented the fact that she and her family had persuaded Dad to become a Catholic. This dislike was a feeling that was powerfully reciprocated by Ann. Today, it is perhaps hard to imagine the importance of religion in everyday lives in the years between the two World Wars. But Aunt Mary and her husband Jim were enthusiastic members of the Salvation Army and had a strong aversion to Catholics.

Dad's career prospects were further threatened when Aunt Mary and Jim's adopted daughter became close to one of the members of the Salvation Army band. Dad did not like the boy from the band and he was angry when Jim said that he was bringing him into the business. The business had been promised to Dad when Jim either retired or died and all his previous hard work had been done on that basis. Never shy of coming forward, Dad said he understood that, if their daughter's husband was in the business, then their first duty was to leave it to him. He said bluntly that he was not prepared to accept that threat to his own future. Aunt Mary and Jim appeared to accept Dad's point of view, but then a month later the band boy, who was called Parton, walked into the shop at nine o'clock on a Monday morning to start work.

Dad was absolutely furious to be deceived and outmanoeuvred, but at first it seemed there was little he could do. He had only about £30 or £40 in the bank and his wife Ann was five months pregnant with me. Dad had spent eight years helping to build up the business and he knew that his skills as a cutter were one of the main reasons for its success. He was horrified that Jim expected him to teach Parton, and he flatly refused to have anything to do with him.

For weeks, the atmosphere in the shop was tense until Dad faced up to Jim Parr and told him he had two choices: sack him or sack Parton, because one of them had to go. Even then, Jim refused to make a choice between his two workers and Dad, who always had a fairly quick temper when roused, stormed out of the shop with the final rejoinder: "Goodbye and bugger you!".

Although he really had burned his bridges, to his considerable surprise, the only feeling he experienced was elation. To celebrate, he walked to the best barber's in town and had a haircut and shampoo. After weeks of tension and uncertainty, he felt really good, until he met his wife Ann out shopping for the family groceries. She wanted to know what he was doing wandering around during working hours and he said he had a confession to make, told her what had happened and admitted, "I am now out of work!". To his considerable relief, Ann's first words of response were "Thank God!".

With scarcely a thought for their suddenly uncertain future, they went to the Fleece Hotel for lunch to mark his new-found freedom. Still elated, they took a tramcar home, only to find a telegram message that brought them both right back down to earth. It said: "Come home at once, father dying".

Dad and Mum took the boat to Belfast that night but my Mum's father lingered on for three further weeks before he died.

After the funeral, it was time for Dad to have a frank conversation with his mother-in-law 'Mazzie', whom he had come to adore. She had realised that Mum and Dad would not have both been able to spend three weeks in Belfast unless something was very wrong between them and Dad's aunt and uncle in St Helens. Dad blurted out the truth that he had left his uncle's tailoring business and he was now out of work. Mazzie had exactly the same reaction as her daughter Ann: she looked mightily relieved and said, "Thank God".

JEFF SMURFIT LIMITED, CREATOR OF GOOD CLOTHES

Both Dad's wife and mother-in-law were sure Dad could do much better working for himself and Mazzie was prepared to provide the money to help him to get started on his own. She hoped that the new business would be established in her native Belfast and, in the early summer of 1936, Dad did look at possible properties there. But he was concerned that he was virtually unknown in Northern Ireland and he decided instead to return to St Helens where he had built up quite a reputation.

Mazzie was disappointed, but still supportive. She handed Dad £215 in cash to help get his new dream off the ground. This was when the Smurfit name went on the window in Harchurch Street, St Helens.

Dad was heartened that many of the friends he had made in the working-class Lancashire town rallied round to help. He had quite a few orders before he started and he had big ideas that he was determined to put into action. He knew every woman tailor in the town and he persuaded four of the best to come and work for him. He had £50 of his own to go with his mother-in-law's £215 and he talked Williams Deacons Bank into granting him an overdraft of £100. So, with his £365 capital and his wife heavily pregnant, he started up in business in his own right for the first time.

Dad's dream to become a millionaire was still alive and well. He worked all day as a tailor and then, in the evening, went out drumming up more business, offering a new service to measure people in their own homes, which went down very well.

However, Dad's return as a rival tailor did not go down well with his old employer. Jim Parr told all the manufacturers and wholesalers who supplied him that, if they dealt with Dad, they were finished with him. This petty reaction hardly helped but Dad was too focused on grabbing his chance of success to let this vindictiveness upset him. Dad made lots of calls in pubs, where he convinced many a publican to invest in a smart new suit. Often, he worked until late into the night and his youthful experience as a debt collector made him insist always on cash on delivery.

Just 11 months after I was born, I had a young brother when Jefferson Junior was born prematurely. Neither my birth nor Jeff's slowed my father down; his ambition and his remarkable natural energy drove him on to make a success of his business.

He must have been doing something right because, within four months, he was making a gross profit of some £60 a week. He invested all of the money in the business and, after about a year, his landlord was taken away to a mental asylum and Dad was able, with the aid of the bank, to buy the whole premises for £1,000.

He wanted to put in a brand new shop-front to let the world know that he had really arrived and his builder friend, Jim Vosse, did the work, after agreeing to take his payment in instalments. Dad was a stickler for paying all his bills on time.

INNOVATION

At first, Dad's business went from strength to strength. Always an innovator, he wanted his shop to be completely different from a conventional tailor's shop and, to that end, he designed his entrance hall to look like a comfortable drawing-room, with a three-piece suite and a gas fire. Customers liked the idea of waiting in comfort and trade increased.

Dad began selling other clothes from recognised manufacturers. He even sold fur coats, thanks to an arrangement with a London furrier, and branched into grey-and-white flannel trousers for some of the cricketers and tennis players of the day.

Business boomed, but he over-reached himself when he opened four more shops. He soon realised that by far the majority of his customers wanted the personal touch that only he could provide, and so he closed down his new branches.

But Dad was colourful as well as hard-working. A famous family story involves an alcohol-fuelled contest with his brawny builder friend, Jim Vosse, over who was the strongest man in the room. Jim claimed that he deserved the title and, when Dad questioned this, he boldly insisted on a test in which each man would hit the other to find out which of them was the stronger. First, Jim Vosse struck Dad with a pile-driver in the chest, which "hurt tremendously". But then Dad had a go in return and thumped his friend with great force in the solar plexus. Jim collapsed on the floor and was violently sick. An ambulance was called and he was in hospital for three weeks, during which time Dad visited him every day. Later he admitted, "It was a stupid act, as Jim was one of my dearest friends. I determined I would never hit anyone again as I went through such anguish!".

CHAPTER 2
BOXING CLEVER

The story of the Jefferson Smurfit Group begins in a small, unprofitable box-making factory in a Dublin suburb.

Dad was learning all the time and, with his energy and overflowing confidence, he even accepted the chance to expand into a completely different business in a completely different country!

This unusual opportunity came from a suitably unlikely source, a Catholic priest, Father Vincent Davy. He was a friend of my grandmother who had helped to officiate at the wedding and had an interest in a box factory that was run by members of my mother's family, the Magees, in Dublin.

Even on his wedding day, Dad found Father Davy inquiring whether he would consider using his business skills to help the troubled concern. Understandably, that day, Dad listened to the stories of management problems at the factory with only mild interest. But Father Davy would not let go.

At first, Dad resisted all of Father Davy's entreaties to step in and help the ailing business. Together with most people in England at the time, he was convinced there was going to be a war with Germany in the near future. Hitler's threat was enough to put Dad off the idea of expanding into Ireland. But then British Prime Minister Neville Chamberlain came back from Munich in 1938, having signed an agreement that appeared to remove all fears of fighting.

With his Lancashire tailoring business running profitably, Dad decided he would take a look at the Dublin factory. Initially, he was not too impressed, although he could see potential, but he knew Father Davy was under pressure from the bishop to get rid of his interest in the business. In the end, Father Davy was so persistent my Dad offered £500 for 51% of the factory. What the priest did not tell my father was that Mazzie had agreed to buy the other 49%.

A FACTORY IN DUBLIN

The Dublin factory was in a lane along the Rathmines Road. There were about 100 employees, mostly young girls plus a few young men, and turnover was around £1,000 a month. Dad knew nothing about box-making, but he'd learned a lot about business and he knew about taking material and making it into a product to sell at a profit.

He set about learning all there was to know about boxes, put his natural sales ability to work and realised that he needed to invest some capital, earned from the tailoring shops, into the box-making business. This was all done on a part-time basis, while he continued to develop his tailoring business in England. He worked 15-hour days, and any time he managed to spend with his family was both rare and precious.

Dad knew the box-making business needed an injection of money. Thanks to his tailoring success, he had around £5,000 in capital available. He offered to invest this to revive the business if Father Davy could do the same. The priest agreed, but again my Dad had no idea that this other influx of money came from his mother-in-law.

From such an improbable and unpromising beginning, the story of the Jefferson Smurfit Group really begins, in a small unprofitable box-making factory in a southern suburb of Dublin.

Dad was determined to make his mark on the packaging business but he was handicapped by his busy tailoring business in St Helens, which meant he was able to spare only one day a week. Thursday was a half-day in the Lancashire town so, every Wednesday night, Dad would board the B & I ferry and be in the factory in Rathmines, Dublin by 8:00 am on Thursday. On Thursday night, he would board the return boat home to become a tailor again on Friday in St Helens.

WAR-TIME

The outbreak of World War II in September 1939 changed everything. Dad was just one of millions of people who had believed Chamberlain's empty promise of 'peace in our time'. His St Helens business was hit hard by the swift introduction of clothes rationing.

Always versatile, Dad turned to making covers for the gas masks that every man, woman and child was issued with.

The war instantly made the whole idea of sailing across the Irish Sea and back every week dangerous as well as exhausting. Dad had a horrifying experience, just two months after war was declared, when the ferry he was on foundered on the cliffs of the Isle of Man and all the passengers and crew had to be rescued by lifeboat. Dad was travelling from Liverpool to Belfast on *The Ulster Queen* and had been to the bar for a few drinks, as he put it, "enough to make me sleep". At 2am, there was a fearful impact, which threw him out of his bunk. Dad was convinced they had been torpedoed, but in fact the boat had run into the cliffs of the Isle of Man.

He learned later that the Admiralty had ordered so many lights to confuse possible enemy aircraft that they had completely bewildered the ship's pilot. The passengers and crew were lowered into lifeboats and later transferred to another ferry, *The Duke of Lancaster*. It was a difficult procedure as the passengers had to lie flat in the bottom of the lifeboat to avoid being struck by the overhanging structure of the boat they were trying to board. Dad said it was a frightening experience because of the freezing cold and the ordeal of scrambling from boat to boat. It hardly helped that British Railways insisted on charging the new arrivals 3d (1.25p) for a cup of tea and 2s 9d (13p) for a berth – and money up front. Some people who had been travelling steerage did not have the money, so Dad paid for them.

Remarkably, even this life-threatening experience did not put him off criss-crossing the Irish Sea to run his two separate and very different enterprises.

OPPORTUNITY BECKONS

In 1940, he was presented with the opportunity to buy the Rathmines factory that, until then, he had been renting. All of a sudden, the landlord was in desperate need of money and Dad quickly agreed to provide it, despite not having any spare funds available.

But the landlord wanted to sell not only Dad's factory but also two neighbouring businesses, Mandleberg's raincoat factory and the

Errislynn factory. Dad knew a bargain when he saw one and, after some hard negotiating, he agreed to buy the three properties for £6,250. Dad admitted later that he did not have 6,250 pence at the time, but nevertheless he agreed to buy all three.

Dad then swiftly went round to talk to his friend Billy Costello, who was the managing director of the raincoat firm. There, he confessed that he had been very 'unethical' and had bought the Mandleberg's factory premises over his head. To make up, he offered a 'fair deal', which was to sell Mandleberg's alone to Costello's firm for £6,250. Billy Costello agreed. Dad could hardly believe his luck. He had bought his own factory, and the Errislynn plant, for nothing – all because the landlord was in a desperate need of ready cash.

DAD'S ARMY

Despite the demands of running his two businesses, when World War II broke out, Dad volunteered for the armed forces, but his age was against him so he joined the Home Guard instead. Dad was desperately moved, like many millions more in Britain, by the gallantry shown at the retreat from Dunkirk and he was determined to do his bit.

By then, he was the self-styled 'squire of Eccleston', the village next to St Helens, and was asked if he would organise the volunteers for that part of southwest Lancashire. He eagerly agreed and Jeff and I would say goodnight to him as he went off into the night, looking smart in his uniform.

He went to the local pub to enrol people to join him. He organised drilling, which took place mainly late at night or at weekends. Dad had an allocation of real guns in the shape of 12 old Lee Enfield rifles from World War I. He would put the rifles in the back of his car and head off to try to get his troops in shape. Dad put a lot of effort into the Local Defence Volunteers but, gradually, the soldiering amateurs like Dad were replaced by old soldiers from World War I and his rank went down from virtually general level towards that of humble private. He was content that he had played his part in helping to get the whole thing started.

THE IMPACT OF WAR

If the war hadn't threatened the safety of his family, Dad might have been content to get the box-making factory on its feet and concentrate on his tailoring business in England. But living so close to Liverpool meant it was impossible to escape the impact of the fighting. Liverpool was Britain's major port for essential imports and it never closed. It was also the hub of the Battle of the Atlantic, and a target for the German bombers that attacked Britain during 1940 and 1941.

At night, we huddled together in the cramped and stuffy conditions of a Morrison Shelter. I remember the steel girder above my head, the wire sides of the cage, designed to protect us from a hit on our house. It was scary and uncomfortable. Sometimes, Dad would be there with us, but often he was out all night doing Home Guard duty or away in Dublin on business.

The German bombing raids were terrifying. We were only seven miles from Liverpool as the crow flies, not that there were many crows flying around on those terrible nights. There would be 500 bombers attacking the city and the shrapnel flying into the sky to try to stop them was an unbelievable sight. Most of the bombers flew through this barrage to attack their targets but some of them kept clear of the flak and dropped their bombs anywhere, which was often around us. My Dad used to call these cowardly bombers 'funky bastards' because they would drop their bombs on farmland and then fly back and say they'd hit their targets.

MY EARLIEST MEMORIES

As a much-loved toddler in St Helens, I was blissfully unaware of my Dad's extraordinary work schedule. At home, my younger brother Jefferson Junior and I had been joined by a baby sister, Ann. My mother must have been just as busy bringing up three tiny children as ever my father was rushing from one side of the Irish Sea to the other. One of my earliest memories is a desperately sad one.

I must have been three or four years old and I remember I was crying uncontrollably. I was not alone in my grief. Everyone in the house was crying. My baby sister, Ann, had died of convulsions and my parents were convinced that it was the effects of living through the Blitz on Merseyside that killed her. Tragically, a baby dying from convulsions was a common thing back then.

Another grim recollection from my earliest days is the time I ran up the street to visit a favourite uncle. I don't think he was an actual relative, but he was a good friend of my parents and he often visited us. He and his family lived on top of a hill not far from where we lived. I arrived at the house to find it had suffered a direct hit and was just a pile of rubble. My 'uncle' and his family were all dead, wiped out. It was a terrible shock.

The only other recollection I have from that time is of my father parading in uniform at the head of the local Home Guard.

Later in the War, in 1942 I believe it was, we moved to Ireland. With the death of his baby daughter, Dad decided England was too dangerous a place to bring up his family. For a while, he kept running the two businesses, but he decided to focus on box-making and appointed a manager to look after his tailors' shops in England.

We first stayed in a hotel and then moved to Castle Park in the Terenure area. Then we went to Killiney to live in a beautiful home. Our fortunes varied through the years; we went from a big home to a small home, a small home to a big home, from rented premises to a lovely house we owned.

JEFFERSON SMURFIT & SONS LIMITED

Following his own beliefs about the importance of a person's name, Dad changed the name of the box factory company to 'Jefferson Smurfit & Sons Limited' in 1942. Clearly, even then, he fully expected me and my brothers to take over the business.

In Dublin, he also appointed a manager. Very unusually for those days, she was a woman. Lily Darcy was one of the best workers and a great 'machine fixer'. According to Dad, the men hated working for her because it just wasn't the thing for women to be in charge of men, but Dad had made the decision and they had to put up with it. And it was a decision that he never regretted.

The arrival of Jefferson Smurfit on the Dublin scene shook up some of the long-established Irish packaging companies.

The kingpin of box-makers in Ireland at that time was P O'Reilly Limited, which was run by a very tough and domineering man called Malachy O'Reilly, who took exception to Dad's arrival. He decided to teach 'this young upstart from England' a lesson and told his sales people to undercut all Smurfit prices by 10%.

Dad was always honest and acted with integrity in his business dealings, but he never took anything lying down. Hearing about the plan to undercut his prices, Dad visited Dublin's main buyers and told them he was able to offer them a good deal. He took details of their requirements and went back with quotes that were 25% below cost price, telling them he was busy and didn't really need the business.

His competitors' sales team did what they had been told, checked what Smurfit was offering, and undercut it by 10%. O'Reilly was inundated with orders that would cost them money to produce and were so busy that they couldn't take on any more profitable work. Dad was able then to take on at a profitable price the orders that they couldn't cope with.

About six months later, a suitably chastened Malachy O'Reilly had the good grace to ask Dad to dinner at his golf club in Woodbrook. Dad said that his rival admitted he had learned his lesson and that, from then on, they remained "quite good friends, without being intimate friends".

Although the Republic of Ireland was neutral during World War II, its people still suffered shortages of goods and basic foods. White bread, sugar, jam and tea were all rationed. Petrol and coal were in short supply. This made life hard for families and tough for businesses. Dad had to take every opportunity he came across and use his ingenuity to keep the business going.

When the business did well, we eventually settled in a house in Mount Merrion, named after my father's Tyneside roots in North East England.

My father, John Jefferson Smurfit, was a genius. I don't use that term lightly and I do mean it literally. He did something that I could never do. He built the foundations of a great business. Much later, I was to learn that I was good at building the house, but I could never have built the foundations. He had no money available to buy machines, so he had to build them – I could never have done that. He had patience and knowledge and great integrity.

CHAPTER 3
GROWING UP

**You can buy brains but you make businessmen, and
I'm going to make you all businessmen.**

My happiest recollection from childhood is the time Dad took me
from our home in Dublin back across the Irish Sea to England to
watch the Grand National. I suppose I must have been nine or ten
years old and the whole event made a huge impression on me. The
noise and the huge crowds were unforgettable. Everything about the
occasion was exciting, especially when Dad put me on his shoulders
so I could see what was going on. He loved horse-racing and the
enjoyment of the day remains one of my fondest early memories. It
was a thrill I will never forget. I trace my love for the sport right back
to that first wonderful trip.

Dad was wearing a peaked cap and a trench coat and I just loved
sitting high up there above the crowd, taking in everything and being
for once so close to my Dad. Times like this were very precious
because Dad often seemed a very distant figure. He worked long
hours, seven days a week, as he battled to make a success of his
business. Even at home in the evenings, he often would be in his
study poring over books or accounts and planning the future for the
factory.

He was a big powerful man who was always in charge of the
household. He was a traditional husband and father who ruled the
roost in every way. To me, he was always a strong and commanding
figure. I think as a boy I was in awe of him. To be honest, I was
frightened of him when I was younger but that fear gradually went
as I grew older, though it was not until many years later that I could
say I loved him. He wasn't the sort of person who came in and kissed
you, like I would kiss my kids.

I think I was in my 30s when I first felt that I really loved my father. He was a profoundly impressive man, a genuine alpha male with an extraordinarily strong personality. It was only much later in life that I really appreciated the strength of character he had helped to instil in me.

My mother was the exact opposite of Dad. She was very calm and quiet and always very gentle. She made sure the house was happy and well-run. She seemed delighted to spend her time looking after all of us children and we all loved her.

I think I was a pretty solitary kind of child. Looking back, I suppose I was always a serious character. I don't even have particularly happy memories of Christmas! We always celebrated it as a family. And I do remember being excited waiting for Father Christmas when I was eight or nine. I'd try to stay awake all night. There's just so much I can't remember.

Certainly, even when I was young, I liked my own company. I read a lot. I loved comics such as *The Beano*, *The Dandy*, *The Wizard*, and any simple books. I really liked fairy tales, particularly the stories of Hans Christian Andersen and, later, one of my special early favourites was *A Tale of Two Cities* by Charles Dickens.

BROTHERS & SISTERS

My brother Jeff was only 11 months younger than me and we were always close, yet different. Even when we were very young, Jeff was much more outgoing and confident than I was. He was the life and soul of every occasion with his cheery personality and quick sense of humour. I was much more cautious and shy as a boy, and indeed as a young man. I always admired Jeff's great natural ability to get on quickly with others but I never envied him. He was my closest friend, as well as my brother.

After Jeff came my sister Ann, who died aged only three months, and then my sister Kay, who is no longer alive. Then there were my brothers Alan and Dermot and my sisters Sheila, who has died, and finally Barbara, who is the youngest of the eight of us.

HOLIDAYS

In the school holidays, Jeff and I often would go and stay with my aunt and her family in St Helens or with my grandmother back in Sunderland.

My Dad's mother still lived in the tiny terraced house where he had grown up. Even to us as young boys, it seemed very small and the toilet was out the back. My Dad wanted to buy his mother something much bigger and better, but she flatly refused to move away from her friends and neighbours and the area she knew, saying she was happy enough there.

My Dad's sister had married a farmer and, sometimes, Jeff and I would go and stay with them on their farm in the village of Cleadon, near Sunderland. We enjoyed being with our cousins in St Helens as well as over in Sunderland, spending the days playing cricket and exploring the Lancashire countryside or the Durham beaches.

I've always had a sweet tooth and that was another reason for enjoying the visits to England. The sweets always tasted better there!

Jeff and I loved our trips to England, though the girls didn't. I don't think our sisters came with us.

SIMPLE LIVES

Life was very different when I was a boy. There was a lot of hardship and people lived simpler lives, without all the appliances and luxuries we take for granted today.

I remember well the days of coupons and rationing after the War. We used to swop coupons sometimes and this bartering was an early opportunity for me to learn the laws of supply and demand, I suppose, but I don't think I was particularly good at trading as a boy. The drive that I had for doing deals came later in life.

With seven children at home, the house was always crowded and full of noise and when I wasn't at school or later, when I wasn't working, I'd escape to the cinema, a place I still love. It didn't matter what the film was – I enjoyed being on my own, watching whatever was on screen. I really enjoyed losing myself in an adventure film. I particularly liked the Lone Ranger, but I was never especially fascinated by America, and I certainly had no childhood dream of going there.

Another reason for escaping to the cinema or going out to play a game of cricket was to escape from the fog in the house. Like most adults at the time, my parents both smoked heavily and I hated cigarettes.

But my parents always meant well. They did everything they could to give us all as full a life as possible. They pushed me in all sorts of directions: to play the piano, to ride horses, to play golf, to play cricket, to play rugby. A lot of them I didn't want to do – though some I enjoyed.

I can't ride now because of back problems but, when I was a young boy, I was taught by Miss Iris Kellett, who was then one of Ireland's famous equestrians. I guess I was around eight or nine years old when she started to teach me. I went on to develop a lifelong love of horses, but parental pushing didn't always work.

One of the reasons I never play the piano, which I could do quite well as a kid, was because every time I made a mistake, the woman teaching me hit me on the knuckles with a pencil.

When I became myself, rather than what my father wanted me to be, I went on to enjoy a number of things that he pushed me into, like cricket and golf. But there were a number of things that I was pushed into that I didn't like and one of those was learning to play the piano.

My brothers and I were involved in the usual boyish scrapes. Dermot, who is eight years younger than me, recalls an incident that I've completely forgotten:

My favourite memory – one of my earliest recollections, in fact – of Michael goes back to when I was about five years old. He was leader of the 'Mount Merrion' gang and he was about 13, I suppose. I was kidnapped by the 'Allen Park' gang. They were our hated rivals and Michael came and rescued me. He was my big brother and I always looked up to him. He was my hero.

A GROWING BUSINESS

Dad's business was always very important in the lives of everyone in the family. By the time I reached my teens, the original box-making business had grown substantially in terms of plant and turnover. Dad was resourceful and totally tireless in his determination to make his business succeed. With his endless ingenuity, he tried all sorts of aspects of packaging.

At one point, he produced a vast quantity of egg boxes. He turned out two different sizes, which were named after me and my brother! The two-dozen box was called 'Michael', while the one-dozen box was dubbed 'Junior', as Jeff was always known. Dad apologised that 'Junior' boxes were always more popular than the 'Michael' brand. But who buys two dozen eggs at a time?

The war was soon behind us and life was beginning to get easier for everyone, including the Smurfit family. We had moved to a house in Rathmines, overlooking the factory at the bottom of the garden, and Dad was looking to the future with great optimism.

Dad was always enterprising. When the business next door went bankrupt about a year after Dad had bought the factory, he decided to move in and use the extra space himself. Not only that, he built over the yard between the two buildings and doubled his manufacturing space. In the freer, less restricted days before the introduction of planning controls, he was able to go ahead and simply do what he wanted. Unfortunately, the new roof was not strong enough and it sagged. Dad said there was no danger of it collapsing but, whenever there was snow, he had a man on the roof sweeping it off, just in case.

Dad always said that, in those early years in Dublin, there was no stage when we were not short of money and only a series of near-superhuman efforts prevented the business from becoming bankrupt many times between 1939 and 1954. He had no money to buy machines, so he spent time reading and researching all about them – and then built them himself. I would never have had that patience or knowledge or ability.

Corrugated board was purchased from Killeen Paper Mills, a well-established Dublin paper and box manufacturer. But after a while, Killeen decided that my father was becoming too serious a competitor and, in the late 1940s, they refused to sell him any more board. His response was typical: he said he would make his own. That is exactly what he did.

Of course, he needed paper to make the board and, remarkably, the paper division of Killeen agreed to supply him. This curious arrangement continued for some time until Killeen ruled that he was becoming an even bigger threat and refused to supply him at all. Once again, Dad's response was, "If you won't supply me, then I will make my own paper".

To do this, late into the night he read all the books about paper-making he could find and then he set about building his own paper machine. This was nothing new; he was forever looking at ways in which he could improve the business.

He carried out his initial trials by making pulp and feeding it through an old clothes wringer. It was a very basic machine – a mangle that squeezed wet clothes between rollers to get some of the water out of them. After a great deal of trial and error, he eventually got the all-important consistency of the pulp right. And then he built a paper machine, the first we ever had.

Money was much too scarce to consider buying a purpose-built machine, so once again, he studied the process and using second-hand parts, he built our first corrugator. We called it 'Mr Clang', because of the loud noise it made. When it worked, we could hear it clanging away and we were very happy because we knew it meant we were making money. When it didn't work, which was very often, we weren't so happy.

Dad also built the company's first-ever milligator, a self-contained production unit where waste paper comes in one door and boxes come out the other.

But there were always plenty of lows to match the highs.

DISASTER STRIKES ...

One of the worst nights of my life was spent looking out of a back window of our house as the business went up in flames. It was 1948 and what started as a small fire quickly spread out of control. We watched as the factory that Dad had worked so hard to create burned almost to the ground. By the next morning, Dad was left with just a few machines and the walls of the factory building. It was terrible.

To make matters worse, he discovered that he was vastly underinsured and could get back only around two-thirds of his losses. He had been so busy driving the business forward that he had neglected to maintain sufficient insurance cover. Typically, Dad blamed no-one but himself.

For a while, it seemed as if everything Dad had worked for was lost, and he found himself fighting for his business life. But with support from his friends, Dermot Barnes and Bill Gleeson, who had joined Dad's Board two years earlier, the business was saved. And within two months, Dad had reconditioned some machines, bought other new ones, rebuilt the factory and was back in full production.

... BUT OPENS NEW VISTAS

Dad began to look around for land to build a new factory and found the site of an old mill, with five acres of land, beside the River Dodder at Clonskeagh. The new factory he built here was made of concrete, including the roof, with the aim of limiting any fire damage.

Dad's friend from St Helens, Alan Yates, owned a 16% holding in the business, and he wanted to raise some cash by selling this back to Dad, who unfortunately had already borrowed more than he should have done in order to invest in the new factory. It wasn't the first time that Dad faced up to the possibility of financial ruin, but Dermot Barnes and Bill Gleeson came to his aid and bought Alan Yates' share between them. Their involvement proved to be a great asset to the development of the company.

INVESTMENT IN OUR EDUCATION

Whatever the state of the business, Dad made sure we all got a good education.

My first school was the Presentation College in Dun Laoghaire. I travelled there by train every day. Then I went to St Michael's College in Rathmines, which was much nearer to home. When I was 12 years old, I went as a boarder to Clongowes Wood College in Co. Kildare, with my brother Jeff. We were so close in age that we were in the same class. The school is just a few miles down the road from where The K Club stands today. The author James Joyce was once a pupil and the school features heavily in his semi-autobiographical novel, *A Portrait of the Artist as a Young Man.*

Although Dad never said as much, I knew that it was a struggle for him to pay the school fees. Jeff and I had pocket money of 1s 6d (7.5p) a week, which was a lot less than most of the other boys. I'd say we were poorer than just about all of our fellow pupils and, while their tuck boxes were full of sweets and chocolates, ours were always empty. We might have considered ourselves upper middle class but we were still the poorest kids at the school.

Clongowes is Ireland's oldest Catholic boys' school, run by Jesuits who were very hot on discipline, but I enjoyed the structure of school life and learning. You might get caned now and then, but only if you did something wrong, and it seemed fair enough to me at the time. I never did anything really bad; I got disciplined for things like not doing my homework or being late for class. It's not something I believe in myself and, as a father, I never used physical punishment on any of my children.

Dad wanted Jeff and me to get a good education. He had converted from Protestantism to Catholicism himself and he wanted us to be educated by Jesuits.

At Clongowes, they gave you a good education and concentrated on building up your character, but they didn't really tell you anything about life, sex, and the modern world. It was a very insular school in many ways and I believe this reinforced my own insular nature. Girls never really came into my life until much later than most other boys and young men. I never had any close female relationships and I found it very difficult to spark with a girl.

While Jeff thrived at school with his natural charisma, I was always quieter in comparison. I got on with the other boys and made friends, but I was forever the quiet one while Jeff was the one who lit up a room. He was also a very bright student. I studied hard and got good results, but it came a lot easier to Jeff, who had a brilliant mind and never struggled to keep at the top of the class, despite being younger than the rest of us.

We both enjoyed sports and I became captain of the cricket team. I would like to be able to say that this showed my early leadership skills. I think it was simply that I was good at cricket. I certainly wouldn't say I was an outstanding captain or led the team better than anyone else. And when I was at school, I don't think anyone would have picked me out as the one most likely to succeed in later life or in business.

Like a lot of children who go to boarding school, I found when I came home for the holidays that I had far fewer friends than kids who went to the local school. I didn't particularly mind. The family was always my world. They were my friends. We were close. We would play cricket together and, often, my brother Alan would be on my team while Dermot would be on my brother Jeff's team. We played a lot of games together.

When Jefferson Smurfit & Sons Limited started to prosper, Dad bought a holiday home beside the beach and he'd drive the family down there. Perhaps because his own father had died when he was young, Dad always had a lot of respect for widows who were working to bring up their families. On the way to our holiday house, there was a shop and petrol station, owned by a widow. Dad would always be sure to stop there to fill up with petrol and buy sweets for us children, along with some holiday supplies. Spending money there was his way of helping her.

For a time when I was at school, I thought I might become a priest. The system tried to establish whether you had a calling. Gradually, I came to realise it wasn't a true vocation for me. It was something we were all encouraged to consider and, at the time, I didn't have any other ambitions. I did have a strong religious faith, which continues to this day.

TRIPS WITH DAD

When Jeff and I were at Clongowes, Dad sometimes would take us to the racing at nearby Naas. I loved that.

Dad once had a horse called *Patrickswell*, which he fancied for the Grand National. The story goes that his trainer, Dan Ruttle, put an amateur jockey on it, the jockey got to the first fence and jumped off.

With his great friend and business associate, Bill Gleeson, Dad began to purchase race-horses. Initially, the duo struggled due to their lack of equine knowledge, but the more they learned, the better they became at spotting a winner. I believe that the second winner the famous trainer Vincent O'Brien ever had was Dad's horse.

Dad once had a horse called *Brooklyn* running in England. It didn't come first but the finish was queried and the judgment went in Dad's favour, so his horse won the race on an objection. A week later, his horse *Rocking* did come first but, again, the finish was queried. This time, the decision went against him. Dad decided to give up racing there and then and never owned another horse or attended another race.

Golf was something else that Dad enjoyed, as it gave him the chance to meet other businesspeople away from the factory. He applied to join the Castle Golf Club near our home, but he was rejected because a rumour had gone round that he was Jewish. Dad was outraged and angrily declared the decision "terribly unfair and completely unchristian". He joined other Dublin golf clubs instead: Elm Park and Woodbrook.

When we were young teenagers, Dad sometimes took Jeff and me to one of his favourite places, the Dolphin Hotel in Dublin. A couple of times, he gave us the tip to pass on to the waiter and we couldn't resist the temptation to keep it ourselves. It was half-a-crown once and a pound another time. I felt very guilty about it afterwards, and I was down to church next day because I couldn't wait to get to confession. That Catholic guilt that you must behave yourself or else you would go to Hell was hammered into me. I had very strong religious feelings in those days – I think most people did at that time. I was an altar boy at church and I used to go in and help the priest to robe and pour the wine.

From the time I was about 12, Dad took me on trips to see other factories and machinery in places as different as Waterford and Morocco, and I had holiday jobs in his factory.

I didn't swan in saying I was the owner's son. In those days, I was much too shy to say "Boo" to anybody. Dad told me and my brothers, "You can buy brains but you make businessmen, and I'm going to make you all businessmen".

I knew that, at some point in the future, I would go into the family business, but I was expecting to continue my studies and eventually go on to university. Dad had other ideas, as I soon found out.

THE UPS AND DOWNS OF BUSINESS

By 1951, Dad's business was doing well enough for him to undertake a trip to the United States. He crossed the Atlantic with Dermot Barnes and, in New York, they stayed in the famous Biltmore Hotel. Even my ever-confident Dad was over-awed by the pace and the size of New York, not to say the height of hotels. He was so alarmed by the view from his eighth-floor bedroom and so frightened that he might jump out of the window by mistake that, on his first night, he confessed later, he tied himself to the bed by his braces.

He certainly came back down to earth on his return when, at Christmas 1952, the Clonskeagh factory was struck by another terrible fire. It happened when the factory was empty during the holiday period and Dad was convinced that the fire had been started by thieves. Although it was a shock and a serious setback, Dad was better prepared this time and production was soon back up to speed.

CHAPTER 4
STEPS TOWARDS INDEPENDENCE

Can you imagine that this capitalist started his career as a trade union member?

Careers advice is sophisticated nowadays but Jeff and I found that our Dad took a rather more direct approach. When we were 16, he took us out of school, handed us some overalls, and put us to work in the family business at the Clonskeagh mill. I suppose I always knew that's where I would end up but I had thought I would go to university first.

I never questioned Dad's decision. If he told me to do something, I did it. Even so, it was a shock to me. I was studying hard for the Cambridge entrance exams. I had taken it for granted I was going to try to get to university. That was what everyone else in the class was doing. Yet I don't think I was particularly upset by Dad's decision.

He certainly didn't do it to give Jeff and me an easy ride as the boss's sons. He always said that he told every foreman in the place to "kick their backsides good" and some of his men took him at his word. Dad wanted us to experience the business at every level and learn everything there was to know from the bottom to the top. He even insisted that we join the union.

Dad was serious about my becoming a member of the union. He was a socialist at heart and, unusually for a factory owner, insisted that all of his workers join the union. When I first joined the company aged 16, we had what was known as a 'closed shop', which meant you had to be a member of the union to work there. I joined the Irish Transport & General Workers' Union. I went to Liberty Hall and voted. I shouted "Up the working man" and "To hell with the bosses"! Can you imagine that this capitalist started his career as a trade union member? Not that I was a very good trade unionist. I remember falling so far behind with my 1s 6d (7.5p) a week dues at one stage that I had to borrow £5 from my father.

For the times, I think my father's decision to put me to work was the right one. These days, I think it is far more important to complete your education: business is much more competitive now. Back in those days, we were still coming out of the war years and there was huge demand for all sorts of goods, and for boxes to package them in. You could achieve 15% to 20% growth a year. These days, you're lucky if you achieve 2%. Back then, there were no computers, no Internet or mobile phones and you didn't need to be technologically clever to get on in business. For years, I never used a computer – in fact, I have only recently started.

My first job was as a fitter's apprentice and that was when I began to learn what made the business tick. Joining the family business meant learning about each stage of production and working my way from the factory floor to the boardroom. To be honest, I did not enjoy it. Many people were very good to me, but a few took the chance to give the boss's son a hard time. I have happy memories of the people, but not of the work. I didn't want to become an electrician or an engineer, so I didn't want to spend my days handing people spanners and screwdrivers. I was bored and, if this was my future, it didn't look good.

DREAMS OF CANADA

By the time I was 19, I was becoming increasingly unhappy. We lived then in a small, crowded house, where I had to share a bedroom with Jeff. At Dad's insistence, we still had to be in by 10pm on weekdays and 11pm at weekends. By today's standards, that sounds absurd but this was the 1950s in Ireland when things were different. I wasn't earning much and didn't feel I was getting anywhere. The Irish economy was failing and around 80,000 young people were emigrating every year, looking for a better future somewhere else in the world.

I was working in the mill's sample-making department at the time and a workmate who was in his late 20s told me he was leaving Ireland and going to Canada. On a whim, I decided to go with him. I didn't tell Dad because I knew he'd be against the idea. So first, I got a job with what was then the world's largest packaging company, Continental Can Company, at a factory in Toronto.

My parents were both shocked and upset when I announced my plans. But my father accepted my decision once I had convinced him I really believed it was the best thing for me. I filled in all the papers and was all set for a new life on the other side of the Atlantic. Then came a bombshell.

I received a letter from the Canadian Embassy informing me that my application to go to Canada had been rejected due to a potential health problem, which had been identified when I had been for the required medical. The letter suggested that I go and see a doctor immediately.

I was shattered. I felt as fit as a fiddle and I was furious that my dreams were in tatters. I didn't know what the letter was all about but I soon found out. The doctor revealed that tuberculosis had been detected, undoubtedly brought on by working in the damp conditions of the Clonskeagh factory. This shocking news allayed any anger that my parents might have felt about my secret plans to go to Canada and the day the boat sailed, I entered the Peamount Sanatorium in west Dublin.

IN THE SANATORIUM

When I went into the sanatorium, I was 20 years old, a slim, fit and healthy-looking young man. Nine months later, I emerged over-weight, pale and seriously out of condition caused by inactivity, but at least well enough to return to work.

My parents visited me often in Peamount and gave me one of the first televisions in the Republic of Ireland. It was just black-and-white in those days, but I was delighted to have it in my small room. Television was just being introduced into Ireland then and the set had a very small and fuzzy picture, but it made me very popular in the sanatorium.

I was still naïve. I remember that it was during this period that I saw a cow giving birth to a calf, which was the first time I knew anything about sex. Somewhat late in life, I learned how babies were born. How times have changed. The young people of today are different. I learned a lot about life in that sanatorium.

Dad's visit to the United States to look at the packaging industry had given him a great love of American cars, to the extent that he imported a huge Buick into Ireland. On Sundays, he would pile my mother and my brothers and sisters into the car for a trip to see me. Mum and Dad would come inside while the others would sit on the bonnet so that I could talk to them through an open window in my room. Their visits were strictly unofficial. Most patients were in enormous wards but I was fortunate enough to have a small private room to myself that Dad got for me.

When Dad came to see me once a week, he would bring me invoices and other paperwork from the business to look through, along with every business book that he could find and magazines like *Fortune*, *Investor's Chronicle* and *Forbes*. This was certainly an innovative alternative to the basketweaving and similar activities that were on offer to other patients to pass their long days. Dad didn't want me to waste my time and neither did I.

Very soon, I found myself consumed with an interest for information about business in general and about packaging in particular. At first, even trying to understand the *Financial Times* had been a major difficulty for me but, slowly and surely, I had got on top of it. I understood what dividend yields and so many other strange terms meant. I was a businessman and I was interested in becoming a successful businessman. I believed I knew early what makes a business tick.

Reading about business really kindled my interest in take-overs. At the time, Jim Slater, with his firm Slater Walker, was the 'king of take-overs'. I was curious about how one company could take over another and I began to study his career in detail. He always seemed to be in the newspapers in the early 1960s, doing something bold and outrageous. He became one of my role models.

In the sanatorium, I also had my first taste of romance. I fell in love with one of the nurses – well, I fell in love with her legs to be honest – but just admired her from afar. I was so very innocent in those days.

Not long after I was confined to Peamount, I was shattered to hear some terrible news from Toronto. My workmate had gone to Canada only to be badly injured in a terrible traffic accident. He was waiting at a bus stop when there was a crash that killed three people and left him so badly injured he was in a wheelchair for the rest of his life.

It made me go cold to think that, if it had not been for my health, I probably would have been with him at that bus stop. I felt that there had been a strange stroke of fate that had altered my life. First, the spur of the moment decision to emigrate to Canada, which led to the diagnosis of tuberculosis. If the condition hadn't been diagnosed, I was told that I would have been dead in six months. As it was, it was found at the early, curable stage and my spell in the sanatorium saved my life. But, on top of that, I had the great fortune of avoiding being in the accident with my friend in Toronto. For the first time in my life, it struck me very forcibly that I was a lucky person.

The spell in the sanatorium brought me into close contact with illness and death. In the time I was in there, I held the hands of men who were dying, usually much older men suffering with cancer or tuberculosis. Suddenly I had become close to death, not just through my own illness but by being with people who were not as fortunate as I was. This was when I first realised the inevitability of death, that it is only a question of 'when' not 'if'. When you understand that, you treat every day as if it is going to be your last, because one day you will be right.

Thus, one important lesson I learned from my time in the sanatorium was never to put off till tomorrow what I could do today. I left the sanatorium with a new enthusiasm for life, for our business and for playing my part in developing the business.

BACK TO WORK ...

When I left the sanatorium, I went back to work in the factory, but this time in the office. Here, I found that I had an aptitude that I didn't have for the factory floor. I enjoyed being in the office and I felt that I was learning something.

Jeff was doing well on the sales side. He was a great character, a great salesman, even in his early days. He was trying to open up the UK market and bring in orders from over there.

My spell in the sanatorium had given me time to think about my life and helped me to decide what to do next. For many years, we had been buying paper from Continental Can, the American company I had been going to work for when my tuberculosis was diagnosed. As the name suggests, Continental Can was best-known as the world's largest producer of cans, but it also produced a lot of paper. Dad said he thought it might be a good idea for me to go and get some experience in America. I agreed that, when I came out of the sanatorium, I would go to America and then I would come back and assist him in the business.

... AND THEN TO AMERICA

Continental Can's head office was in New York. Dad arranged for me to go and work there. I was a quiet and shy young man at the time, still very much under the shadow of my father. Ed Garcia, one of their young managers, was assigned to look after me and be my mentor. That was a real stroke of luck. Ed took me under his wing and he's still a great friend of mine.

My first placement was at Continental Can's plant in Portland, Connecticut. There was no accommodation in Portland, so I ended up staying in the YMCA in nearby Middleton. It was a pretty soulless, scary kind of place. I had to block up holes in the door of my room with chewing gum to avoid the prying eyes of some of the other young men. I had no real money to go out and enjoy myself as Dad only gave me around $5 a week pocket money.

I used to walk the two miles to work, and then the same two miles back home again at night. I had no money for a car and there was no decent public transport. In the winter, this was no fun at all. It would take me about an hour to do the journey because the roads were icy. The wind would be howling and the rain pouring down and I felt pretty sorry for myself.

It was a lonely time. Every night, I went to the movies on my own. Sometimes, I saw the same movie three or four nights running, but there was nothing else to do. There was not even a TV to watch. The movies helped me to keep warm and pass the time. It was very hard, but I guess I was determined to make a go of it.

One day, the plant manager saw me walking along the road to the plant and pulled up to ask, "What happened to your car?". I said, "I don't have one". He couldn't believe what he was hearing. He asked how I got to work and I explained that I walked. He said, "You've been doing that since you arrived?". I said, "Yes," and he replied, "That's crazy!". So he contacted Ed Garcia, who got in touch with Dad, and said I needed a car.

My Dad came up with the money and, for $90, I bought an old Chevrolet coupé. I called it 'Blue Streak', because it burnt more oil than it did petrol, creating a big blue streak out the back. Having my first car was very exciting and changed my life. I drove thousands of miles in that car. I went all the way from Connecticut to Savannah, Georgia and worked in a number of kraftliner mills on the way. The first one was in Hopewell, Virginia and the second was in Port Wentworth, Georgia: two plants that we were later to own.

America opened my eyes about so many things. I had grown up in a family business where most of the machinery was home-made by my father. Some days it worked, some days it didn't. When I went to America, I was working in a modern corrugated box plant and saw how modern machinery worked and what it could do. I was staggered when I realised what we could do with that machinery in a rapidly developing Irish market. I learnt about management techniques, about how to cost correctly, how to plan production through the plant. I soon discovered that just about every single aspect of production and delivery was a whole lot more efficient in America than ever it was in Ireland.

Gradually, despite my shyness, I got to know one or two people and I celebrated my 21st birthday in Manhattan at a party thrown for me by a friend. People must have thought that I had a keen interest in music as I spent the evening changing the records. But, in fact, I became the permanent disc jockey because I was too afraid to ask anyone to dance with me.

But I did get interested in jazz and, one time, I took a Trailways bus from Savannah to go and listen to the trumpeter Al Hirt, who was appearing with a band in the Blue Room at the Roosevelt Hotel in New Orleans.

The journey took me four days, because I got arrested and thrown in prison for sleeping in what many white Americans from the Deep South often offensively referred to at that time as a 'nigger seat'. I was tired, so I found an empty seat at the back of the bus and fell asleep. The next thing I knew, I was being roughly woken up by a very unfriendly policeman in Alabama. I was arrested because I was in a seat that was designated for non-white people. I was taken off the bus and put in jail for 24 hours. When they explained the reason for my arrest, I told them I didn't know anything about segregation. I still don't understand it and we have never allowed any form of discrimination within our companies.

After a day's unhappy incarceration, I was let out of jail, and eventually got on another bus and ended up seeing Al Hirt in New Orleans. I enjoyed myself, although I didn't meet anyone or make any friends. I came back by bus but, this time, I was careful not to sit in the wrong seat.

Sometimes, I can hardly credit my own naïvety. I drove the 'Blue Streak' up to New York for a weekend and was delighted when I saw a sign that said "Parking". I drove into the parking lot and it seemed very efficient: a guy took my car and gave me a ticket and I thought it was fantastic service. But when I went to collect my car on the Monday, they wanted $27. I couldn't believe it. The car only cost $90 and I was being asked to pay $27 to park it! I was so unworldly that I thought maybe I'd have to pay a dollar for parking. I had to go to the Continental Can office to borrow some money.

When the time finally came for me to leave America, I sailed back across the Atlantic on *The Queen Mary*. I drove the 'Blue Streak' to the port and parked it on the quay, this time without caring about the possibility of any parking fee. In fact, I left it with the keys inside and a note on the windscreen: "I hope somebody enjoys this car as much as I have". It wasn't worth anything.

Recalling my time in America, I was preoccupied in learning as much as possible about the business. I realised I had to make the most of this opportunity. I took copious notes and worked hard at learning as much as I could, but socially I was completely hopeless. I came back home still anything but confident, yet fired with an enthusiasm for realising my business potential.

HOW I GOT MY E-TYPE

Dad dominated just about any room he ever entered. He was such a commanding personality that it always seemed to be him talking and everyone else listening. And there was never the slightest doubt that whatever he said went. He ruled his world with an iron fist. But there were ways to get round him and I learned one of them from my mother: "If you really want your Dad to buy you something, tell him he can't afford it."

As a young man, I loved speed. I used to race motorbikes at Dunboyne and at Long Kesh, the old airfield that later became a prison. And I always loved fast cars. When Jaguar brought out its beautiful E-type in 1961, I wanted one very badly. It was the ultimate fast car and I set my heart on getting one.

I took Mum's advice and I told my Dad that I didn't suppose the business could afford to buy me a company car. He was outraged at the suggestion. Of course, the business could afford a company car for me, he insisted!

But there was much more outrage when he saw me drive up in a wonderful new white Jaguar E-type. "What are you doing driving that?", he said angrily. "But Dad, you told me we could afford a car",

I replied, with as much innocence as I could manage. "Not that car!",
he snorted furiously. I think he realised that, for once in his life, he
had been outsmarted, and he allowed me to keep the car, which I
raced from time to time over roads in Ireland, primarily Dunboyne
and the Phoenix Park and also at Long Kesh in Northern Ireland.

II
BUILDING APACE

CHAPTER 5
STARTING OUT ON MY OWN

**Now you can put your own ideas into effect and show
what you're really made of.**

During my time in the US at Continental Can, I had worked hard and
had learned a great deal about the packaging business: about
equipment, planning production, finance and how to get accounts
done quickly. I believed I'd really got to know the business.

I had lots of great ideas for developing the family business, but
Dad didn't go along with them. I didn't like the way he was running
things and I knew that he was wrong. He had taken opportunities
and battled to achieve what we had. Now, I wanted to look at things
strategically and plan for growth but he didn't like my ideas or
understand them. This frustrated me.

Things were changing in Ireland in the early 1960s and we were
faced with a number of difficult issues. I believed that the biggest
challenge was that Ireland had entered into a free trade agreement
with the UK covering a 10-year transitionary period. I knew that this
would spell the death-knell for our business, because we would be
faced gradually with more competition from companies like Reed
Corrugated Cases and Bowater, much more highly capitalised and
better resourced than we were. We were protected by the tariffs that
existed at the time, but free trade threatened Irish businesses.

But, with our business growing at 15% or 20% a year, Dad
couldn't see the problems looming ahead. I knew we would lose a lot
of customers because the tariff barriers were coming down, but I
couldn't convince him of the difficulties we faced.

Dad and I argued a lot and he regularly told me: "Every time you
open your mouth, your brains drop out!". I remember one time I was
pushing him to invest in new machinery that he really didn't want to
buy. Suddenly, he banged the table and asked me, "How the hell do

you think your father ran this business before you came along?". I looked at him calmly and replied, "Do you know, Dad, I often wonder". To his credit, he laughed. But he still refused to see my point of view.

I was frustrated but, at least, I could drive my car and the motorbikes as fast as I liked, even if I was held back from driving the business forward.

A LESSON LEARNT IN LONDON

Further confrontations with my Dad were avoided when I left Ireland again for a while. This time, I went to London for six months to study time and motion techniques and business methods at Associated Industrial Consultants in Richmond.

I had to find myself an apartment and couldn't believe my luck when I found one in Buckingham Gate, right near the Palace. It was half the price of anything else on offer. I soon found out why. I fell asleep on the first night and, at about 5:30am the next morning, I was woken up to the deafening sound of a military bugle! My apartment was right over Horse Guards Parade and, every day, I was woken by their reveille and the sound of horses clattering along the road. I didn't get a good night's sleep for six months – to get eight hours sleep, I had to go to bed before 9:30pm.

That was one of my first important lessons in life – one I have never forgotten. If something looks too good to be true, then it probably *is* too good to be true. If it's cheap, find out why. There's always a reason. But not all of the surprises I encountered in London were unhappy ones.

INDEPENDENCE

Once the six months in London were over, I went back to Ireland, but the relationship with my father continued to get worse. My Dad still wouldn't accept my ideas for the business. He was Chairman and Chief Executive and I was a Director in charge of the factory, but I didn't have any real power and couldn't implement any of my plans.

Dad would always say we would do it, but nothing would get done. I was bursting with plans and ambitions and I became frustrated by his attitude – and so I decided to leave.

I wouldn't say I fell out with my father exactly. He had sent me to America to learn the most up-to-date techniques of corrugation, which I did. I came back and wanted to apply them: he wouldn't apply them. He was used to doing business his way and I was frustrated as hell. That's when I decided to do my own thing. It was more frustration than anything else. We didn't fight about it.

I told my Dad I was going to leave the business and start up my own company and I was surprised to find he was right behind me. He reacted very positively and gave me tremendous support. I remember he said, "Well, now you can put your own ideas into effect and show me what you're really made of".

It was an amazing time. I was full of enthusiasm for getting started on my own. I went over to England and started to scout around to find suitable premises. Dad gave me invaluable backing.

In 1962, I found a possible business base in Bryn, near Wigan in North West England, and Dad came over to have a look. Although I was very young when I left, it was still an area I knew well and it felt like my 'ancestral home'. Dad had a good contact, Philip Jacobs, a successful businessman based in nearby Liverpool, another good reason for the location as he was to become one of our most important customers.

The owner of the premises showed us around and he obviously took to my father. Dad asked how much he wanted for the buildings. He named a large amount and Dad smiled and said that sounded reasonable. Dad walked around and started stamping his foot on the floor in different places. The owner was bemused and asked, "Mr Smurfit, if you don't mind me asking, why are you doing that?". Dad gave him a friendly smile and said, "Why, I'm looking for the shafts, because surely, at that price, this must be a gold mine?". The owner laughed and brought his price down to one that we could agree: around £7,000.

As it happened, the joke about shafts wasn't too far from the truth as the factory was built above disused coalmines and not really suited to the heavy machinery that we used. Later, we had to strengthen the floors to avoid our business disappearing into a hole in the ground.

Dad helped me buy the factory and gave me some money to start me off in business on my own. Of course, he also helped me with contacts, as my first deal was with Philip Jacobs. I think he was just curious to see what would happen. But the relationship between my business and his was to become complicated because, not long afterwards, he took his business public – against my advice.

JEFFERSON SMURFIT (PACKAGING) LIMITED

My business, Jefferson Smurfit (Packaging) Limited, was set up with myself as the majority shareholder. Dad, Bill Gleeson and Dermot Barnes also invested in it, as well as Philip Jacobs. He was a big supplier of garments to Marks & Spencer and used a lot of cardboard boxes. At the time, I was looking for some security of orders and he took a 25% share in the business, put a lot of orders my way, and eventually made a lot of money when he sold his share. He was a nice man and a good businessman. I listened to him and had a lot of time for him. I was glad when his investment paid off so well for him.

As an aside, Philip Jacobs' nephew was Brian Epstein, who became well-known as the manager of The Beatles. I met him at his home two or three times. I went to see The Beatles in Liverpool when they were nobody and I even saw them in Hamburg. This was before they took off. But I was much too busy worrying about setting up my packaging business to worry too much about a new group. I had my own *Hard Day's Night*! Lots of them.

My brother Alan came over to Wigan to help me with sales. I still had the E-type Jaguar at the time, but we often just parked it at the front of the factory to look impressive because we couldn't afford the petrol for it. Like my brother Jeff, Alan is a warm, sociable person, and he proved to be a good salesman.

The relationship with Dad changed now he was Chairman of my Wigan company and I was Managing Director. I didn't grow to really love him until I was in my 30s, but I always respected him and began to see that what he had done for me was tremendous. He had given me a set of values, a set of standards, and an ambition that I didn't realise was burning so much inside of me. I was always going to make a success of my life.

A FRIENDLY INVESTMENT

Good friends were thin on the ground when I was a young man, but one arrived in the simplest of circumstances. At Bryn one day, a young man called Maurice Buckley came to see me. He had just set up his own business, making rubber dies for box printing and he wanted to supply my Wigan plant. I was impressed by his approach and his enthusiasm and asked if I could visit his factory. He said, "I don't have a factory. I work from an attic in Warrington". So I said we'd go off to his attic and we'd go in his car, which was a small battered old Ford Popular parked next to my E-type Jaguar. Maurice apologised for his car and I gave him a piece of advice that came from the heart, "Never apologise for yourself to anybody. You are what you are".

It was one of those grey Lancashire afternoons with heavy rain and we set off down the East Lancs Road to Warrington. I asked Maurice about his business, "What is the capital of your company?". Maurice seemed perplexed and said, "Look Michael, I don't understand these things. I don't know what the capital of a business is and I don't know about return on investment. I just know what I want to achieve".

I said I liked the cut of his jib. I sent him along to the bank manager to get a loan. I said I would pay £250 for 25% of his business.

He was happy, I was happy and we became friends. We shared the same roots, being born in Lancashire and growing up in war-time. We also both had a fascination with America and the American approach to business, and a hunger to make something of ourselves. We went on to share a lot of business interests, one of which was to cause us both major problems, but that happened much later.

Maurice's memories of our meeting and early times together as pals are interesting. He recalls:

It was a miserable Lancashire day when I met Michael. He had the same charisma as his father, who had previously impressed me a great deal. Michael had a desk as big as a Hollywood producer. There was a picture of JFK on the wall. It was magical; we chatted and quickly there was a chemistry.

I didn't understand what the capital of the business was or return on investment, I just wanted to start in business. He said he'd give me £250 for 25% of my business going forward and I said "OK". It was a lot of money then. We became friends and met every week.

It became evident to me that Michael had the basic ingredients to go a lot further than where he was at the time. Michael was very, very sharp, very energetic and very disciplined. He was a real tiger. People loved him but he was tough to work with. He was very demanding and very ambitious. I believe that Michael was driven, the same as I was. I know what drove me early on was anger and I would say a lot of anger drove Michael, too. I was angered by the iniquities and inequalities of British society, the way people talked down to you and the golf clubs kept you out.

Michael eventually became friendly with the managing directors of Bowater and High Grade and Reed Paper Company but, at first, he was looked on as just another Paddy opening up in England in a little box factory. He wasn't seen then as the hero he is today.

If we had been out for dinner, he would always go into the factory afterwards to see the night shift. The people who worked for him loved and respected him. They were frightened of him but he had the ability to know when to pat them on the back and when to kick them up the backside – and that is the art of management.

He had the ability to take risks but also the ability to understand the consequences of risks. I was more of a gambler, which cost me dearly at different points of my life. Whatever Michael would gamble might hurt him, but it would never destroy him.

Years after we met, Michael admitted that the £250 was a steal. But I asked him where else I could have got the sort of education I got from him. He said he had never thought of it like that. I would happily have given him £250 just to learn all the things he taught me.

Maurice became a close friend but, back then, I was more concerned with trying to build a business. My first ambition was to get some decent machines because basically I was dealing with clapped-out equipment. I was so proud to get my first new corrugator. Packaging was all I knew and hard work began to pay off as we secured contracts to supply top-flight customers like Heinz, Kellogg's and United Biscuits.

HARD WORK PAYS OFF

We moved the business from Wigan to St Helens, following a fire at the Bryn factory. As the business began to make money, I was able to reward everyone involved in it through a system of bonuses based on production and performance. I believe that money motivates people. People work because they need money: money to raise families and for themselves. If you create an environment conducive to happiness and contentment, with cleanliness, good conditions, and good food in the canteen, then you create a social environment with a family atmosphere – which is what I set out to achieve – and then good people don't leave.

I knew by now something of the importance of choosing the right people. Good people are always hard to find, while bad people are easy to find. If you pay people well and create a good atmosphere for them to work in, then they'll stay with you. That's why so few people ever left Smurfit. We had an atmosphere of something special.

But moving from Bryn to St Helens also gave me an early experience of the power of the trade unions. Bryn was then part of the Newton le Willows branch of SOGAT, the trade union for the paper and packaging industry in the UK. It was very docile and gave us little or no trouble but St Helens, I soon discovered, was very different. Here, we had to deal with the much more militant Liverpool branch and we soon found that dealing with the union could be much, much more difficult. Compared to Bryn, the troubles with the union turned our experience in St Helens into a disaster.

But it didn't put me off. I was still very optimistic about the future. My business in England was going well and I was happily settled there. We were the first company in the UK to install an 87-inch Martin corrugator, significantly increasing our output, and I was looking at expansion through opening other factories.

CHAPTER 6
A FAMILY MAN

**I don't think that I would ever have succeeded as I did
if I hadn't met Norma. She was fantastic.**

As a young man, I was very naïve in many ways, particularly
sexually. I had very little confidence and I didn't see myself as good-
looking. I hadn't been to university or had the chance to meet people.
I didn't have many friends from school. I had no real mates.

NORMA

One night, during the time I was in London studying with Associated
Industrial Consultants in Richmond, I went to a party at a local hotel
dance-hall. I still felt very shy and awkward but I was determined to
try to meet people and make friends. There were three pairs of legs in
front of me and I asked the owner of the best pair of legs to dance –
she became my girlfriend and, later, my wife.

This was Norma Triesman, who was a hairdresser working in the
centre of London. Driving her home one night, I asked her what
church she attended. We were just going past The Angel, Islington,
when she told me that she was Jewish. I nearly crashed the car, as I
had never met a Jewish person in my life before.

To be frank, I don't remember too many of the details of meeting
the woman who was to become my wife or much of our early time
together, but Norma recalls:

*I was with my sister and a girlfriend one Saturday night when I first
met Michael. We used to go dancing most Saturdays, to
Hammersmith one week and the Lyceum another. I've no idea why we
went to Richmond, which is miles away down the Piccadilly Line. We
were all standing around waiting to be asked to dance, as you did in*

those days. This Irishman came up and asked me to dance. It was Michael. He said later that he'd asked me because I had the 'slimmest hips' or something! Then he asked me out a few nights later. I remember he had very short hair, which I hated. It was in a sort of crew-cut, and shaved up the back of his neck.

The first night we met he had his first drink. He had never drunk in his life before and he had a lager and lime. He hadn't a clue about anything, and neither had I at the time really, although living in London taught you a few things. Men in Ireland only ate steak and chips, but I introduced Michael to other kinds of food. We went out to different restaurants and drank the old Mateus Rosé! I was working in Knightsbridge, hairdressing, and we went out to all the jazz clubs like Ronnie Scott's and Humphrey Lyttelton's. I think for our first date he took me to see Lawrence of Arabia *somewhere in Victoria.*

I knew nothing about Ireland then. My perception of Irish people was the guys who dug the roads. The relationship was all very secret at first. When he had gone back to Dublin, I went over for a weekend and we didn't stay with the family. No-one knew. Then he used to come over for weekends. It was quite romantic, he used to 'phone every night and send me letters, which I still have. He could never spell 'Wednesday'!

Quite honestly, I don't know how we drifted into getting engaged. There was the religious difference; my family was horrified at first, all except my grandmother, who said, "Oh, just do what you want!". My father was troubled that Michael was not Jewish. Not that he was very religious himself. Although we would observe the Passover, we didn't go to the synagogue or anything like that and I never attended Jewish schools. I went to Church of England schools.

Michael's family were horrified as well. But, in Ireland, in those days they didn't understand anyone who was not a Catholic. They just didn't meet non-Catholics.

Meanwhile, I had still been seeing a lot of Norma, despite our parents' disapproval. I took her all round Europe in my convertible E-type. It was a wonderful time. I had a beautiful woman to go with my beautiful car. At last, I began to conquer my crippling shyness.

MARRIAGE

We had been going out together for 18 months and, before moving to England to open my factory, I asked her to marry me. Norma was a city girl who had never heard of Wigan. All I could offer her was a life in a rented home far away from her family and everyone she knew, but she accepted.

We had a small private wedding in a Catholic church in London. There were only four people at the wedding, just Norma's sister Gillian, my brother Jeff and ourselves, as none of our parents would attend. Norma agreed that our children would be brought up as Catholic and they were. She always kept her word.

Our marriage was followed by a four-day honeymoon in Gibraltar, as that was all the time I could spare when I was busy setting up my business.

Norma was very shy, too. She was always very quiet, but she gave me a lot of confidence and we were great together. She came from a very working-class background. Her mother had died very tragically some years earlier and Norma lived with her sister and father. With strong echoes of my own Dad's experiences, her father was against our relationship because I was Catholic, though in the fullness of time he became a great friend to me. My parents were equally against us, as they objected to me being involved with a Jewish girl. I wasn't accepted by Norma's Dad, and Norma wasn't really accepted by my Dad. However, in time, they got to know and really like her.

Moving to Wigan from the middle of London was a big wrench for Norma. We knew nobody in Lancashire when we arrived there, apart from a few relations of mine down the road. We rented a small bungalow opposite the factory. It had one sitting-room, two bedrooms, a bathroom, a kitchen and a mouse and was situated right behind a filling station. There was a slag heap, a pub and the bungalow, then my derelict factory. Down the road, there was Reed's corrugated plant, which was one of the biggest factories in England in those days, just a short walk from my little 'Irish' factory.

Again, Norma recalls:

I never thought that Michael would become such a good provider. When he said, "We've got a bungalow", I was so excited I was showing the plans to everyone in the hairdresser's. I was so thrilled at the prospect of a two-bedroomed bungalow right opposite the factory in Wigan! I had never been north of Watford. It was all very strange, but when you're in love you don't think about things like that.

I became pregnant pretty quickly. Michael's aunt and family were in St Helens and they were the only people I knew. It was hard to understand what everyone was saying to me in Wigan but everyone there was charming to me. Michael was always working a lot and he would come in at night and talk about it a bit but really I was busy with the baby. He gave me £8.50 a week for the housekeeping, which was a lot of money in those days. I liked cooking and I always had his meal ready for him when he got home.

Starting up on my own just outside Wigan was probably the single most exciting period of my life. At last, after years in my father's shadow, I was in charge of my own company. I was on my own – it was exhausting yet exhilarating. And I found my crippling early lack of confidence had virtually vanished as I did everything I could to grasp this great chance with both hands.

In fact, my self-esteem and confidence grew very rapidly after my marriage. Once I came out from under my father's wing, I quickly found that my whole outlook on life became completely different. For such a long time, Dad had been a very dominating and controlling figure in my life, but now I was making my own decisions and running my own show.

Crucially, I also had the perfect partner by my side. Norma played a huge part in my sudden self-assurance. She was very supportive and loving, always there with her quiet but steadfast backing. She was a wonderful woman, a wonderful mother, a wonderful everything. She created a comfortable home and was a tower of strength to me.

I even stopped racing the cars and motorbikes that had been my earlier passion. When I got married, my Mum said I ought to give up racing because of the dangers it brought into my life. I decided she was right and that was the end of my racing days. I don't think I really missed it.

CHILDREN ARRIVE

We didn't make many friends in Lancashire. With a young family and each other, we didn't need anyone else. We just had each other and we were very happy.

Within two years, we had two sons. Our first son, Tony, was born in 1963 and I was delighted to be starting a family. It was what I always wanted. What was the point of creating the business I was creating, and would go on to create, if there was no one to leave it to? In those days, fathers weren't expected to attend births, which suited me fine. In fact, the only birth that I have been present at was the arrival of my youngest son, Christopher, and that one birth many years later was definitely enough for me.

Our second son, Michael, was born prematurely in 1965 in St Helens Infirmary, the hospital I was born in. Michael nearly died at birth. He was given the last rites and it was a terrible time for us, but mercifully he pulled through. He grew into a healthy child with an excellent brain who excelled at sport. Now he's over six feet tall and married with a family of his own.

The arrival of Tony and Michael in quick succession was followed in due course by the arrival of our two daughters, Sharon and Tracy.

When our children were small, I had little time to spend with them during the week, but I saw more of them at weekends and we had great holidays together.

I remember one time we planned to go to Newquay in Cornwall and were looking forward to this wonderful holiday. We'd booked a cottage – just 100 yards from the beach – and it was fantastic. The only problem was that the 100 yards was straight down a cliff. We checked into the cottage, but checked out the next day because it was too risky with small children. We booked into a hotel and I learned to check things thoroughly in advance.

SUCCESS DAWNS

Everyone of a certain age remembers exactly where he or she was when the terrible news came through that President John F. Kennedy had been fatally shot in Dallas on 22 November 1963. I was in the bath in our little bungalow in Bryn. John Kennedy was such an inspirational young leader that Norma and I had really identified with him. Suddenly, we felt we had lost someone who would have achieved so much for the world.

At the time, I had come to admire a great deal about the whole go-getting American lifestyle. It seemed very positive and forward-looking. I wore US-style button-down shirts and had a big office with a big desk built by my joiner, Harold Foster. On the wall, I proudly hung a large picture of John Kennedy. The charismatic President had been my hero and I was surprised to find I was very emotional about his death. Somehow, with his youthful energy and zest for life, he symbolised the future to many people of my generation and I still believe his assassination was a tragic loss. Not that I had much time for reflection about the American dream or any other kind of introspection, as I threw myself into the hectic task of getting my new business off the ground.

In the early days, I used to work really hard. I couldn't wait to get up in the morning to get to work. I would work up to 14 or 15 hours a day, often seven days a week, and it was only every now and then that I would take some time off. I got so involved in the business sometimes, I almost felt as if I hated coming home. I loved running my own show. I had so much energy and there was so much going on. I kept a notebook and pen beside the bed as I often woke in the night with an idea that I wanted to write down. I've always been disciplined about writing things down.

I enjoyed every second of it but I did take the occasional Sunday morning off and, every month, I would take Norma out for a slap-up dinner in the Adelphi Hotel in Liverpool or the Piccadilly Hotel in Manchester. Anywhere they had Mateus Rosé, which was all I drank at that stage. I didn't know anything else.

Within a year of starting the business, it was beginning to make money and we were able to move from the bungalow in Bryn to 40 Forest Grove, St Helens. This was a semi-detached house and the first house I ever bought. I took out a mortgage to buy it and I was very proud when we moved into the first house of our own.

CHAPTER 7
TAKING CHARGE

Dad said, "I'd like you to come back to Ireland and run the business" and I replied, "Thank you. When do you want me to start?".

Back in Dublin, Dad was keen to raise some capital. He had always had an income, but he never had capital. So, in 1964, Jefferson Smurfit & Sons Limited was floated on the Irish Stock Exchange in Dublin.

On 30 June, the opening share price was 10s 6d (52.5p). The price shot up to 13s (65p) and it closed at 12s 10½p (63p). Family, friends and employees had been given shares and it was surprising to find that a number of them promptly sold their shares in order to make a quick buck. I was annoyed because I believed that the shares had been undervalued and I was determined that it was the last time this would ever happen. I also believed that too many shares had been given away, particularly to those people who did not return our loyalty but quickly sold. It was the people who kept their shares who gained the most in the long-term and they made a lot of money. I believed that Dad should have been better advised. From then on, I questioned all the advice that I got and, in the end, I always did my own thing.

"COME BACK TO IRELAND"

Towards the end of 1965, I had to review my plans following a phone call from Dad. At first, he just said that he'd like to come over and see me on Friday afternoon in a pub that he used to go to for a pint whenever he visited us in St Helens. That was the only time I ever went into a pub and I'd never had a pint in my life. Even today, I've never had a pint in a pub.

The pub was opposite my factory. When I went over, there he was, smoking and enjoying his pint, ready for the conversation that was to change both of our lives.

I said, "Hi Dad" and we exchanged the usual pleasantries before I asked, "To what do I owe the honour?".

Dad said, "I'd like you to come back to Ireland and run the business" and I replied, "Thank you. When do you want me to start?". "Monday" was the answer.

Dad was then 56 years old and he had been working very hard ever since he was 12. He was worn out and he knew it. He admitted that the edge had gone from his adventurous business spirit. He said he had seen what I was capable of in the UK and he was at a stage when he was ready to step back and let someone else take on the responsibility for developing the business in Ireland.

It was agreed that I would become Joint Managing Director together with my brother Jeff, with Dad as Chairman and Chief Executive. Jeff and I would both receive a basic salary and a bonus related to profits.

This was a fair deal. If the company performed well, we would be rewarded with increased bonuses. If it didn't, then this would be reflected in our pay. Everyone was happy with the arrangement at the time, but it was to cause controversy in the future.

It was also agreed that Jefferson Smurfit & Sons Limited would purchase my company, Jefferson Smurfit (Packaging) Limited. By this time, my business had already expanded to two factories and it was worth more than my father's – about £1.5 million to his £1 million.

I agreed to move to Dublin and to run both businesses from there.

THINKING OF TAKE-OVERS

The year 1966 was the start of a time of great change, both for the family and for the business.

I very quickly pushed ahead with a second factory on land in Walkinstown that Dad had bought in October 1964. The plant at Clonskeagh was fast becoming too small as the business expanded.

At the end of 1966, production began at Walkinstown, allowing us to turn Clonskeagh into a dedicated paper mill.

This was progress certainly, but with the Anglo-Irish free trade agreement now into its third year, enormous change was on the way. I was concerned that we were too small to survive against competition from the big UK packaging companies. I came to the conclusion that the only way for us to survive was to attack.

Once I felt firmly in charge, I went to see Dad – he was still Chairman and the controlling shareholder – and said, "You know, Dad, regarding this Anglo-Irish free trade agreement, when the tariff barriers come down, two things are going to happen quickly. We're going to lose a lot of customers, because they're going to go out of business. We're going to face an increase in our bad debts. Secondly, we're going to have massive competition from Reed in Northern Ireland and somebody will set up in Ireland against us".

"OK, that's the problem – what's the solution?", he said with characteristic bluntness. I said that the Irish packaging industry was pretty much fragmented and I thought that we should be the ones to rationalise it. Dad wanted to know how we'd do that, and I said we'd take over the other companies.

"How are we going to take them over?", he wanted to know. I replied, "I don't know, but I'm going to find a way".

MERGER NEGOTIATIONS

In the meantime, there were tortuous and distracting negotiations involving the sale of my UK business to the Smurfit family business. Martin Rafferty of Allied Irish Investment Bank acted for me. Charles Rawlinson, Richard Hooper and Kevin Wylie of the Investment Bank of Ireland acted for the public company. Martin Rafferty later became a director of Smurfit, while Kevin Wylie acted for Smurfit again in our first take-over deal.

It was difficult for the public company to expand before these negotiations were concluded, because I had the rights to the Smurfit name in the UK. So what had started off as a natural thing between father and son became a quite contentious and difficult situation. It was fraught because, on the one hand, I couldn't be seen to be blocking the public company shareholders from doing something and, at the same time, I wanted to defend my own rights. To make matters worse and infinitely more complicated, as the discussions went on I was very busy running both companies.

Reaching agreement on the value of my company was problematic. I put my value on it, but those acting for the public company couldn't agree to it because I was looking at what it was going to achieve in the future. It would certainly have become as big as or bigger than LinPac became – at the time, LinPac was a comparably-sized UK family packaging business that was eventually sold in 2004 for £700 million. I wasn't looking for anything like that. The accountants involved were looking only at the current valuations and couldn't agree to my figure, which was based on future valuations. It looked like stalemate but then I came up with an idea.

I said, "I'll tell you what I'll do. I'll take B shares with no dividends for 15 years and, in 15 years' time, the B shares will become A shares and have dividend rights". This allowed the accountants to discount the future dividend flow into the calculation and agree to my valuation. This made me the largest stockholder in the company, owning more than my Dad. The deal had brought our family stockholding back up, but I was about to change all that when I embarked on my mission to take over other companies.

DAD'S SECOND SURPRISE

Dad seemed happy to take a back seat, while I relished being in charge. He had certainly earned the right to take life a little easier, but he still retained the ability to spring a surprise.

Early in the autumn of 1969, he called me and my brother Jeff into the Boardroom. He asked us to sit down and said, "My sons, when I sign this document in front of me, I will effectively transfer my entire shareholding and all of my wealth into your hands". We were shocked. It was totally unexpected, because even back in those days this represented a considerable sum of money.

My father's solicitor, Oliver Fry, was clearly alarmed and protested that he could not advise such a step because effectively my father was destituting himself. Back then, you had to live on for another seven years to make such a gift tax-free. My father did not take any notice of Mr Fry's warnings. He turned to the concerned lawyer and answered his protests with words I will never forget. He said, "Mr Fry, if my sons cannot look after me, it is better I should never have lived".

Needless to say, Jeff and I were gobsmacked. Dad had no pension. Back then, there was no pension provision for business owners. So the first thing Jeff and I did was to arrange to buy Dad an annuity. We wanted to make sure he would be OK if anything happened to us or the company.

I was shocked by my Dad's decision and, afterwards, I reflected that it must have taken foresight and courage to do what he did. It was just typical of the man.

But it was that transfer, plus the sale of my own company to the Group, which made me the largest individual stockholder, still the position today.

Incidentally, my father passed away exactly seven years and five months to the day after he signed the document.

CHAPTER 8
MAKING A LIFE IN IRELAND

It was an exciting time. I felt really alive. I might have been a late starter, but I was catching up fast.

When I went home from that chat in the pub with Dad and told Norma that we were off to Ireland, there was not even a moment of questioning. Her attitude was simple, down-to-earth and entirely typical of her: "You're my husband. If that's what you want to do, then that's what we'll do".

By then my youngest brother, Dermot, had joined the family business. He started at 16, making samples, and at 19 he was managing two machines and a team of eight women. In his early 20s, he became assistant mill manager. My sisters, Kathleen (who was always known as 'Kay') and Sheila, also worked in the business, undertaking office duties. My sister Barbara was the baby of the family and too young at that stage to be working.

Dad also had said that his house at that time was too big for him and he'd like to sell it to me so that Norma and I could live there with our family. He sold it to me for £12,000 and I had to take out a 25-year loan to raise the money. By the time the last day of the mortgage arrived, I had forgotten all about it as by then I was earning very good money. Today, it is worth a great deal more, especially after my daughter Tracy had it completely remodelled.

Norma and I moved into Dad's home with our children and he moved to an apartment. My mother had not been well for some time: she suffered from Alzheimer's disease and required constant care. She moved into a house near us where she could be looked after and we could all visit her regularly. Towards the end of her life, she didn't recognise anyone except me. She shared my love of horse-racing and died peacefully while watching a race on television.

SOCIALISING IN DUBLIN

After we moved to Dublin, Norma and I began to have much more of a social life. I met a guy called Joe Murphy of Tayto Crisps. He was the man who invented cheese and onion potato crisps. He was a big customer of Smurfit and became a good friend of mine. He was very gregarious and introduced me to a lot of people and he and his wife Bunnie were very good to Norma and me. Joe and Bunnie introduced us into Irish society. Sadly, Joe died a few years ago.

The late John Reihill had been a friend from my youth. His family lived near our family and, when we moved back to Dublin, Norma and I became friends with him and his wife Emer. She was a lovely person who had a way of putting me in my place if she thought I was getting above myself. I could always take it from her. Sadly, she died of cancer and left John with a young family. Norma and I missed her.

The days of restricting ourselves to a monthly outing for a meal were over. We started to go out to dinner more with others and we built a good group of friends. Every Saturday night, we'd go to the Intercontinental Hotel in Dublin, which became Jury's, and have a dinner with friends. Along with Joe and Bunnie, there would be another friend, Eamon Donnolly and his wife, Joan, along with John and Emer.

Eamon helped me to learn about wine in an unusual way. He got me involved in a poker game every Monday night. It was an unusual type of poker game. There were seven of us and we'd meet in a different house every week. We had a four-course dinner, which started and finished promptly at a set time, and then we played poker. If you were late for dinner, you had to pay a fine of something like £1 for every minute you were late. During dinner, we had wine tastings. Each person would try four different wines, so over a couple of years of doing this I learned to tell the difference between good wine and cheap wine.

I was only ever an average poker player, unlike my brother Alan, who is considered one of the world's best. That's not an idle boast: he has won a world poker championship. But it was always a fun evening and a great way to learn about wine.

BROADENING HORIZONS

My horizons were being broadened in other ways, too. I also developed an interest in art, thanks to Norma, who always had a great eye and a real love of art. We began to buy paintings and I think we bought our first Yeats for £500. At the time, this was a fortune and it was not easy to find the money. Today, I believe the painting is probably worth more than €500,000.

My head office was very near my house and I was able to jog home most nights. I had recognised that physical fitness was essential for the job that I was doing because with the long hours, the fitter I was, the less fatigued I was. I still use an exercise bike every day for about an hour.

Most nights, I ate out for dinner. I used to attend as many as 200 business dinners a year and Norma often came with me. I loved it – I still do.

I was earning a good salary now and we could afford some help in the house, but we never had a lifestyle with a lot of home-help. We both preferred to keep our home life as normal and relaxed as possible, for ourselves and for our children.

When I wasn't going out for dinner, Norma would cook and I was happy to sit and eat dinner in front of the TV. I was away travelling a lot and didn't see much of my children during the week, but I had a very contented home-life and Norma supported me brilliantly in everything we did.

I had so much self-confidence at this stage. I had gone from being the shy and retiring boy to become an assured and fulfilled man who had found his place in the world.

Of course, I was still learning about business, about new business ideas, about how to hire people and how to motivate people. At the same time, I was learning about the world, learning about wines, learning about art, and learning about all sorts of other things. It was an exciting time. I felt really alive. I might have been a late starter, but I was catching up fast.

TIME FOR THE FAMILY

Building a business is a demanding occupation but, however hard I worked, I always managed to find time for the family. I was fortunate that Norma was such a wonderful mother, so when I was rushing around trying to clinch some deal or other I always knew our children were in the safest of hands. But, although some people might think I was a total workaholic, I did believe in enjoying myself as well. And I didn't like anything getting in the way.

Maurice Buckley recalls:

We were staying in a hotel with our friend Leo Reynolds and his family. It was not that long after the children had started to arrive and we had five little kids between us. When we arrived, we found the hotel had not provided the cots we had ordered. We didn't know what to do and we were all busy complaining until Michael came up with the answer. He walked to the reception and said to us: "Put the babies on the counter". Then he said to the staff: "Right, you look after the babies, we're going for dinner". We had the cots within 30 minutes.

I loved all of my kids very much and I always made sure we had a summer holiday together. We'd have beach holidays in Ireland and then we started going to Majorca, sometimes with Maurice and his family. He likes to tease me by recalling:

It was none too grand in those early days. We laid on lilos on the sand because we only had one deckchair. And who should be sitting on our solitary deckchair but Michael? There's a picture of him somewhere sitting down with a newspaper – the Financial Times, *of course! That was Michael, 100% engrossed in business. But he did still find time for the kids.*

Indeed, our holidays were always important times for us to be all together as a family. I can remember taking up skiing, because I realised it was something I would be able to do with the kids as I grew older. I was in my early 30s when I thought it through very carefully. I asked myself, "What can you do with your kids all your life?". The answer was skiing and golf.

SKIING

I already could play golf, but I had never tried skiing. I am self-taught in just about every other area of my life, so naturally I just thought I would pick up skiing all by myself.

I didn't know there were such things as skiing instructors. I went out onto the slopes at St Moritz without any preparation. It sounds pretty naïve, I know, but I never thought I'd need anything like skiing lessons – I didn't even know they existed. I just wandered in and they said, "Do you need boots?". "Yeah," I said. "Do you need skis?" "Yeah." I was just in my ordinary clothes. Some people showed me how to put the boots on. I got on the ski-lift and the next thing I know I'm being dragged up a mountain! I didn't know how to get on. I didn't know that you had to sit on it. A guy was yelling at me in German – he was trying to help me, but I don't speak German!

When I got to the top, I was all battered and bruised. I came back down somehow and, back in the hotel, when I was getting my key from the reception, one of the other hotel guests noticed how I looked. He asked me if I'd ever skied before and I said, "No". He explained that everyone needs some kind of instruction and offered to take me out the next day and teach me. He became my first ski teacher. Then I got a full-time teacher and learned to ski properly. I enjoyed it and became serious about it.

Norma and I tried to get into a particular hotel, the Suvretta House in St Moritz, when the kids were young. It took me three or four years before we managed it, because they were always booked up years ahead. We ended up going there with the family for 15 years or more, every Christmas and New Year for a fortnight. You had to stay for at least 14 days, although many times I had to come back early due to business. We made a lot of friends there from all over the world, and we would meet up with them each year. Many of them are still friends today. I also learned to play bridge and curling there.

It was a nice time, a family time.

'TROUBLES' AT HOME

But back home, life was not so idyllic. The Ireland of the 1970s and 1980s was very different from the Ireland of today. The 'Troubles' raged north of the border as the IRA was violent in promoting their cause of a united Ireland. People from all backgrounds faced danger and I had to be particularly careful to ensure that my high profile did not put my family at risk.

There was a newspaper story at that time written by a journalist about the notorious Irish criminal, Martin Cahill, who was known as 'The General'. He was supposed to have set out to burgle our house, but when he saw the homely domestic scene, with Norma sitting knitting beside the fire, he decided not to rob us. For many reasons, this story seems highly implausible. We had excellent security at the time and it is unlikely that anyone could have broken in undetected. Also, Norma had fantastic hearing: she would know if a child's breathing changed pattern in the night, and if anyone had been walking around our house, I am pretty sure that she would have heard them. We led a normal life and were in no way ostentatious – but it made a good story.

In 1977, I appointed ex-policeman Pat Dempsey to take charge of our personal security arrangements. He was an Irishman who had been working in England in the Manchester police force. He wanted to bring his family back to Ireland. I moved him into a house next to mine and blocked off the entrance to my home, so anyone wanting to come to our house had to come past Pat's house.

Ireland was then a poor nation in deep recession, with high unemployment. I remember one of my daughters, who has always had a very pressing social conscience, being very upset that she was driven to school by a chauffeur in a big car while many of her friends' parents were out of work and their families were struggling.

In the 1980s, there were several kidnappings of prominent businesspeople who were held to ransom for huge amounts of money. Ben Dunne, then head of the Dunnes Stores business was kidnapped, as was Don Tidey, head of Associated British Foods, and the Guinness heiress, Jennifer Guinness, along with others.

In my own case, I'm not sure how I would have been viewed by the people engaged in this activity. My mother was a Catholic from Belfast in Northern Ireland, while my father was from England. I was considered English by some, Irish by others, Catholic by some, Protestant by others. No-one knew what I was, but I was a high profile person so I made sure we had security.

I received two threats in letters that were considered genuine by the authorities. Both messages said that the sender would kill me. Both originated in Northern Ireland. I didn't waste time worrying about these threats and just got on with my life, with security firmly in place. My only concern was that, should I be unfortunate enough to be killed, proper provision had been be made for my family.

The security arrangements didn't intrude into my life at all. I would get into a car to be driven somewhere and I would get out papers and work while I was being driven around. I could never just sit in the back of a car and do nothing.

There were two attempts to blackmail me. A guy who worked for us threatened to burn down one of our factories. He wanted money. We called the Gardaí (the Irish police). I took a phone call and arranged to meet the blackmailer in the Phoenix Park, Dublin, to hand over the money. The Gardaí arrested him, but he skipped the country and was never charged.

Another time, a safe was stolen from our house. It didn't contain anything of great value to anyone but the family. A message was placed in *The Irish Times* by the thief insisting "Meet me in the Berkeley Court Hotel", and, when we got there, a phone call told us to "go round to Jury's Hotel", where there was yet another phone call. The caller wanted money and said he was with the IRA. His threat was that he would publish the safe contents. They were of no interest to anyone, so we just told him to go ahead and publish them. And that was the last we ever heard from him. The safe eventually was found up in the Dublin mountains.

I would have more concerns now than when I was living in Ireland at the time of IRA activity, when I had actual death threats. I see the world as a much more dangerous place today than I have ever seen it, and that's because of the terrorism factor. I don't think this is something to do with me getting older and feeling that things are not as good as they used to be. There's never been a period before when there were people willing to put a bomb on their body and walk into a place and blow themselves up. How can you stop a suicide bomber?

To be honest, back then, I simply ignored the threats and the security concerns, which never bothered me.

CHAPTER 9
TAKE-OVER TIME

**I walked through the front door one day – a Catholic
walking into a Protestant company – and told them,
"I'm here and I ain't going away".**

Before I went into the sanatorium, I didn't know a corporate take-over from an apple turnover but, by the time I came out, enthused by poring over the exploits of flamboyant and innovative financiers like Jim Slater, I had developed a drive and a real passion for business that was to help me to go on and create the biggest paper-based packaging company in the world.

In fact, it was very early on when I was in the sanatorium that I first became captivated by the idea of taking over other people's businesses. It soon became evident to me that it was the only way our family business would really be able to grow. With a single box plant, our balance sheet was limited and our capital base was very small.

I wanted to understand every detail of how take-overs worked and so I started reading all about them. The more I read, the more fascinated I became. Back then, mergers and acquisitions seemed to be taking place all the time and I tried to learn everything I could about getting control of another company. Even then, I could see that the opportunities for the future were incredible.

I started to buy shares in the second-largest Irish traded company, the Hely Group. It was very badly run, but I knew the business was full of potential if it could be properly organised. I was able to buy shares secretly because, in those days, you were not required to make share purchase disclosures, even though it was a publicly-traded company.

ON THE TAKE-OVER TRAIL

At the time, the Hely Group was much bigger than Smurfit, probably five or six times our size, so initially I went after smaller fry. I picked up CR Bailey, E Pak Cartons, Wood Rozelaar & Wilkes and Irish Paper Sacks very quickly. I also started Pakrite around that time.

The first larger company that I made a bid for was Temple Press Limited, a business that produced folding cartons. It was mainly owned by the Jauncey and Lamb families and my interest was not well received. The Temple Press directors themselves owned over 50% of the shares and, without giving due consideration to me and my proposals, they more or less kicked me out of the Boardroom. It was the first hostile bid in Ireland. The Irish Stock Exchange gave the directors hell over their rejection because they were abusing the rights of the minority shareholders.

Temple Press had just built a factory and had fallen on hard times. Things were not going well for them. The pressure on the directors to accept the deal eventually became so great that they gave in because the minority shareholders wanted to take the offer. And we wouldn't make the deal unless we had more than 50% of the shares.

To my surprise, we won that particular battle and I felt as if I was on a roll. Buying Temple Press for around £350,000 doubled our size at a stroke. Then the dominoes started to fall.

I made a £1 million bid for Browne & Nolan Limited, a privately-owned factory next door to ours, and they accepted our offer, with Alan Nolan joining our Board.

As part of the Browne & Nolan deal, we acquired an interest in a banknote printing company in nearby premises. It was a British company called Thomas De La Rue, which had a contract to print banknotes for the Irish government.

Thomas De La Rue wanted to set up in Ireland and was looking for premises. Dad and I met the Chairman, Sir Arthur Norman, and the chief executive, David Rowe-Beddoe, in the Shelbourne Hotel in Dublin and the deal they set out was so good for Smurfit that I remembered saying to Dad, "I'm sure when these gentlemen get back to London, they will realise that they are offering us too much". So I cleared the table and I wrote the bones of the deal on the tablecloth and I got Dad and Sir Arthur Norman to sign it, so we had evidence of the agreement.

I had been right to strike while the iron was hot. Thomas De La Rue soon did realise how good the deal was for us, but they accepted it.

I followed the Browne & Nolan deal with a bid for Gibson, Guy & Smalldridge, which was very much a Protestant-dominated business. The purchase deal was agreed and we shook hands on it.

A few days later, they got a bid from Clondalkin Group, another Protestant company, and even though our bid was higher, we lost out to Clondalkin. It was remarkable that the shareholders of Gibson, Guy & Smalldridge preferred to take a lower offer from a Protestant company rather than accept Catholic cash.

So that just left the Hely Group for us to target.

THE HELY GROUP

The potential synergy between Browne & Nolan and the Hely Group at that time was fantastic. I knew that, if I could follow the Browne & Nolan acquisition with Hely Group, then we would have a strong position in the cigarette packaging market, the printing market and the securities and banknotes market.

I was now one of the largest shareholders in the Hely Group, but they didn't know anything about it. However, I knew it was still too big for me. Even with all our acquisitions, the Hely Group was about four times our size and it was a very traditional Establishment company. The board was full of Kilroys and Hetheringtons and it was all very Protestant. They were in many businesses: printing, packaging, retailing, TV manufacturing, toy distribution and property. They had a lending company and were the first company in Ireland to use computers.

Of course, this was at a time when the majority of Irish businesses were run by Protestants. In many large companies, Catholics would be employed, but they could never make it into management, no matter how good they were at their job or how considerable the contribution that they could make to the success of the business. In the 1950s and 1960s, there were many companies that Smurfit couldn't sell boxes to, just because we were Catholic and they were Protestant. Up until the 1970s, 5% of the population of Ireland controlled a huge percentage of the wealth. That control extended in some measure to the professions. A lot of the land and large estates and many of the big companies in those days were Protestant-controlled. That was the way it was, and it was generally accepted that this was the way it would stay. It was a situation that I didn't like and, in order to achieve what I wanted, I had to fight against it.

My motto was "I must, I can and I will". And I did.

In December 1969, I was appointed Deputy Chairman of Jefferson Smurfit & Sons Limited, shortly after Smurfit shares were first traded on the London Stock Exchange. In 1970, the name of our company was changed to Jefferson Smurfit Group plc, just as the break I had been waiting for miraculously arrived.

Hely got an order to print millions of greetings cards. It seemed like a real boost to their business, but it was a scam. The guy who ordered the cards never paid for them. The cards were shipped to England, but very few were sold. He kept the money from the ones he did sell and his scam cost Hely a fortune.

The result of this scam was that the Hely Group was left with massive unexpected debts and a management whose credibility was widely questioned. The value of the shares quickly collapsed and the company's image was seriously damaged by the publicity surrounding what had occurred. It didn't take me 24 hours before I was knocking on their door. We were able to buy enough shares to bring our stake quickly up to 25% of the company. I walked through the front door one day – a Catholic walking into a Protestant company – and told the directors, "I'm here and I ain't going away".

It was a shock for some of Ireland's most senior businessmen when I walked in, aged 34, and told them we were taking them over. They couldn't believe it. I said we were a substantial stockholder, then we bought some more stock and made a bid. They didn't want us, but by then Smurfit was the largest stockholder and, although they tried everything, there was nothing they could do to get out of our clutches. I was the brash new guy on the block wanting to take over one of the longest-established companies in Ireland. They tried very hard to find a white knight, someone who would buy the company instead of us, but they couldn't because we had got a block on the shares. In the end, they had to embrace us.

We ended up owning a business with a wonderful head office near Dublin Airport, with computers in the back of it. It was much bigger than Smurfit's head office, so we moved out there. But I didn't push them out. I found it written in the company records that no Catholic should be a director of the Hely Group but I was after growth, not revenge for a policy that was simply a sign of the times. The directors were gentlemen and that is how I treated them. After the take-over, the Chairman said, "I presume you want to take over my office". But I didn't want to rub their noses in it. I used the Boardroom for a number of years as my office. I went onto their Board and eventually became close friends with several of the Hely directors. I won them over just by sheer persistence.

Smurfit buying the Hely Group was the biggest acquisition in Ireland at the time. I learned about the company and how it operated before I started to make changes. They had a lot of money. We sold a number of units that didn't fit in with our plans. This was a defining moment for me, when I really knew I could run a big company.

Hely had all these little companies. They were into printing, cigarette production, accountancy, books, magazines, finance and distribution. They had shops all over Dublin. Every time I dug into what they did, I found a new piece of gold. Hely had working capital coming out of their ears. I think we got the bulk of our money back in two years. I knew that there would be a huge growth in the need for packaging. Paper was taking over from the tin cans and tin boxes that everything used to be sold in previously. Even biscuits were moving to corrugated packaging. It was exciting when I pulled it off. Even now, all these years later, I get animated when I talk about it.

Then I knew the principle worked. I could target other companies. I saw I could run a big business. I knew exactly what to do. I knew how to motivate people. I showed them what they could do and showed them how to do it. I was very demanding and I suppose some people might have been intimidated by me but I didn't set out to scare people. It wasn't like that. I kept strictly to business at all times. The shyness that had dogged my early years had long gone. My confidence and self-esteem grew rapidly as I was forced into the public limelight by virtue of the take-over. People were writing about me and I became known. My father was amazed. I don't think he believed I could do it.

DOMINATING THE MARKET

I remember going to Dad's office after the take-over of the Hely Group and telling him that we were now the second-largest company in Ireland. I was proud of our achievement and I said: "We can now have a great future. I've now got a base from which I can build".

He asked, "Well, how big do you want to grow?", to which I replied, "As big as they'll let us". Dad asked, "Who's they?". "The competition," I said. I knew that the future expansion I dreamed of was not going to be easy, but I was always confident of success. I felt elated, as if the world were my oyster. I was ready to take on any challenge.

As soon as I had sorted out the Hely Group, I knew we were really on our way. We were making money hand over fist because we had control of the marketplace. If I hadn't rationalised the print and packaging industry in Ireland and put them together as a large, strong business, they either would have gone out of business or would have been taken over by a large British business or someone else from outside Ireland.

We were now the fastest-growing business in Ireland and other sectors began to see what I was doing and take-overs and mergers began to happen there as well. Small family businesses were disappearing and larger groups began to appear and more businesses were becoming public and raising capital. It was a fast-moving time.

The Smurfit business was now a conglomerate. My brother Jeff was still Joint Managing Director of our company, handling sales, but I needed to build up our size in Ireland so that I could expand into the UK. I knew we had to keep growing for my plan to work.

TAKE-OVERS IN THE UK

The first company that we picked up in England was WJ Noble Limited, a small public company in Pudsey, near Leeds in the North of England. It was a small folding carton business that was run by an extremely formidable lady, who was something less than approachable. We thought Noble would be a first good move into the UK and made a take-over bid against her wishes.

It took us some time and a great deal of effort, but we finally won the battle for control. Then we got a big shock when we took it over because we never made any real money with the company. We found out that most of their profits were made by the way that they revalued their stock every quarter. They revalued their stock upwards and took it into the profit and loss account, which in those days you could do. We would never have done a thing like that. We were always conservative in our accounts and wrote stock down, not up. We discovered that, while we had taken over the company based on it making certain profits, in fact the profits were illusory.

We had to set about sorting out the company. We put it into corrugated box production and brought over a guy called Sid Moorhouse to run it. He came from the St Helens plant that I had originally owned. Eventually, we made a reasonable return on our investment, but it was anything but easy.

We now had a small foothold in England. One day, I read in a newspaper some interesting news about the Alliance Alders Box Company, which had been one of my main competitors in Lancashire. It had three box factories, in Tamworth, Warrington and Glasgow, and two paper mills. I read that Jim Slater's company, Slater Walker, had bought 25% of Alliance Box. Consequently, I watched developments very carefully and later I met with Slater Walker in London. They wanted me to buy shares in a glass company in the North of England called Foster's Glass, which was a customer of Smurfit. I declined that offer, but I eventually bought their stake in Alliance Alders, which again was a much bigger company than we were.

Pretty soon, it was 'knock, knock, knock' on the Alliance Alders door: "Here I am, we own 25% of the company and we want to bid for the rest". In the cosy inner sanctum of this very established British company, I was about as welcome as an Arctic breeze. This was an upper class and traditional firm run by Colonel This and Sir That. Suddenly, these mainly elderly and staid directors were confronted by a brash young Irishman whose company had just bought a quarter of their company. We had some very protracted negotiations, which were eventually concluded to my satisfaction and – bingo – we had arrived in the UK in a pretty significant way.

I started to attract the attention of large competitors – Bowater, High Grade Container and Reed Corrugated Cases – although we were still small in the UK compared to them.

We followed up the Alliance Alders take-over with some other acquisitions.

GROWTH IN THE UK

We soon had six factories. One of them was Cannon & Clapperton, a fine paper mill just outside Oxford. A few years after we acquired the mill, it landed a big contract to make 'play papers' for all the London schools. The schoolchildren used the paper to draw on – about 4,000 tonnes a year of it, which was about half of the business. It was a great contract until some genius in the Greater London Council decided that the kids should draw on both sides of the paper. This halved the contract and, eventually, led to the closure of the mill. We sold it off and beefed up the paper mill operations in Tamworth, and soon started to make a lot more profit out of the business.

We kept the same people on from the original Board. They were genuinely decent people – Robert Fairclough became our Human Resources Director and proved himself very good at the job and Alan Meades, the Chairman and Managing Director of Alliance Alders, went on to join the Board of Smurfit Group. I liked them and got along well with them all and I think eventually they liked me, too. After a while, they could see that I was simply doing business in a different way. I wasn't antagonistic towards them and I respected them, but I did things my way, running the business in a modern, correct and efficient manner.

While I was busy building the business in England, I also had been out to Japan. I had heard that, in Japan, there was a thing called a continuous running corrugator owned by the Rengo Company. I got in touch with them through Saburo Seki, a Japanese businessman who became a good friend. I went out to see Rengo and met the Chairman, Reiji Kato, who became another good friend, as did his successor, Kaoru Hasegawa. Rengo was a very big company in Japan, far bigger than Smurfit at that stage. I was mesmerised by their factories, because they were so far ahead of the game – they were ultra-efficient. I ordered my first continuous corrugator, which was the first machine of its kind to be installed in any factory anywhere in the world outside Japan.

In those days, to run the standard corrugators, you needed about 14 people. The continuous corrugator brought the manning level down to six or seven. I had negotiated an agreement with the unions for the reduced manning on the new machine, but when it was installed in our UK plant at Tamworth, the unions promptly reneged on the agreement. They could see that, if many more of these new-style corrugators were introduced into England, they were going to lose half their members.

I ended up in the worst of all worlds. Instead of being a low-cost producer, I was now a high-cost producer because I had a capital investment that I couldn't get a return from, because I still had too many people running it. I couldn't afford a strike because they would have taken out all the staff in all the factories, so this time we decided just to live with it. This was the early 70s, when unions were very powerful, the time of Arthur Scargill, the strikes and the riots, the blackouts and three-day weeks.

I remember saying then, "There's no future for me in the UK with the union situation and the way I want to do business". I really was angry. Here I was ahead of the game again and I was being blocked. I remember going back home and saying to Norma, "I am going to make my future and it is not going to be in England".

Nonetheless, in the spring of 1973, I bought the print and packaging division of a UK company, Tremletts Limited. Although by then I'd decided our future was in the US and not the UK, the deal with Tremletts was too good to pass up.

Tremletts was owned by an extraordinary Jewish entrepreneur from London who eventually ran into financial difficulties. Although we ended up paying considerably more than we had anticipated paying for the company, the Tremletts deal turned out to be a good one for us. It was a unique opportunity, because it gave us a number of diverse businesses in the UK and gave us much more scope.

NIGERIA PROVES PROFITABLE

The Tremletts deal resulted in again doubling the size of the Group. And with it, we had the chance to acquire an interesting Nigerian business. While we were doing the deal, the seller offered to include a plant just outside Lagos for another £1 million. I asked for the weekend to think it over, but I didn't reveal that I spent the weekend flying out to take a look for myself. It was well worth the money, so I agreed.

Expanding into Africa was never in my plans but Nigeria proved to be a very profitable area for a number of years and, in time, we extended our interests there from one factory to four.

We built a new factory way north of Port Harcourt, which was deep in the territory of the Ibo tribe. I felt I needed to see this remote new outpost of the Group for myself so I travelled out with a full Smurfit management team to visit it. It meant taking a pretty scary trip, but we had to go. We flew out to Lagos in a private jet, which was fine, then from there we had to travel by helicopter over large tracts of jungle. It was a memorable journey.

Fortunately, we landed safely and the visit became a great adventure. I was made a tribal chief and, during the day that we dedicated the new factory, the tribal leader gave me my chief's stick and robe and asked me to adjudicate as chief on some tribal issues. I sat on the chief's throne and a couple came forward with problems about a divorce on which I was supposed to make a decision, although I didn't really understand what was going on. Happily, I later learned that it was just a ceremonial occasion so any comments or decisions that I made didn't have any real impact on the relationship.

We also got used to coming up against corruption in Nigeria. At that time, a lot of business in Nigeria was dependent on bribes and underhand dealings. I took the decision early on that this was something that we would not get involved in. This was not only because we were a public company responsible to our shareholders, but also because it was simply not the way that Smurfit operated. It was the same underlying principle that stopped us ever seriously considering any move into other countries where corruption was rife.

We soon discovered that there were many Nigerian companies that we just couldn't deal with because of our anti-corruption stance. Fortunately, there were also a lot of large multinationals who, like us, did their business in a legitimate way and who became our customers there.

Nigeria proved to be a very good investment for us. For five years, we enjoyed good earnings of up to 15% to 20% from our investment. During this time, we built up a 40% share of the Nigerian corrugated case market.

The Chairman of Smurfit Nigeria was Chief Christopher Ogunbanjo, who did a fine job for our company and his country. I visited Nigeria regularly and John Coleman, who was the executive responsible for our interests in Nigeria, spent a great deal of time there. However, in those days, Nigeria had a fundamentally unstable economy and was experiencing considerable political uncertainties.

Later, in 1978, the government decreed that foreign companies no longer could own more than 40% of a Nigerian business. This was followed by a number of changes to government, which was mainly under military control. We decided to withdraw completely from the country but we never received the money the government promised to pay us for the 60% of our interests it took over. In the end, we had no choice but to write off the Nigerian business.

BRINGING HOWARD ON BOARD

My brother Jeff came to me one day. He knew that I was looking for a top financial executive. Alan Jeffers, who I had taken from the businessman Paddy McGrath, had gone back to his old boss, so we were short of a really effective Number Two. Jeff said, "I know this man called Howard Kilroy, who is related to the Kilroys of the Hely Group. He's the nephew of Desmond Kilroy, who's on our Board. He's brilliant and he's working with Corn Products in Brussels. I've sold packaging products to him and he's a very hot guy, you should meet him".

We had a small office in Sloane Street in London, and we arranged a meeting in the Carlton Towers Hotel. I had lunch with Howard and he was very affable and clearly very able. We got on well and I decided to make him a job offer. He turned me down flat. I was shocked. I was in shock for about a week. No-one had turned me down before. He said, "You're too small. You're not big enough".

After the Tremletts deal, I re-approached Howard Kilroy, which was something I had never done in my life. This time, he said, "Yes, you're now a good size".

Howard Kilroy was to prove himself a key appointment. Indeed, he became an invaluable ally and a great friend. But perhaps I should let him tell the story himself:

> *My uncle was on the Board of the Hely Group. He and my father ran a company called Kilroy Brothers within Hely and they both joined the Smurfit organisation. I lived overseas at the time but I had watched Michael's progress from the outside with interest.*
>
> *Michael had been brought back in the late 1960s because he was the right man to succeed the father in running the business. Without Michael, the business would probably not have expanded or gone anywhere. The father was a man of his time and he made the first £100, which is the hardest one to make. But he did not have the vision or the get-up-and-go to make it the sort of company that Michael saw was possible.*
>
> *He was a brash young man who upset the Establishment by acquiring traditional companies, which were very often part of the Protestant*

ascendancy. In certain circles, the fact that Michael was a Catholic was a problem. He was resisted considerably and sometimes not given the rightful credit for what he was doing. Michael resented this and planned to show them what he could do – and, of course, he did. He was very much the brat on the block. I think Michael thought the Catholic community he represented had been disadvantaged over time. It didn't have the history of education or the opportunities in business. I think he believed that the Protestant community corralled a lot of the opportunities in Ireland between the 1940s and the 1960s.

My father and my uncle were concerned for me when they heard I was joining Smurfit because they thought I might be joining a bit of a roughhouse. At the time, I was making a career with an American company and this change did not appear to be a smart thing to do.

I was in my 30s then. I was born in 1936, so I was the same age as Michael. I went away because Ireland was then a poor country with limited job opportunities. It wasn't a place where you could easily get a job and make a significant career for yourself. I went overseas for that reason. At that time, if you wanted to make it, you had to go away. In a sense, Michael did that by going to St Helens.

Michael wasn't a great mixer. He wasn't a clubby kind of person. He ran his own show. He became a part of the Establishment eventually, just by being successful at what he did. He commanded attention because he was so successful. He was the first leader of a multi-national in Ireland. Lots of other businesses in Ireland have gone on to become multi-nationals but Smurfit was the first. No-one had gone abroad from this little tin-pot country and built an international business before Michael did it.

The first time Michael approached me I said the company wasn't big enough. That was a bit tongue in cheek but he came back to me, which he jokes about because he doesn't go back to anybody. At that time, he had Tremletts in the pipeline, and two or three months later he asked me again. He felt this acquisition was a substantial company, which changed the scene and enabled him to make me a more substantial offer and interest me in being part of the start of something. I knew he would get bigger. He had it in his bones.

He said, "Come and help me build this business". I think he felt he could trust me because he knew me and my family and he thought perhaps I had some talent. So much of the chemistry was right between us. So much of working with people is about the chemistry. I think he felt we could get on well together, which we did. We worked together well, but it was because we were different. He could do a lot of things that I couldn't do. And he did a lot of things I didn't care to do. I was patient and administratively sound and he was like the front end of a sonic boom. I cleared up all the debris and put it in neat piles. Sometimes, we disagreed. Mainly, I was tidying up while he was pushing ahead. Also we had a very different approach to people and thus compensated each other.

He worked like a dog. He read and read. He knew more about the industry than anybody else I've ever met because he was a voracious consumer of facts. And he developed from that knowledge-base so many ideas. Often, some of them were crazy but that was partly my role in life to say which ones to follow up. You only need one great idea in 10 to be successful.

I have always been very pleased he came back and asked me a second time to join him, even though it was not the most promising of starts. I came in at the middle of the Tremletts deal, to find that it would cost us about three-quarters of a million pounds more than we had anticipated. I had only been in the place about a week and I had to bring this message to Michael. He was not very pleased or impressed but, fortunately, I was just the messenger. In the end, we agreed the price but Michael got his money back later. He has a happy habit of being a winner.

BACK IN IRELAND

In Ireland, it was an exciting time for Smurfit. From being a small cog within the industry, we had become the industry. We had created a very nice business and we ran it very effectively.

Time to turn our attention to the States.

III
INTO AMERICA

CHAPTER 10
INTO AMERICA

An effective team: me, Howard Kilroy and Jim Malloy.

Nigeria was not the limit of my global ambitions and the early 1970s was a time of intense activity on many fronts. The pace of change in the company was speeding up rapidly and I was helped in many ways when my brothers Alan and, a little later, Dermot, joined Jeff and myself on the Board. With their support and that of trusted colleagues like Howard Kilroy, I had the confidence to press ahead with expansion plans. We opened an office in the United States to seek out growth opportunities over there.

CONTINENTAL CAN COMPANY

Way back in 1972, the mighty Continental Can Company took a 20% shareholding in Smurfit. The reason behind the investment was to enable them to sell a type of paper they produced: kraftliner. We didn't produce kraftliner at the time and, in those days, most boxes were made of it. Generally, kraftliner mills tend to be in places where there is a lot of wood. There's one in France, in Austria, and several in Scandinavia and in Russia, but the bulk of the kraft mills in the world are in the southern states of America. Continental Can had three or four mills and wanted to export.

They couldn't compete on price because the kraft export association was a cartel, but an associate company could sell at a much lower price. So they took a 20% holding in Smurfit to give them a source of sales and to give Smurfit a discount on the price of the material. This was the start of a long association with Continental Can, in whose mills I had worked as a young man.

One day, I got a call saying that Robert Sherman Hatfield, who was Chairman of the Continental Can Board, wanted to come to

Dublin to see me and to play a round of golf. I was intrigued. He was a very tall, aristocratic American, educated, poised and polished. He got off the plane and we went to Portmarnock. He went around in six over par, beating my eight over par: it was unbelievable, the guy just got off the plane and played like that.

We went to dinner that night in Le Coq Hardi, which I used to frequent at that time. During the course of the meal, he explained to me that he had been impressed with my career and with me as an individual, and with the way the company was growing. He was impressed with the way that we were trying to get into America, and he had come to the conclusion that we would make a very good member of the Continental Can family, so would we like to join them?

I was both flattered and concerned because the notion of selling the business had never occurred to me and the thought of working for somebody else definitely had never entered my head.

I reported the conversation back to my father, who was Chairman at the time, and being a public company, we felt that we had the obligation to explore all the avenues. Our stock was sitting at a reasonably good price but I didn't want any speculation to get out so we kept it very tight with just the directors knowing about it.

Robert Hatfield then invited me to America and I went over to see him. I'll never forget what he said, "You know, Michael, I'm setting up an office and, if we can come to terms, what I'd like you to do is to become one of the three officers of the company in what I am going to call the 'Office of the Chairman' and one of those people will succeed me. There will be yourself, Warren Heyford and Bruce Smart". I knew Warren and Bruce: they were senior guys and they were totally different to me. There was nothing bad or wrong about them, but I just knew I couldn't work with them. Robert said, "I want you to come to the 54th floor and become part of the Continental Can family". I thought about it very carefully and then said, "No".

If he had offered me the top job in Continental Can Company, guaranteed it to me, I would have put Smurfit into Continental Can's stock, and I would have taken stock in Continental Can, and two years later I would have become Chief Executive Officer. But I wasn't going to become one of three. I would have had to move my family and my life to America, and we would have done that. But I felt that I would probably be the underdog in a three-sided contest, because I hadn't grown up in the Continental Can system the way the others had. That might count heavily when it came to decide whether I was the best man for the job. I had no doubt about my own abilities but I could see myself floundering there in a second or third position. I didn't like the idea at all.

I was very clear back then what I was and was not going to do with my life. I was absolutely sure that I wasn't going to work for anybody else. The difference between someone who wants to work for himself and someone who wants to work for somebody else is the entrepreneurial aspect. I knew where I was going, and I knew I was going to get there. I also knew that I couldn't get there if I had to report to somebody else.

I couldn't stop Continental Can bidding for the company. That was a right they had. But I was the biggest stockholder and I said I wouldn't be tendering my shares for a bid, even at a substantial premium, because I figured I was going to get there in any case as we were growing at 25% a year. So even with a 30% or 40% premium, in two years I was going to beat that with the growth pattern that I had laid out for the company.

Robert Hatfield said that, as I was such a large component of the Smurfit company, unless I joined Continental Can, the company had no value to them. I said that was gratifying for me personally, if not for the shareholders, but we couldn't strike a deal.

About a year and a half later, Continental Can Company had a bit of a rough time themselves and they came to me and said: "Listen, we need some earnings for this quarter, we want to sell our stock". And so they made $54 million profit on the sale of their Smurfit stock. That's the story of how Continental Can Company came into Smurfit, and how, in 1978, they left.

HOW THE SWEDES FUNDED OUR US EXPANSION

I was at the FEFCO (*Fédération Européen Fabrique de Carton Ondule*, the European Federation of Corrugated Board Manufacturers) conference in the lakeside resort of Montreux in Switzerland when I came up with the idea that gave us the money to go into the US.

At the conference, I met two people who were to become important figures in my life: Jim Malloy, who was then running International Paper Company's paper and packaging division in the USA and later became a key part of our US expansion, and Anders Carlberg, who was running Svenska Cellulosa's paper and packaging division. Both men became close friends as well as trusted colleagues.

At the time, everybody was mad keen to get Smurfit's kraftliner business as we were buying a lot of it. We had three or four different people supplying us and I got the idea that we should go to Svenska Cellulosa (SCA) and offer a large contract to buy kraft paper from them, in return for their purchasing 49% of Smurfit's Corrugated Division. This would give me enough money to go into America big-time. Like many significant ideas, it was refreshingly simple and direct. I think I even said to myself, "My God, what a good idea!".

So I approached Anders at this conference and said, "Mr Carlberg, would you be interested in acquiring 49% of Smurfit's corrugated holdings? But far more important, would you be interested in having a contract for 40,000 tonnes of kraftliner?". This would have been about 10% of their kraft output, which meant SCA would have no downtime, when the machines weren't producing, and we would pay market price. I could see he wasn't that keen on the 49%, but he was dead keen on the contract.

Eventually, we agreed a deal and the £20-odd million that SCA paid for a share in Smurfit gave me the capital to go to America. With that amount of money, I could borrow another £20 or £30 million, so I had a war chest of $50 or $60 million.

Not that this was as easy as it sounds – deals seldom are. It was not completed until Howard Kilroy and I flew to Sweden to conclude matters. Howard's devotion to duty was never more exemplified than when he and a fellow called Kjell Brandstrom from SCA stayed up all night to do the final nuts and bolts of the deal. Next morning, I found Howard asleep in the shower in his room, with the shower still running. I think Kjell Brandstrom was in much the same condition. He and Howard became lifelong friends.

The deal with SCA gave me the cash and the credibility. Selling part of the company and using the cash to go to America, where I multiplied it 100-fold, was a masterstroke. Nobody had ever done that before in the history of the paper business.

When SCA later bought Reed in the UK about 10 years later, they had to sell us back their 49% of the Group for a fraction of what they had paid for it.

I can't say where the idea came from. It was just intuitive.

TIME INDUSTRIES

Although things were going well for us in Ireland, not all the news was good.

I learned that an American company, Hanson Scales from Chicago, had set up in Sligo to produce weighing scales. The owner brought over his good friend Don Hindman of Time Industries to set up a sheet plant to supply Hanson Scales. This was the first sheet plant ever in Ireland, up until then there were only corrugators. I didn't like this development at all: I could see where it could lead to, because Time Industries had some corrugators in America and they also had paper mills. This would definitely not be good for Smurfit. What could I do?

I decided I needed to get to know Don Hindman so, over the next couple of years, I got to know him very well.

I was having dinner with him one night and asked if he had ever thought of selling his company. He said that, if he got the right price, he would sell it on the spot. Don was that kind of entrepreneur: he worked hard building up his company but he definitely wasn't in love with the businesses.

Based in Chicago, Time Industries included Time Packaging, the O'Connor Drug Company, a laminating and coating plant, a flexo packaging business, a paper mill, a corrugated box plant – a whole host of little industries. It was capitalised at around $30 or $40 million. I decided to make a run for it so we bought a 45% share, using funds from our deal with SCA.

Once we had got control of Time Industries, I discovered it was a bit of a junk heap of companies with nothing of size and I couldn't work the usual 'Smurfit magic' on it, because it was a diverse set of businesses. So I set about selling them off.

To run Time Industries, I brought in Ed Garcia, who had been my mentor at Continental Can Company, and the guy who introduced me to Saburo Seki in Japan.

BUSINESS GOES ON

I always had the ability to concentrate fully on the job in hand and put everything else out of my mind. That ability was never more important than after the death of my father in March 1977. Of course, it was not easy to focus on business then, but personal matters would be dealt with in personal time, business matters would be dealt with in business time. The sudden loss of my father brought me to a halt, and I had to catch my breath. But, even at a time of tragedy, when some people go to pieces, I go to work.

Following Dad's death, at a meeting on 29 April 1977, I was elected Chairman of the Group by the Board of Directors, in addition to my role as Chief Executive. My brother Jeff became Deputy Chairman. My brother Alan was then in charge of UK sales, while my youngest brother Dermot was Managing Director of the UK Paper & Board Division. All four of us had learned and inherited a great deal from our father and I believe Smurfit has always drawn strength from having a rock-solid family team at its heart.

International expansion was then very much in my mind but there were also important deals to be done closer at hand. Investment in Ireland continued: in the second half of 1977, we acquired the equity of Goulding Industries Limited, a plastic film and sack manufacturer from Waterford. We also bought 50% of the Eagle Printing Company Limited in Cork and took full control of Irish Paper Sacks Limited.

The agreement with SCA also helped to provide the cash to back further expansion farther afield. In 1978, I bought 51% of Mistral Plastics Pty Limited, a company specialising in extrusion and conversion of high-density polyethylene, based in New South Wales, Australia. This was followed up three years later with the acquisition of 70% of Clearprint Limited, a specialist print company.

BACK TO AMERICA

But Australia was a sideshow compared to America, which was to be a key part of the Smurfit future. I knew we had to make it in the richest market in the world and I knew it was not going to be easy.

I had already set my sights on my next major target, the Alton Box Board Company in Alton, Illinois, near St Louis. My experience with Time Industries had given me the chance to familiarise myself with US business practices and had improved my perspective of the packaging industry in America. By now, I was well aware that the US either was going to make us or break us.

At the time, I was spending about a third of my life on the other side of the Atlantic so the arrival in service of the supersonic jet Concorde was a boon to me. I soon became one of Concorde's best customers. To assist my planned expansion into America, after a meeting at the FEFCO conference in Montreux, I had very quietly hired a remarkable executive, Jim Malloy, for a suitably remarkable salary.

Jim came from Boston, USA, and was of Irish descent – sadly, he passed away not long ago. He was tall and straight in his looks and exactly the same in his dealings. His father had owned a corrugated box business, which he had sold to International Paper. Jim had built an impressive career in International Paper, starting as Personal Assistant to the Vice President and rising fast to become one of the youngest and most able executives in the whole company. He was highly regarded within the business and no one knew the US packaging industry better than Jim.

We were lucky to get him as he had been managing a $1 billion business and we were then only a $40 million company. But we had got on well together and he liked the idea of being in at the beginning and seeing a company grow.

He was my secret weapon in the States when he joined us. For a while, I kept Jim in the background so that people didn't know he was working for Smurfit. I was buying companies in the States and, if the industry had known that Jim Malloy was part of my management team, they might have been watching us more carefully. When the time was right, I unleashed Jim and he ran the American business for us. In time, Jim was to help us to grow in America way beyond what anyone would have predicted for this young company from Ireland.

Jim's recollections of this time are interesting:[1]

When I first met Michael in Switzerland, it was his personality that attracted me to go and work for him. It was a very difficult period for me, leaving as I did a very secure position with International Paper and having to be kept hidden for nearly a year, but I sensed early on what he was trying to achieve in America, which was very different from the culture that I had grown up in. I knew he was going to be a success and I wanted to be a part of that success.

One of the most outstanding things about Michael was his razor-sharp memory. He never seemed to forget anything, not even the smallest detail. He also knew the industry back to front: he was more knowledgeable than anyone I had ever met. And very important to me was that he gave me complete freedom and his support to put my own energies and abilities to work and help establish the Smurfit company in America. As we expanded in size with new acquisitions, my responsibilities became greater and much more to my liking.

Howard Kilroy, to whom I related so well, was a wonderful colleague and a very sound man in every way. His feet were firmly planted on the ground, while you could say that Michael, at that time, was 'flying'. It was take-over, consolidate and build. I was responsible for

---

1   Sadly, Jim Malloy died after these comments were recorded. He made an enormous contribution to the development of the Smurfit business in America, both from his intellect and his work ethic and also from his deep knowledge of the US paper and board industry. I know that his son has started on his own in our business and I am delighted that he is doing well.

putting the cement blocks into place. And we succeeded beyond our wildest dreams. These truly were the most fabulous times of our lives. Michael always said we were the 'A-team'. We were the dynamos of our industry in the 1980s and 1990s and I was very proud to be at the centre of that.

Michael always treated me and my family with the utmost respect. When I had the tragic loss of my first two wives (more or less with the same problem), he was so supportive of me during those difficult times. I shall never forget it. He was a wonderful boss to work for and I am proud to say he is my friend as well.

We were an unstoppable team: me, Howard Kilroy and Jim Malloy. Jim was an outstanding appointment and Howard Kilroy was simply the best person by far I ever worked with.

I knew we needed to be at our operating peak in the United States, the land of the entrepreneur. It was a huge market with massive companies. Smurfit was just a little 'peanut guy' with a couple of box factories and a sheet plant in the States. I lined up Alton Box Board, which was a $70 million company. At the time, it was all that I could afford and I decided to go for it.

ALTON BOX BOARD

Alton Box Board was the right size and scope. It had a kraft mill in Jacksonville, a paper mill in Alton for recycling and virgin paper and a number of box plants. The Chairman of the Alton Box Board was a gentleman called Ed Spiegel, who was well-known in St Louis and on the Board of a number of companies in the city. A powerful kind of corporate 'Mafia' existed in St Louis, where a small and exclusive clique of businesspeople all sat on each other's Boards. I was well aware of the kind of welcome I could expect.

The controlling shareholder in Alton Box Board was the Williams Company of Tulsa, Oklahoma, which owned 25% of the stock. We looked at the numbers and saw that Alton clearly was not performing. We didn't understand what Williams, which was an energy company, was doing in the packaging business in the first place – especially since it had received no dividends for years.

We made direct contact with Mr Williams, the Chairman and Chief Executive of the Williams Company, and he agreed to see us in Tulsa. Howard and myself flew out there, arriving on a Sunday. In those days, Oklahoma was a dry state: there was no alcohol to be found anywhere and both Howard and I were dying for a drink. It had been a long flight and a long day.

We met Mr Williams and, after some discussion, he agreed to sell us his shares. It was as simple as that. We shook hands on a deal and, there and then, he called up Ed Spiegel and said, "Mr Spiegel, I want you to meet Michael Smurfit and his colleague in Jacksonville". We had said that we would consummate the deal only if we were happy with the Jacksonville mill. It was a huge asset and I just wanted to touch and feel it before I sent a cheque. We weren't allowed to do due diligence of the company because this was a direct purchase of the shares, but I wanted to make sure of the main asset of the company.

First, we insisted on having a good look around in Jacksonville. We went to the mill, saw that indeed there was a bit of a problem, but we still thought this was a gamble worth taking. We'd spent a day looking at the property and had seen that they needed a new boiler and various other things. I calculated all that in my mind and, that afternoon, late on, we met Mr Spiegel in a hotel room in Jacksonville and told him that we had an agreement to buy 25% of his company. He was totally shocked. He simply couldn't believe what was happening and immediately got on the phone to Mr Williams, who told him that, yes, he had agreed to sell us the shares.

Ed Spiegel was completely taken aback. He called his chief legal counsel, a lawyer called Karl Hoagland, who turned out to be a very tough adversary. Every time, we tried to increase our stockholding, he found ways to block us legally and tie us up.

There was a pre-emptive clause in which they had 90 days to find somebody else, which we didn't know about and which Mr Williams didn't actually recollect. It was a familiar scenario. They went on the hunt to try to find a white knight. Anybody but Smurfit, that was what they wanted. It's always the same story with take-overs. The first person through the door is always the bad one, even though they might be the best person to buy the company.

I tried to be patient because I knew from experience that you could win them over after you'd got them as part of your team, through charm and through work. I was the villain and we had to sit on our stake. In the meantime, I had been paying Jim Malloy to do nothing for nearly a year. Finally, the deal went through. We had 29% of Alton Box and they couldn't find anyone else to come in. At the last minute, they nearly did, but it didn't happen and we got the stock.

I remember my first Board meeting at Alton Box. The company was losing money hand over fist and one of the items on the agenda was the purchase of another corporate jet. I thought, "I'm living in cloud cuckoo land!". I didn't have a corporate jet at this stage, and I was making a lot of money, and these guys were losing a lot of money and they were buying their second one. I think their original plane was a Hawker Siddeley 600. It always left every Friday to take Ed Spiegel down to his place in Florida. It just went from St Louis to Florida and then flew him back every Monday.

Alton Box had had a bad year and we went in for the kill, immediately setting about changing everything. I went round all the factories and what I found out was that we had to spend more on the roofs than we did on the take-over. They hadn't repaired the roofs for 40 years, which was another important lesson I learned along the way.

Howard Kilroy remembers this important deal:

Alton Box Board Company was the beginning of Michael's large moves in the US but it was not exactly the big-time. We did a tour of facilities. I'd get off the plane with Michael, who didn't have a suit but had borrowed one for the day. First, Michael would ask: "Where's the nearest McDonald's?". The driver would be shocked, but Michael would make him stop the limo that we'd hired for the day and we'd all go and have a McDonald's for lunch with some of the Alton Box workers. Traditional American management had little interpersonal connection with the guys in the ranks and they couldn't get over this. It worked very well. Michael could inspire great warmth with people about the business – not about families or the ball game, but about the business. He would extract more information from a manager over a Big Mac than you would learn in a month's reports, even reading the small print. He would know very quickly whether or not they really knew their business. You couldn't con him when he got into talking about his own business. If you didn't know your business, he would identify it straight away and write you off in the process.

After we acquired the company, I discovered that the office of Hoagland, Hoagland & Sons was in the Alton Box head office building in Alton, Illinois. The day after we had made the take-over, I called Karl Hoagland, who had so assiduously blocked our efforts to buy the company at every stage, and asked him to come up to my office. We had a brief conversation.

Hoagland started it with: "I suppose I'm being fired".

"Well, you gave me a very hard time," I replied, and then the conversation went:

"It was my job".

"Yes it was, and no, you're not being fired, you're being hired. I want you to become general counsel to Smurfit in the US".

"Why is that?"

"You're a tough son of a bitch. Now I want you to be my tough son of a bitch!"

Karl Hoagland and I became good friends.

With the acquisition of Alton Box Board complete, I could bring Jim Malloy out in to the open and fully into play. Alton Box Board was full of overheads and Jim's energy and executive expertise helped enormously as we trimmed down the working capital, made a big success of it, renamed it Jefferson Smurfit Corporation and later used that to tag on other acquisitions.

I remembered that, at a seminar in the United States in the early 1970s, an analyst told the industry's leading executives, "There's a young Irish fellow come over here called Michael Smurfit. You've never heard of him. This guy is going to be number one in America one day". They all laughed.

They were not laughing as we got to work on Alton Box. We put into practice the 'Just in Time' system, which was something I learned in Japan when I visited in the early 1970s. Japanese box manufacturers supplied boxes to Panasonic, Sanyo and similar companies literally on the hour, whereas we were sending truckloads to our customers several weeks in advance. We had paper coming out of our eyeballs, paper everywhere in storage. I did away with all that. I got stocks right down to the bone, but we made sure that we never ran out. We always survived and had some paper somewhere, but we tightened up so our working capital was 7% or 8% at a time when the industry standard was double that or more. So I had all that debt-free cash to use.

CHANGE EVERYWHERE

In Ireland, I was now being viewed a little differently from the upstart who had gone in and taken over so many companies. *Business & Finance* magazine made me their Man of the Year. I think the first time I was on the cover was in 1977. I was being written about and noticed, but I didn't pay any attention. I am not interested in personal publicity and I hardly ever gave any interviews because I was just too busy.

Financially, I was doing very well. Money is not the be all and end all, but you have got to have it to live. Life was still very exciting. I saw opportunities all over the place and there weren't enough hours in the day. I worked 12 or 14 hours a day, every day of the week, and it didn't faze me at all. I enjoyed every second of it.

There was so much travel involved with my job that, when we acquired our own company jet, life became easier and less of my time was wasted.

It came in handy in other ways as well. Some years earlier, I used to go running with Fred Tiedt, a very fine amateur boxer who had represented Ireland in the 1956 Melbourne Olympics and who was then working for us in one of the Hely subsidiaries. When I heard later the sad news that Fred's son was terminally ill, I wanted to know what I could do to help. The only thing Fred's stricken son wanted was to go to Lourdes, but he was too ill to fly on a commercial airline. I was glad to be able to offer Fred the use of the Smurfit jet and his son got his wish to go to Lourdes.

In the US, there was much more of an acceptance of take-overs once the deal had been done than in Ireland or the UK, perhaps because Alton Box Board itself had previously taken over other companies and absorbed them. Its Jacksonville mill used to be owned by National Paper Company, for example. Assets changed hands more easily than in the UK.

In the US, there is a tradition of movement. People will move from one coast to the other and it's not seen as a big deal. In England, to get a person to move from Wigan to Bryn, just a few miles, or 30 miles from Llangollen to Liverpool, is like asking them to move to another planet. "But what about my football team?", they ask.

To get people in the UK to change, even in the higher echelons of management, was difficult and still is today in many parts of Europe. In the UK, it's not as bad as it was. Motorways have changed travel patterns and people can move around a lot more quickly, but it's a European cultural thing: "We like what we have – we don't like change".

With the acquisition of Alton Box, Smurfit became a medium-sized company, maybe 10th or 12th by size in the US industry. I was hunting for more things to do because we had turned the company around, cut costs, and the company had become quite profitable. We didn't have to wait long before another opportunity for US expansion came our way.

CHAPTER 11
MORE DEALS

That's one of the things I am proudest about the Smurfit business: the ethics and the integrity of all of our dealings.

One of the great strengths of the Smurfit Group was that, while I was in overall charge of a talented management team, I had my three younger brothers Jeff, Dermot and Alan in key senior positions. They each helped me greatly: Jeff was a salesman with a charismatic personality; Dermot was a great executive with a good brain; and Alan had some of both Jeff and Dermot's qualities, but he was also a little different.

In fact, he was so different that, as a gifted gambler, he had played backgammon with Lord Lucan and earned a considerable living from his gaming skills. Known in gambling circles as 'French Alan', his real identity was not widely known. Once he became seriously involved with the family business, he and I decided it might be wise to keep it that way. Alan explains:

> I never told people who I was because, in those days, there was a stigma attached to gambling and we had just gone public. After I had joined the Board, I didn't think – and Michael agreed – that it would be a good idea for my gambling activities to be highlighted because of my new role as a director of the company. In the time I was a director, I didn't gamble. I decided 'French Alan' had died and gone to poker heaven.

Throughout the 1980s, we continued to expand by acquisition, in Ireland, the UK and America. And *Forbes* magazine recognised our success, placing the Jefferson Smurfit Corporation number 1 in its survey of 1,000 top US corporations ranked by earnings growth over five years.

DIAMOND INTERNATIONAL

I was in a meeting in Dublin early in 1982 when I got a call from Alan. He just said, "In five minutes, Jimmy Goldsmith's going to call you". My interest was instantly aroused. I knew that Alan knew Sir James Goldsmith, who at the time was someone I had only read about. I was aware that he was a very charismatic character, and a real anti-Establishment person whose life seemed to be always well-publicised. We had never met, but I respected him because he had achieved a lot in business.

He called me and he said straight away that he was going to "make me a lot of money" and asked to meet me very soon. He was in New York and we agreed to meet and have lunch in the Carlisle Hotel there the following Tuesday.

In the meantime, I did some research and found that he had recently bought a company called Diamond International Corporation, which he now wanted to sell. It was a conglomerate: in paper, packaging, playing cards, specialised labels, bottle caps, plastic mouldings and a lot of other different businesses.

I met Sir James for lunch and he said, "Look, I've taken this company over, and I need a quick deal. And I've heard that you're a guy who can do a quick deal. I know that, because I want a quick deal, I won't be in a strong negotiating position".

I said, "Well, Sir James, I want the deal to work for both sides".

We went for a meeting with his people and they had divided the business into four different packages. They wanted me to buy it all if I could. It was like being a bee in a honey-pot.

I arranged to meet Sir James again, this time at his home in Richmond, London on a Saturday morning. I took Howard Kilroy with me and we planned to mix business with pleasure by discussing the deal in the morning and then going to the England-Ireland rugby match at nearby Twickenham in the afternoon. Sir James had his associate Roland Franklin with him and the four of us sat down to discuss the possible deal in detail. We talked until around 1:30pm, then stopped for lunch. By then, it was too late to drive on to Twickenham, so we asked if we could watch the match on TV. Sir

James kindly agreed, and left us to it while he went off to spend some time with his family. Towards the end of the match, he joined us, bringing a couple of his youngest offspring with him. Howard and Roland Franklin were left literally holding the babies, while Sir James and I continued discussions in his kitchen.

A huge and varied range of companies made up the Diamond International group and, if I could have bought all the businesses, I would have made an eventual profit of around $2 billion, but I didn't have the money. So I gathered what resources I could, which was about $130 million, and I made him an offer for straightforward book value. That was at a time when assets like this were trading between one-and-a-half and two times book value, but he needed that money fast.

We did the deal pretty quickly and I bought 12 plants: two mills, three corrugated paper plants, three folding carton plants and four printing plants. Sir James agreed to carry the cost of 150 redundancies, which he already had been planning to implement before we took over. By the time we'd shaken hands on a deal, Ireland had beaten England 16-15 and were on their way to winning the Triple Crown – a good omen.

We made a fortune from these companies. Straight away, they were worth double what we paid for them. I moved a management team in and we diversified them again. That gave me an increase in size. The Middletown paper mill had been losing a fortune; we turned it round from losing $40 million to making $12 million a year in two years.

A little bit later, as part of the deal, Sir James and I together personally bought Diamond Match. The company was one of the largest match producers in the world, producing toothpicks and dental floss as well, all using wood from a factory in Minnesota. God, it was cold up there – minus 35 degrees at night! We owned that company for about 10 years and then we sold it on.

Sir James Goldsmith and I did a few more deals over the years and, every time we did a deal, it was straight down the road. I liked him and I found him to be 100% straight in his dealings. He was a man of his word.

With the completion of the Diamond International deal in 1982, two-thirds of the Smurfit Group's operating assets were now located in the USA and we were in the top 250 companies in Europe, with annual sales of almost $1 billion.

It had been a great year for us, but we were all saddened by the death of Bill Gleeson at the age of 77. He had been a friend of my father from the days when the family moved to Dublin and he had made an important contribution to the development of the Group as a Board member for over 30 years. His son Peter was an astute businessman, who had already joined us as a non-executive director, continuing the role of the Gleeson family in the success of the business.

MIXING WITH MAXWELL

Unfortunately, not all well-known figures have turned out to be quite so impressive. The publisher Robert Maxwell also wanted to do business with us at one time, but I never wanted to do business with him. I always thought he was an out-and-out rogue. I just used my nose: it twitched and I knew he was a wrong 'un. He came over to Ireland twice to see me to try to sell me one of his businesses in Ireland and I wouldn't even negotiate with him.

Maxwell was a bully, and I was never in for being bullied. I was not rude to him. Both times, I listened to what he said, and I said I would write to him with a decision. I didn't say to him what I was actually thinking, "I think you are a rogue and a chancer". At that time, I didn't know that for a fact. I just sensed something was very wrong with his empire. I had no idea what he was doing, but now we know that he was a mean and ruthless character. What he did to his employees – raiding the pension fund – was unforgivable.

There will always be rogues in business and there will always be apparently respectable guys to be steered well clear of. There will always be bad guys out there. That's one of the things I am proudest about the Smurfit business: the ethics and the integrity of all of our dealings. For me, it goes back to my father's simple code of honesty and the all-important reputation.

BANKING

Times were changing in all sorts of ways and I learned early on that it is important to be adaptable and open to new ideas.

In the 1980s, it was harder to make £1 in Ireland than to make £1,000 somewhere else. However, we were still an Irish business and we always looked at the opportunities at home. So, with our financial acumen, we decided we should develop our financial services interests.

When we purchased the Hely Group in 1970, it included a financing subsidiary called Standard Trust, which we sold. It was the right thing to do at the time, but many years later I did think that, if we had kept it, we could have developed it into one of Ireland's largest financial institutions.

I had gained an insight into banking as a director of Allied Irish Banks and we had moved into financial services with a company called Smurfit Finance, which dealt in second mortgages. We also owned Strongbow Finance, which undertook hire purchase and leasing, Eurofinance, a car hire purchase company, and Belgrave Lease, which was an in-house operation doing business for other Smurfit companies. Developing our financial services seemed a logical and potentially profitable move for us, and also demonstrated our commitment to Ireland.

In 1982, the Irish Central Bank granted a banking licence to Smurfit Group and Banque de Paris et de Pays-Bas (Paribas). We tossed a coin to decide whether the bank should be named Paribas Smurfit or *vice versa* and Smurfit Paribas won.

Smurfit Paribas Bank opened for business in 1983 in what had been the Methodist Centenary Church, a fine building on St Stephen's Green. We had a capital base of IR£2 million and a staff of 20. Having traded for a year, it became the first Irish bank to move into stockbroking with a 20% holding in Doak & Co. The Board was half-Paribas and half-Smurfit, with Dr Ivor Kenny, a fluent French-speaker, as the independent Chairman approved by the Central Bank.

Once you've achieved some success and made some money, resentment starts in certain quarters. The Smurfit Paribas Bank was seen by some critics as a mere vanity project on my part, as if I'd achieved everything else and all I needed was a bank with my name over the door. These detractors overlooked the fact that, as Chairman and Chief Executive, I reported to a very strong, informed and capable Board. Any proposals that I had for the development of the Group were placed before them and the directors' priorities were the good of the business, its investors and the people who worked for it and the communities where we had operations. My ego didn't feature anywhere on the list. It didn't even feature on my own priority list. As it worked out, my belief in the potential for financial services proved to be right, but it wasn't something that Smurfit went on to develop in a big way. This challenge was undertaken – and spectacularly achieved – by a businessman called Dermot Desmond.

Dermot Desmond was born in County Cork. He worked in the financial industry outside Ireland for a while and returned to set up his own stockbroking firm. The established stockbrokers probably thought it was a joke, this young man coming from nowhere to challenge them. He came to see me and I liked the cut of his jib, so I gave him 50% of the Smurfit stock business. When I told our existing brokers, they were shocked, but it proved to be a good decision for us, and for Dermot. His brokerage house was struggling against the Establishment, and by then we were the Establishment. Not only did he benefit directly from our business, the kudos of having the Smurfit name on his client list was fantastic for him. I always thought very highly of Dermot and we became good friends. He was key to the establishment of the International Financial Services Centre in Dublin and developed many other business interests.

REVIEW & RE-ORGANISATION

The year leading up to the 50th anniversary of the business in 1984 was a time for reviewing and restructuring our organisation.

In Ireland, I spoke out against the crippling rates of business and personal tax that were detrimental to our country and to our people. Businesses were under pressure from the government to create jobs, but weren't getting the support from the government that would enable them to do this.

The UK accounted for about a quarter of the Group's turnover, but our British-based business was operating at a loss. We decided to close the St Helens corrugated plant, which had been my original business, plus a small paper mill near Oxford and two paper machines at the Tamworth mill. The UK corrugated industry was in need of rationalisation and it was in our best interests to participate willingly in the process. SCA, which owned 49% of our corrugated division, bought the number one player in the UK, Reed International. We therefore decided to become the number two in the UK, by merging Smurfit-SCA's plants in North West England and in Scotland with corrugated container plants in the UK that were owned by MacMillan Bloedel, a Canadian company, to form UK Corrugated. Then MacMillan decided to sell out, leaving the Group with 100% and a free hand to sort out the business.

Whereas until then we had been something of an also-ran in the UK corrugated industry, the merger gave us a significant share of the market at around 17%, and we had outlets for our raw materials. I had to admit that it was a merger of weaknesses rather than strengths and we didn't have an easy time ahead of us.

In the USA, we re-organised operations, with most becoming subsidiaries of Jefferson Smurfit Corporation. We employed 6,500 people in the US and had annual revenues of $700 million, making Jefferson Smurfit Corporation much larger than our European interests. For the business, the year ended with a 37% growth in turnover, but a fall for the second year running in pre-tax profits.

With Irish and UK markets in recession, the wisdom of our expansion into the USA was left in no doubt when in January 1985, the American business magazine, *Forbes*, ranked Jefferson Smurfit Corporation as the fastest-growing company in the previous five years with average earnings per share growth of 139%. The Smurfit parent group was identified as the top performer in the packaging industry with a five-year average sales growth of 56% and an average return on equity of 54%.

We were about to mark our 50th anniversary and, unbeknown to us, one of the best deals in the history of the Group was waiting to be done.

THE SMURFIT GROUP HITS 50

We celebrated the Smurfit Group's 50th anniversary with record pre-tax profits of IR£50 million and a party for 700 guests at the Burlington Hotel in Dublin. Smurfit was now the second-largest company in Ireland by market capitalisation and our sales were equivalent to 6% of Ireland's national income. We had produced the highest recorded earnings of a private sector industrial company in the history of the Irish state.

Lots of people recognised the success. The Taoiseach (Ireland's prime minister), Dr Garret FitzGerald, spoke of the "tradition of exceptional leadership, dedication and hard work established by members of the Smurfit family". Tony O'Reilly paid a fine tribute to my father for establishing the company and also generously praised my own "courage, foresight and skill" for achieving the all-important move into the vibrant American market.

They were kind words indeed. I was just coming up to my own 50th birthday, and it was great to mark my half-century with business success. Professionally, it was a very proud time for me and all the family but, in my personal life, things were not going so well.

CHAPTER 12
AMERICAN EXPANSION – NORTH & SOUTH

Effectively, this was the transforming deal that made the Smurfit business – and the family fortune. We went from being well-off to being extremely wealthy in the blink of an eye.

As my personal life underwent great changes (see **Chapter 13**), I found that my business life also offered huge new challenges.

In early 1985, the opportunity came along to buy a newsprint operation in the west of America. I had got to know the Chairman of the Board of Times Mirror, Robert Erburu, very well. Times Mirror published eight newspapers in the States, including the *Los Angeles Times*. They had a newsprint operation, Publishers Paper, in Newburg, Oregon, but they really didn't want to be in the newsprint business. They wanted to concentrate on what they did best, which is publishing. So I made them an offer, which they accepted, and we had a 10-year contract to supply them with paper.

Again, we turned the business around and I think we got our money back in three years. One of the keys to the success of the Publishers Paper deal was that we found they were over-paying for electricity – something like $48 million a year! Of course, we knew that this price was extortionate, so as soon as we owned the company we brought in the electricity supplier, which was a privately-owned utility, and informed them that we were thinking of installing our own plant which would be big enough not only for our mills but also to supply other huge users in the area. They quickly caved in and reduced the price by something like 50%.

Our timing was good. Newsprint is a commodity, so it goes up and down in price – but we had a good cost structure and the Newburg mill became the most cost-effective mill in North America.

We renamed Publishers Paper as Smurfit Newsprint Corporation. It included two newsprint mills, 12 reclamation plants, four sawmills and two particleboard factories. This acquisition made the Smurfit Group the largest collector of waste paper in the world.

Newsprint was a total diversification for us as we had no knowledge of the industry, no history in the industry and it was away from our core competence, but I saw that part of our competence, in fact, was running paper mills. We had great experience from the old Clonskeagh days and knew about paper-making. We knew about energy efficiencies, moisture content going into driers, and all the countless other essential details. So I was confident that we knew the business and its purchase gave us more size and scope.

But the interesting part of the Publishers Paper deal was the strategy that underpinned it – both when we bought it and later when we sold it.

What made me buy it in the first place was the guaranteed contract for 10 years from the *Los Angeles Times*. That was critical to the acquisition because they were a huge customer. But I knew that we were going to get out of the industry because I had determined that newsprint was a sunset industry. It's still in decline and, one day, it eventually will disappear. How long that will take, I don't know but, in the meantime, of course, the last man standing can make a lot of money. In England, we were the last people producing waxed wrappings for bread loaves before plastic wrapping came in. We were making 30% on sales for a number of years. We knew we were going out of business but we made a fortune in the meantime. The strategy in Publishers Paper was to make a lot of money in the short term to use to buy other companies, which we did.

The end for our newsprint division came some years later when I realised the potential of the Internet, and the effect it was going to have both on newsprint and on deliveries of products. That happened by accident. I was walking from my hotel in Chicago to my office and I saw a sign, 'Internet Café'. I had heard about the Internet but I didn't know much about it so I went inside. The guy asked me for a dollar to sit down and use the computer. I started asking people in there, "What newspapers do you buy? How do you get your information?" and found none of them bought newspapers. Then I was in London about four weeks later and saw another Internet café near Bond Street. I went in there and got the same story.

I went to the Smurfit Board and said, "We're getting out of the newsprint business. We've seen the best of it." The Board agreed with me. We sold very well. We sold the two mills for a lot of money. Over time, I believe that the companies that bought them had good reason to regret their decision to buy.

On the other hand, I believe the Internet will have a very positive impact on our business. How will products bought online be shipped to the customer, other than in a corrugated box? Presumably the emphasis on transportation graphics will be high, so high-graphic coating is likely to be a growth area. In some cases, products bought online may be boxed three times – once in the manufacturer's packaging, then in an Amazon box for computerised storage and then in a FedEx box for delivery. Certainly single, probably double and possibly treble upside potential.

But, then, the Internet was barely in its infancy. After Publishers Paper, I still wanted something bigger and better, but I had to wait for that to come. I always talk about the old tiger in the long grass. He can't go hunting for his meat like the young tiger, he's got to wait. So I was waiting for the opportunity to come, and I knew it would.

Meanwhile, I had been fitting together the smaller pieces of the jigsaw. There were little add-ons to the Group. They were good and some of them were great, but they just weren't the scope and scale I really wanted.

THE BIG OPPORTUNITY

I recall the occasion very well when the big opportunity first revealed itself. In 1985, I was in Los Angeles. I had spent the morning with Bob Erburu. Some analysts had invited me to lunch and, during the course of the meal, they asked me what our next move would be. I replied cautiously that I wasn't altogether sure. I had just bought some mills and was planning to upgrade them.

One of the analysts turned to me and said, "Have you thought of approaching Mobil Oil?". At that time, Mobil owned Container Corporation of America. I responded that I didn't think CCA was for sale. Privately, I also had a concern that some members of the board of Mobil Oil might not be too keen to let me have it.

Afterwards, I went back to the house I had rented in Los Angeles. When the telephone rang, I picked it up and a voice said, "Don Brennan of Morgan Stanley here. Would you be interested in joining with Morgan Stanley Leverage Equity Fund in a joint buyout of Container Corporation of America, because I think that we can buy it, and we would provide you with the necessary funds if need be?".

I had never met Don Brennan before but I knew about him. Jim Malloy had hired Don to work for International Paper. Eventually, Brennan, who was an extraordinarily clever executive, was promoted in IP over Jim Malloy and later was headhunted by Morgan Stanley.

I agreed to meet Don Brennan and he outlined the deal to me. I thought it was just an incredible opportunity. It was going to cost over $1 billion and he figured that all we had to put up was about $150 million. He couldn't do it on his own because he wanted management and he figured we were the best management team available because he knew Jim Malloy.

So Don trundled off to see Allen Murray, who was Chairman and Chief Executive of the Board of Mobil, and the message came back that Mobil did want to sell CCA. But they were not prepared to take less than book value, and they were not prepared to give us the opportunity of full due diligence because we were a competitor. If we wanted to do the deal, we had to take the company as we found it.

In the end, I was given limited due diligence but, with the way I ran the numbers, I saw this thing was so fat that it was unbelievably irresistible. There was working capital coming out of their ears, they had overspent huge sums of money on capital items and they had a huge depreciation stream, much bigger even than we were. I figured we could make some very serious money out of this company – even buying at book value.

I flew down to see the first mill in Bruton, Alabama. The plant manager had arranged the visit for me and the first thing I said to him was that I wanted to look at the roof – I had learnt that from my experience at Alton Box. So I went up on the roof and then toured the mill. It was a very impressive mill, the only mill making any real money in the whole system, about $40 million a year.

As we were leaving the mill, I spotted this very large building, perhaps 100 yards in length and 50 yards wide. I asked what was in there and was told it was for storing spare parts. I said I wanted to take a look. There were gears, pulleys, motors, pipes – it was unbelievable. I asked how much value was there. My guide, who was called Gary Trimble, had shaking hands and smoked like a trooper. He said, "It's all on computer". He was nervous about my visit, though he later proved to be a good manager. We took a look and the parts turned out to be worth $20 million. I thought, "Oh my God, $20 million". There were 10 other mills and we were going on to the next mill in Jacksonville. We called the Jacksonville mill from where we were and asked about their spares. They had about $21 million. I calculated there must be about $150 to $200 million in spare parts across the CCA mills.

I was disappointed because I knew this was a deal-breaker. There was no way we could take a deal based on book value. I was notorious for buying below book value, but Murray had insisted that we buy at book value. They weren't making the earnings to justify this, but that's what they wanted – and we had accepted that precondition before we were allowed to look at the mills.

I was having a cup of tea back in Gary Trimble's office. I was a bit down and Gary said to me, "Mr Smurfit, you seem very low". I said, "Yes, Gary, this is a deal-breaker". He replied, "Why would it be a deal-breaker? Mobil write all the spare parts off. That's why we buy plenty of them". I said, "You mean they are in the books for nothing?". "Yeah, I mean that". I could hardly believe my ears.

So now I was getting $200 million worth of spare parts for nothing! I got on the phone to the Chief Executive of Mobil and he wanted to know if everything was OK. I told him it was going well. I came back after my due diligence, went to see Don Brennan and he asked me what I thought. I said, "Don, this is a home run to such an extent we don't have to put up hundreds of millions. We only have to put up $10 million equity each". I got the preferred stock, $50 million of preferred stock, and that was the deal, the rest we borrowed.

We were just about to close the transaction when Mobil, to their horror, found that the book value of CCA that we had been given, and on which we did our calculations, was different from that in Mobil's books, which was a higher figure, amounting to $50 or $60 million more. We figured that we couldn't get more from the banks and the alternative was that we would have to put more equity in, and we were not inclined to do that, because on the surface the deal was tricky enough as it was.

But I remembered that, on my trip to the mill in Bruton, I was told that the largest producer of telegraph poles in America was a subsidiary of Mobil's in the same town, which was in the books at about $30 or $40 million, but was worth considerably more. So we took that out of the deal – which meant that Mobil made no book loss – and closed the deal on the rest.

The reason that Morgan Stanley were there was that they had to go in with the letter of guarantee that the money was good. The bank wouldn't have given me the letter until I had done my due diligence. Morgan Stanley, being the bank they were and the money they had, with their name behind the deal financially, it was money good.

I didn't have the $1 billion – that was a step too far for me, but the $10 million, and the $50 million was just right. I think we took out $250 million of costs in the first year and we turned it into a cracking business. Effectively, this was the transforming deal that made the Smurfit business – and the family fortune. We went from being well-off to being extremely wealthy in the blink of an eye.

TWISTS IN THE TAIL

But there was a consequence to the story. Morgan Stanley Equity Partners II was our partner in the CCA deal and they had a sharp executive working with them called Alan Goldberg, who was based in New York. I have a lot of respect for him. At the time, he was Morgan Stanley's tough man, a real enforcer.

Don Brennan and Alan Goldberg asked to see us in Dublin a couple of weeks after the CCA deal was consummated and we had a dinner in the Berkeley Court Hotel in a private room, which I thought was going to be a celebration. During the course of the dinner, Brennan and Goldberg explained that they were going to charge us $35 million in transaction fees for doing the deal. I was dumbfounded and said, "You're my partner. You're going to make a ton of money!". They said the leverage fund was one thing, Morgan Stanley Bank was another and that we always knew there would be a transaction fee. "We always knew?", I said. "If we always knew, why didn't you tell us? If you had told us before, we would have told you to get stuffed. But we're telling you now, we're not going to pay you". Howard Kilroy took me outside and said he thought we were going to have to pay it, or most of it. I told Howard that it didn't sit well with me. They were fair, I suppose, but in my view, they didn't properly appreciate what we were going to do for them, because ultimately we made them $500 million.

I came back into the room and I said, "You guys told me that you aren't all that interested in the Latin American and the European interests – the whole deal is a dollar-based deal basically, based upon the North American business". Whenever we talked to them, their focus was the North American businesses, because that's where the debt was, that's where the main factories were. They really didn't want to talk so much about Latin America, or the Italian, Dutch or Spanish plants.

So I said, "OK, if we pay you the $35 million, and it's a big IF, I want a two year option to acquire at book value (because we had paid book value for everything) the Latin American interests, which you say that you're not interested in anyway, and the interests in Europe, for the Jefferson Smurfit Group. The Group owns 50%, but I might want to own 100%, if the book value makes sense for us". They agreed, the fee was paid, and Smurfit Group obtained an option to acquire at book value the European and Latin American interests of CCA.

INTO THE FIRST DIVISION

In footballing terms, the CCA deal took us from the top of the second division in America up to the middle of the first division. My PA at the time of the deal was Peter Cosgrove. I remember, very clearly, waiting in our hotel in Chicago for a call from New York to say the money had been paid and the company was now ours. Naturally, we were all raring to go.

The call came through and we went over to the CCA offices in the Sears Building. There were about 65 floors to the building, so Peter Cosgrove and I got in the lift, and Peter had completely forgotten which floor the CCA office was on. He was rummaging around in his papers while we both stood there. I said, "Punch 54 and see what happens". So he punched 54 and, sure enough, it was the main floor for CCA, which had a number of floors in the building. We were met by the Managing Director, a guy called Cooper, who couldn't wait to clear his desk and get back to Mobil. I think he was out of there within an hour.

Where did the "54" come from? Years earlier, when Continental Can Company offered to make a bid for Smurfit, Robert Sherman Hatfield had tried to persuade me to go and work for him along with two other people and he had said, "Michael, please come and join me on the 54th floor of the Continental Building in New York". Even though – perhaps because – the deal for CCC to buy Smurfit didn't go ahead, I never forgot his mention of the 54th floor. So it was pure coincidence that I suggested to Peter he try "54", since we were in a completely different building.

But, as they do, coincidences multiply: Madison Dearborn, who were later to take the Smurfit Group private (see **Chapter 22**), also had offices in the Sears Building.

SUCCESS IN LATIN AMERICA

The reason I took the option to acquire CCA's European and Latin American interests, rather than simply buy them straight out there and then, was that I didn't know at that stage what the companies were worth. Subsequently, however, it became apparent that they were very valuable businesses and Smurfit Group was able to exercise the options it had obtained to acquire them on very attractive terms. I remember Howard saying to me, "How did you know?". I said, "I sensed something but I also thought 'I'll be damned if I'm going to let these guys go back to America with a fee of $35 million without us getting something in return'. It was just against my entrepreneurial nature".

That's how Latin America became an important area of growth for us, and still is today.

My brother Alan was the perfect candidate to head up the Latin American operations. He knew the industry and he knew the Smurfit approach. He was already fluent in French and the first thing he did was to go off and learn Spanish until he became fluent in that as well. Alan wanted to know what was going on at all levels. He wanted to be able to talk to people on the factory floor as well as in the boardroom. He wanted to be able to talk to our customers and to our suppliers. He did a superb job in bringing the operations and the countries together and developing a strong management team and business for us there.

The Latin Americans are a very proud people. They are very emotional; they hug you and kiss you when you arrive there. It's not like Germany where they say, "Welcome" and stand back and salute you. In Latin America, the people shake your hand, hug you and say, "It's nice to see you". I love going down there and I love the people.

Even so, they were very wary of us at first and it took us a while to 'Smurfitise' them. They had hardly heard of Ireland and, all of a sudden, these guys from the middle of nowhere were at the front door, saying, "Knock, knock … Michael and Alan Smurfit here. We're taking you over. We now own the company. This is how we are going to operate". They were amazed because they had never seen anybody from CCA.

We lived down there at first and then I would go to Mexico four times a year, Colombia two or three times a year, Venezuela four times a year. We were totally involved in developing the companies from the very first year we had them.

For example, the Venezuelans had no raw materials because they had stopped planting trees, so I gave them a lot of money and now they are harvesting those trees. In Colombia, I doubled the tree plantation programme the first year we were there and the second year I went back and doubled it again. I gave them huge resources because I could see the future for them. Now we are nearly self-sufficient in fibre. That means we've reduced high-priced imports from America and increased our quality. Before, we were in a position where someone could have come in and taken half the market away from us. Now no one can take the market from us, because it would take them 15 years just to grow the trees.

In Latin America, one of the things we instituted straight away was that, to get a position at a certain level in the company, you had to be able to speak English, because we communicate in English. Some managers who learned English said that it was like going back to school and was a bit boring and they didn't like it; some said it was something that they had always wanted to do; others didn't tell you what they thought but, because it was mandated, they just got on and did it. Whatever they thought, they knew if they wanted to progress in the Group, it was something they had to do. I didn't want to sit in meetings where people couldn't understand what was going on.

I think it is true to say that, in Latin America, there is a genuine love for the family and for the company. The proof of the pudding is that I don't think I've lost an executive from Latin America for as long as I can remember.

Alan did a great job and, as he says himself:

Michael gave me a lot of support. He often visited us to keep an eye on what we were doing. He was always interested in Latin America. For every tree we chopped down, we planted seven, so we became the good guys.

One of the nicest letters that I received on my eventual retirement as Chief Executive of the Smurfit Group was from César Gaviria, Secretary General of the Organisation of American States and a former President of Colombia. He wrote me a very moving letter, about what I had achieved, and how many Colombians were grateful to me. Many years ago, he gave the company the Order of Boyaco and the Star of Colombia Grand Cross, Colombia's highest distinction. This is an honour that I had great pleasure in accepting on behalf of the Group's employees.

But the final word on the CCA deal goes to my brother Dermot:

Container Corporation of America was the jewel in the crown. To go to America, put up $10m in cash, $50m on tick, buy a business for $1.1bn and, three and a half years later, arrive back in Ireland with $1bn in cash and still own 50%+ of the business. It was the greatest deal the paper business has ever known.

IV
LIFE OUTSIDE SMURFIT

CHAPTER 13
PERSONAL UPHEAVALS & INTERESTS

We had four great children and Norma was always the perfect wife in every way. But I had fallen in love with somebody else.

Of course, life is never smooth sailing all the time. Along with the many ups and downs of my business life, there were some downs in my personal life too.

DAD'S DEATH

Although Dad was still Chairman of the Smurfit Group and still involved in it, he was free of the worries about business and money that had dominated so much of his life. He spent a lot of time in Spain and travelling around the world. He had many friends, he visited his children and grandchildren, and he often called in to the offices in Clonskeagh. He was still a big part of all our lives. He was always keen to hear about what was happening in the company and I would talk through the deals that we had done and the ideas I had for our next move. He was a great source of motivation and encouragement for me and a "Well done, Michael," from my Dad meant so much. The end, when it came, was shocking.

I was in Stockholm on business in March 1977 when I received the news that Dad had died. It was devastating. In many ways, I was still doing it all for him. Every time I walk into the Grand Hotel in Stockholm, I think of him. I was just checking in when I heard. I couldn't find my pilot to fly me home so I had to stay the night.

Dad had been into hospital for a routine check-up and, within a few days, he had a stroke and died. It was a tough time for us all.

Dad had wanted to be cremated, but this was not an accepted practice in Ireland at that time. We arranged for the cremation in St Helens in England and brought his ashes back to Dublin for an official burial the following day.

To the end, he was so proud to see what had happened to the company. When you think of his background and the poverty he came from, to have Smurfit become so successful, accounting for 25% of the total value of the Irish Stock Exchange, and his name over the door, was remarkable. I know he couldn't have been more chuffed. I remember walking into his office one day and saying, "You know, Dad, as of today, we are the biggest company in Ireland". It was a marvellous moment between us.

But, all these years later, it still angers and upsets me that he was denied a huge honour from the Roman Catholic Church that he richly deserved. Back in the days of Pope Pius XII, the Vatican decided that the *Breviary*, the prayerbook read by priests as part of their daily ritual, was to be updated and translated from Latin into English for the first time. The Educational Company of Ireland, which was owned by the Smurfit Group, won the contract to complete this difficult and delicate task. The contract was complex and expensive for Smurfit because the Church had a committee in Ireland and a committee in the Vatican and both of them literally had to dot every 'i' and cross every 't' to make sure there were no mistakes in the translation.

Eventually, the task was successfully completed and Pope Pius XII granted Dad the honour of being made a Knight of St Gregory. My father bought his robes and a date was fixed for him to travel to Rome. However, such a knighthood had to be confirmed by the local archbishop in Dublin and he refused to endorse the Pope's recommendation on the grounds that my father had been born a Protestant and not a Roman Catholic. Dad was bitterly disappointed when the rejection came and took it very personally. To me, it seems a clear injustice. I swore there and then that I would get decorations myself in life that I would accept at least partly on behalf of my father. His rejection is one of the things that drove me on to acquire the varied awards I hold.

A great deal of what I was doing was for Dad; that did not change even after he was no longer with us. I shall never forget his strength of character, his utter determination to succeed, his advice and his warmth both as a father and as an employer. He was unique and simply irreplaceable. It was hard to believe that we had lost this strong, powerful man. His influence is always with me.

ANOTHER SHOCK: JEFF'S DEATH

Sadly, before we celebrated the Group's 50th anniversary, my brother Jeff had to resign for health reasons. He had been very involved throughout the growth of the business, so I felt his loss very deeply.

Jeff had worked hard for the Smurfit business since he was a teenager. As a salesman, he was unbeatable and he was a warm, outgoing and popular man. He had done an incredible job in building sales and no one knew the value of his contribution to the Smurfit success better than I did. All our lives we were close, although there were times when we'd argue, particularly about which of us was contributing most to the business. I would scream at him, "It's the bottom line that counts!" and he would scream back at me, "Without the top line, there is no bottom line!". But it was all in good humour and I know he was happy with the directions in which I was taking the business.

However, he had become an alcoholic and was in poor health. He had earned a break from the pressures and responsibilities of being a senior executive and, at the age of 46, he resigned as Assistant Chief Executive and Deputy Chairman of the Group, remaining as a non-executive director and a consultant. Alan and Dermot were appointed Joint Deputy Chairmen.

In 1986, he sadly became ill again, suffering a heart attack. He underwent a quadruple heart by-pass operation and, with new arteries, he appeared to be making a good recovery and enjoying a more relaxed lifestyle.

We celebrated his 50th birthday with a massive party on the Isle of Man where he lived. It was a wonderful occasion, but four weeks later the people who had assembled for his birthday were back again to bury him. No-one expected such a sudden end. One day, Jeff was in Marbella playing a round of golf with Sean Connery. He still had the card in his pocket recording how he won that particular game. He packed his bags and flew off to the Isle of Man to go to his daughter's wedding the next day – and keeled over and died. It was a terrible, terrible shock.

Jeff and I had grown up together, been through school together, worked together and we always saw each other a lot. He was an irreplaceable friend as well as a much-loved brother.

A NEW WOMAN IN MY LIFE

I met Birgitta Beimark in St Tropez. I was only there for the weekend and was introduced to her by a friend of mine, Malcolm Aw. He's originally from a wealthy Hong Kong family who own the famous herbal treatment, Tiger Balm. Malcolm had a film showing at the Cannes Film Festival and had borrowed my car. I met Birgitta in a hotel bar with Malcolm and we had a drink.

Next day, he said, "You know, you should call Birgitta, she liked you". So I did. I hadn't been thinking of leaving Norma, but I fell for Birgitta. She was tall, blonde and Swedish. She was very attractive and a very nice girl.

It was traumatic, because I still cared very much for Norma. I felt like a right heel, but I also believed I really loved Birgitta.

I don't know whether Norma suspected I was seeing another woman but I took her to a restaurant and, over dinner, I told her that I had met someone else and wanted a divorce. She threw a glass of wine over me and left. This happened on 1 April, 1985. It was April Fool's Day but Norma knew I wasn't trying to play any kind of joke on her.

My biggest concern was for my four children. It was really tough for them. I knew that. Deciding to leave somebody for someone else is a selfish decision and it's horrible for the people who are affected by it. Even for the person who's doing it, it's horrible, but you have to live your own life. You only live once and this is what I felt was the right thing for me to do. I've never regretted that decision.

I talked to each of my children individually and explained things to them but, to a child, there is no justification for a father to leave their mother. There is no way that that is acceptable to them. It took time for them to understand.

Of course, they didn't like Birgitta, and I understood that. I didn't push her in front of them and I didn't bring her to Ireland very often.

At the time we split up, divorce was not possible in Ireland. There were lots of people 'living in sin', who had left their wives or husbands to live with someone else but couldn't divorce. But we had been married in England, so we were able to divorce. It came through in six months and shocked a lot of people – and there was a lot of public comment. Some people took Norma's side and others took mine, but most people sensibly tried to keep up a relationship with us both. And, fortunately, time is a great healer.

Norma remains one of my best friends and she does amazing work running the Jefferson and Michael Smurfit Foundation in Monaco. I think the world of her and I was very sorry to hurt her. But it was a decision I had to take and I took it.

I married Birgitta and we have two sons: Alexander and Christopher. Sadly, our marriage did not last, but I have never regretted my decision, particularly as I now have my two youngest sons, and a great relationship with all of my six kids.

I was delighted to be able to help Birgitta start her children's foundation, which has been extremely successful in helping disadvantaged children, especially in Romania and Sri Lanka.

A NEW LIFE

At the time, I didn't want to live with my second wife in Ireland, as this would have been distressing for Norma and our children. So I decided to make a new home abroad.

I just focused on a new phase in my life with a new lady in my life. We had a fantastic home in St Tropez in the south of France and then we moved to Cannes, and then to Monaco. It was a change of pace and a change of life.

Moving to Monaco was nothing to do with taxation, as some people seem to assume. I was paying most of my taxes in the United States, so moving to Monaco did not alter that.

In fact, I found it was very hard to move away from Ireland. All my friends were in Ireland. Even years later, I still miss many things about Irish life like the Christmas parties and seeing old friends.

NORMA'S SUCCESS

However, there was one very positive thing, in my view, that came out of my break-up with Norma. Although it was a big shock for her at the time, after the first couple of years she really came out of her shell and developed very independently in her own right. I don't think she would have done that if she had remained married to me.

When she saw the kids were growing up, she developed her own friends and rebuilt her own life, and has been very successful. She is probably one of the best-known women in Ireland for raising money for a variety of different charities and she gives poor people practical help herself on the streets as well.

She started a wonderful organisation called First-Step, to help people take the first step into starting their own business. She is Chair of the Arthritis Association and on the Board of many other organisations and the driving force behind numerous charity events. And she does excellent work in running the Jefferson and Michael Smurfit Foundation, which I set up some 20 years ago and which has quietly done great works in helping many people.

I don't think all this would have happened had we not split up. Maybe it would, but my sense is that it caused her to say: "I'm Norma Smurfit and I'm somebody who is going to do something with my life". And she did and she has been a great success. I'm very proud of her for that.

Norma was always a lady and she remains a lady.

PERSONAL INTERESTS

Although building the Smurfit Group was a complex and time-consuming job to which I devoted most of my life, I have always been aware that there is a world outside the company. From my earliest days in charge, I had my own business interests outside the Smurfit Group, all with the knowledge and approval of the Smurfit Board to ensure that there was no conflict of interest. The Board also had first refusal on any new business interests that I was investing in and, if it was thought that they would benefit the Smurfit business, then the Board had the option of taking them up.

I formed a company called Tyne Villa Investments. Basically, people would come to me for advice and to talk to me about all sorts of projects, or with a specific idea for which they wanted to raise capital. If I believed in the person and thought the plan had potential, then I would invest in it.

Most of my investments were confidential and private, and I have been involved in some great success stories that have never been told publicly. I've taken 10% equity here, 15% there, 25% in another, and just let them get on with it. I always liked the idea of getting in at the ground level. If someone had a good idea and wanted my advice, I enjoyed helping them. Sometimes, I would direct them how to raise money and, other times, I would assist directly. This was back when it was very difficult to raise money. I knew how to raise capital and, obviously, I was a very good entrée to the banks.

I've always said that I made more money outside Smurfit than ever I made inside, from very early times, just by backing certain people and doing certain things.

TROUBLE AT TMG

One of my non-Smurfit interests was the TMG Group, which I invested in with my old friend from my time in Wigan, Maurice Buckley. We had stayed close friends and, as Maurice's business prospered, I made a bit of money on it from my stake in it. In the meantime, I moved back to Ireland, and Maurice expanded into

Ireland to follow us because he could supply us with dies. For many years, he was Smurfit's sole supplier, although as a public company, we had to do everything at arm's length: it was never a question of him being my friend or business associate, he had competition and he beat the competition to get our business.

Maurice and I saw an opportunity to do for engineering in Ireland what I had already done for packaging. Through Tyne Villa Investments, in 1972 I had picked up a company called Tonge McLaughlin Holdings, which was to form the basis of the TMG Group. There were two parts to it: one was a foundry, manufacturing manhole covers and fabricating water mains; the other was one of Ireland's premier structural steel engineers. The highlight of the firm's achievements came when it was responsible for constructing the huge cross for Pope John Paul II's celebration of Mass in the Phoenix Park, Dublin in September 1979. It was a great business, one of the top performers on the Irish stock market, and up until 1980, it delivered unbroken profit growth.

I asked Maurice to join me in Tyne Villa Investments, which he did. I encouraged him to run TMG and he proved to be a stunning success for quite a number of years. We put together a great board, which helped us to get off to a good start. We brought Kevin McCourt's son, Declan, back from America. Kevin was on the Smurfit Board and was also Chairman and Chief Executive of Irish Distillers for many years. Declan was a brilliant Harvard-educated guy and he backed up our entrepreneurial skills with great discipline. James O'Dwyer, my lawyer, also was on the Board. He was then Managing Partner of Arthur Cox, a large Dublin law firm. I had met him some years earlier when he had dealt very effectively with some difficult issues on behalf of TMG. We made a number of acquisitions and it was a nice, comfortable company.

Half-way through our expansion, I said to Maurice, "Now is the time to take some money off the table. We have a lot of money in here, with maybe £20 or £30 million invested between us". Back then, this was serious money. Maurice disagreed with my judgement that this was the time to draw back. The company was growing very quickly and Maurice said he'd like to buy another company, Pierce's of Wexford. I said, "Maurice, it's time for us to slow down, we've got too much in this sector". But it was very hard for me to fight against the Chief Executive, which Maurice was at the time, even though I was Chairman of the Board and controlling shareholder. When the company's record was so good and the trend still upward, it was very hard to say, "No". Of course, I knew that companies can't go on like that forever. The outlook for trade in Ireland was difficult, the Anglo-Irish free trade agreement was having more effect, and government spending was being reduced. TMG was heavily dependent upon the farming community for a lot of its sales. But Maurice was against the idea of selling a few shares.

That was a decision that Maurice came to rue bitterly because, eventually, he lost almost everything, including his home. He almost went bankrupt and he was forced to go to America.

TMG was well-structured, and I believe it was well-run, but events overwhelmed us. Ireland went into recession, TMG went into serious decline, profitability disappeared and the company had to be rescued eventually by the Jefferson Smurfit Group. I was concerned, of course, about the effect that TMG's bankruptcy would have on my reputation and on myself. I went to the independent directors of Smurfit Group and talked the matter through with them. I said that TMG faced an impending disaster, but that I thought there was money to be made in it for the Group. TMG had to be taken in and sorted out, and I had the man to do the job of cleaning the company up and selling off all the pieces – my brother Dermot. The directors agreed that this was probably the best course of action because of the potential damage if it collapsed. Smurfit Group was growing very rapidly and had known nothing but success. The Smurfit directors figured that, for the small sums involved in the investment in TMG, it should not be allowed to fail.

Jack Lynch, who was Taoiseach from 1977 to 1979 and who joined the Smurfit Board as a non-executive director in 1980, took it on himself to champion the cause of the rescue of TMG. I had to excuse myself from the Board deliberations on the matter because I was involved on both sides.

There was no gain for either Maurice or myself personally. The equity in the company was gone: it was the jobs and the reputation that we wanted to save.

Maurice and I lost our investment, but we didn't put too much in to begin with, so we didn't lose too much. But, at one stage, if you said we were worth £20 million, then we lost £20 million.

Dermot took charge and sorted it out. It took about two or three years and he sold off the parts bit by bit, until it was all sold. The irony is that some of the properties once owned by TMG, which were used by scrap metal merchants, were in the Dublin docklands. If we'd kept those properties, they probably would have been worth €200 or €300 million at the height of the Celtic Tiger property boom, because they were in what later became prime sites – but, at that time, no one wanted to know the docklands.

The rise and fall of TMG was a saga in itself. If there is a moral to this story, it's that when things are going right, things are fine; but when they go wrong, you had better know what you are doing. It brought home to me the truth of the old saying, "No one ever became poor by taking a profit". And throughout my business career, I always focused on profit, not turnover or growth.

Because I was non-executive as Chairman of TMG, the papers didn't hold me responsible, although it was still a difficult period for me personally. Publicly, Maurice was blamed and he received a lot of bad press at that time because he had rubbed too many people up the wrong way.

When TMG went down, Maurice was in real financial trouble. But he went to America, started in business again and re-built his life. Although our friendship took a big knock with the end of TMG, we re-built that as well. Today, he is active within the Ireland Chamber of Commerce in the USA.

Maurice is a very interesting character. He would come with me sometimes when I was looking at businesses. On one occasion, I had a meeting with a guy who just wouldn't give me a straight answer to any question that I asked him. Eventually, the guy turned to Maurice, and said, "What do you do?". I said, "It's very simple. He's going to tell me how much bullshit you talk". The guy did a double-take and said to Maurice, "Are you a psychiatrist?". Maurice said, "No, I'm his friend" – which he still is today.

YOUR MAN IN MONACO

After I had been living in Monaco for a while, and continuing to spend time in Ireland and travel around the world on business, the Taoiseach invited me to become the Irish Honorary Consul to Monaco. It was something I had never even considered and I was honoured to accept.

It's a role that doesn't bring too many responsibilities, but I deal with whatever comes along. Every so often, I host an Irish night, bringing in Irish musicians. I'm on the board of the Princess Grace Foundation in America that raises money for actors and actresses and I have become a close friend of Prince Albert.

Previously, there was no Irish Consul in Monaco. The Irish Honorary Consul General in France is Pierre Joannon, based in Cannes. He is also Chairman of the Ireland Fund de France and has written many books about Ireland, which is his country of 'adoption'. He is an extraordinary Frenchman who speaks Irish fluently and knows more of Irish history than any other person I know.

CHAPTER 14
TELEPHONE TROUBLES

I wanted to find out what worked and what didn't work. I discovered it just didn't work at all.

It's always been my view that everyone should do a little 'National Service' at some point in his or her life. As the Smurfit group grew and developed, I had never been slow to let the leaders of the Irish government know exactly where I thought they were going wrong or how they could improve things for Irish business and for the Irish people. Possibly as a result of my persistent and unasked-for advice, one day in 1979 the Taoiseach, Jack Lynch, asked to see me.

He came straight to the point and said, "Look, Michael, you've been very critical of the government and of the telephone system and the postal system, which have been in the State sector for years. Would you come in and run one of them for us?". He told me that the government was going to set up separate companies to take over the two utilities and he gave me a choice of taking charge of either the telephone company or the postal company. I didn't like the postal idea so I decided I would become Chairman of the Interim Telecommunications Board, which was later to become Telecom Éireann (and, in time, eircom). Little did I know I was to spend the next 12 years fixing it. The civil service had made a disastrous job of running Ireland's telephone system but I was soon to find that putting it right was a considerable task.

I insisted on the highest salary ever paid to the Chairman of a Board of this type: IR£7,000 a year, which was a lot of money at the time – up to IR£2,000 a year was probably the going rate. I wanted to establish the importance of the job and to establish the principle for my successor that the job was a good-paying job. But I gave all the money to charity and didn't even take any expenses. I didn't want to be paid for what I was doing.

I have never been one to boast about the Smurfit name and how much we have done for charity. We have given tens of millions to good causes and charitable institutions that we have never publicised. In my view, nobody else needs to know if you're doing good deeds.

But David O'Reilly insists that the following story be told:

In the late 1970s, St Gerard's, the school Michael's two older sons, Tony and Michael, attended, had the opportunity to purchase adjoining land. The field in question was for sale for IR£60,000, although St Gerard's Board of Governors wanted to minimise the school's outlay by buying just enough to add a couple of sports fields. Approached to assist with funding the purchase, Michael said, "I think you should buy the lot because you never know when you might need the extra land. Or there might be a re-zoning play". He agreed to put up IR£30,000 if the other parents made up the balance.

Fast-forward 25 years ... St Gerard's has two extra pitches ... and sold the additional land for €30 million or so at the top of the property boom. That was strategic thinking!

REFORMING TELECOM

I got an office, took on some executives and appointed a PA, Leslie Buckley, who was seconded from Smurfit specifically to work on the Telecom project.

I wanted to change things quickly, but it took three years before Telecom Éireann was extracted legally from the Department of Telecommunications. The government told us it would be done in one year, but it took three.

So, for those three years, I found myself running a company that did not exist. I was in charge of an organisation that wasn't in operation, but I stuck with it and I used the time to learn about it. I wanted to find out what worked and what didn't work. In fact, I discovered it just didn't work at all.

I learned about the choking bureaucracy, which was unbelievable. I learned how many thousands of people were employed and how demotivated and undervalued most of them were. I realised that, as it was, the organisation *couldn't* work. The people in the organisation were ashamed to go home and tell anyone where they worked, because they knew what they would get: "You work for the telephone company? Jesus Christ! Where's my phone?".

I also used the time to learn about phone systems and all the technical aspects that I'd known nothing about before. I was heartened that we had a fantastic Board of directors, one of the best Boards that I was ever involved in and one of the most confident. On the Board, we had worker directors who are still friends of mine.

WORKING WITH THE UNIONS

Harold O'Sullivan was my Deputy Chairman. He was a senior executive of the Irish Transport & General Workers' Union and of the Irish Congress of Trade Unions.

When I said I wanted him to be Deputy Chairman, he said, "I'm your enemy, I'm not your friend. Why would you want me as your deputy?". I told him, "Harold, this is a people business. You're a trade unionist, I'm not a trade unionist. It's about doing what's right and you're there to make sure we do things right. You're there to look after the people. That's why you're a director and why I want you for my deputy".

Harold could see the sense in what we were trying to do. If I had tried to talk to the unions, they would have seen me as someone from the wrong side of the tracks, and they wouldn't have listened. But they saw Harold as someone from the right side of the tracks and when he explained the problems and the solutions, people listened and understood.

Everyone respected Harold and we had no people problems, no strikes. We had to negotiate with the unions, but we were just talking logic and common sense. We weren't talking BS, and they saw that. We said that we didn't need 24,000 people; we needed something like 8,000 or 9,000. It was a time of very high unemployment in Ireland, so cutting numbers from the telephone company wasn't popular. Half the exchanges were based in post offices and were still hand-operated. Some of the equipment went back to the 1920s and a lot of it to the 1930s and morale in the place was in the gutter. Yet the only solution that anyone could see for the problem was to hire more people.

The first thing I did was to let the government know that we wouldn't be hiring more people. Instead, we were going to let people go because they were falling over each other and getting in each other's way. One Minister, Albert Reynolds, thumped the table and said, "You are going to take on 3,000 more people in the telephone company!". I told him, "Over my dead body. We'll be letting 3,000 people go. Unemployment is not my problem. My problem, my task is to give the Irish consumer an efficient telephone service that is cost-effective. At the moment, we have one that is losing millions, even as a monopoly".

How can you lose millions of pounds in a monopoly? Well, Telecom did. But by the time I left, our employee numbers were substantially reduced, we had introduced a system that worked and we were making millions instead.

HOW THINGS WORKED (OR DIDN'T)

When I became Chairman, it took anything up to two years for someone to get a telephone installed. The whole organisation was hopelessly incompetent. People selling their houses in Ireland at the time could add significant value if they had a phone installed. And it wasn't just private individuals who had to wait, it was the same for businesses. It was a disaster, and getting worse because Ireland was expanding and people had a bit more money and more of them were demanding phones.

It took years, but we changed all that, slowly but surely. It was like a big ship; it took time to turn it around. We didn't go after everything at once. We fixed one problem and then moved on to the next.

I had to start at the very beginning, so things got worse before they got better. I was digging new foundations and encountering shocking new situations. For example, I found that typically a worker would clock on at 8am in a depot. He couldn't leave to start working until 9am or 10am, because the foreman had to check him out. He had to be back by 12 noon for the foreman to check him in and then check him out at 2pm. So I figured that he was working four hours a day maximum, and that included the driving time to wherever he was going.

When I was asked to be Chairman of Telecom, I think some people thought I would be a figurehead. They certainly didn't expect me to go around looking at exchanges and going into depots to discover the truth about what was going wrong – but that's what I did. Often when I was driving around, I would see a Telecom van and I would ask my driver to stop, so I could have a chat with the workers and see what they were doing. I wanted to go down the manholes and see how the connections were made. I learned all about the problems they faced, such as systems being destroyed by water, and what they were doing to repair them. I was determined to discover every possible detail of what we could do better.

Initially, some of the managers were annoyed that I would go straight to the workers and talk to them. But, in the end, they understood that what I was doing was learning, so that I could relate to them, and become able to talk to them about the issues. That was always my style in the Smurfit factories: if I went on a factory tour, I wouldn't just talk to the managers or the people they picked for me to talk to. I would take the route around the factory that I wanted to take and I would talk to the people behind the machines so that I could get a good feel for what was going on in the place.

I wanted to understand precisely what I was involved in at Telecom. I was there to do a job of work and that job was to get the phones working. How could I get the phones working if I didn't understand how a phone actually worked? So I went to the depots, I went to see the systems, I went to the stores area, where we stored our equipment and found that, in addition to providing a telephone service, we were doing odd things like issuing uniforms to An Garda Síochána, the Irish police force. We were also responsible for providing nurses' uniforms and boots for soldiers in the army. No wonder the phones weren't being installed on time.

I got rid of all the things that were not our business. I stripped it down to telephones and focused on our job, which was to get the telephones at the lowest possible price that we could to the customers. Customers are vital for any business because it is the customer who pays.

I remember going into Telecom's head office in Marlborough Street, where there was a counter you went to in order to apply to get a telephone. I became a member of the public and politely queued up. The clerk asked me to fill out the form, so I did as I was told and filled it out. Under 'Title', I put 'Chairman of Telecom Éireann'. I handed it back and the clerk didn't read it. He just said 'Thanks', so I asked him what he did with the form. He replied unambiguously, "It's none of your f****** business!". I said I really wanted to know and asked him if he would read the form.

So I went through the whole process from start to finish as to where this piece of paper went. The bureaucracy was simply stifling everything. I put up a map in Telecom's Boardroom for all the executives to see. It showed with diagrams and demonstrations why you couldn't get a telephone in six months if you tried, because it had to go through so many absurd procedures and so much preposterous paperwork.

So I said that what we were going to do was simple: reduce the form-filling to application, installation and payment. We tore up ridiculous regulations that had been built up over 50 or 60 years. It was not the fault of the individual workers. The people in Telecom only knew to do what they had been taught to do. They didn't know any different. No one had ever actually sat down and gone through the whole thing.

It was not just the bureaucracy. I was determined to find out exactly how the telecommunications service worked and insisted on inspecting everything we could think of, but I was not prepared for the terrifying moment when my enthusiasm almost cost me my life.

RISKING MY LIFE

I wanted to visit each of the Irish telephone exchanges personally and see for myself how they operated. The only way to do this in the time that I had available was to travel by helicopter. Leslie Buckley had arranged a packed series of visits.

We were due to fly from Dublin across to the west of the country. Leslie had booked the helicopter to depart at 8:30am and he arrived early to make sure there were no problems. It was a beautiful, clear morning. He phoned our destination and confirmed the weather was excellent there as well. But strangely, the helicopter didn't arrive. So Leslie phoned the helicopter company, who said that due to fog, they wouldn't be flying that day.

Leslie was furious. He had checked the weather conditions himself and knew they were perfect at both ends of our planned journey. He guessed that they had made a mess of the bookings and that our helicopter had been allocated to someone else. He told them in no uncertain terms that we would be flying and they should get a helicopter over straight away.

Then I arrived, and was none too pleased to find that there was no transport and already my busy day was running late. After about 15 minutes, the helicopter arrived and we set off into a clear blue sky. I settled back to go through some paperwork, still annoyed about the delay.

As we got towards the midlands, the cloud set in and, before long, we couldn't see a thing. The pilot was forced to manoeuvre desperately and to jump telegraph lines as they suddenly appeared before us. On we went, flying blindly up and down, all three of us grimly silent and doubtful that we would live to see another day.

Finally, the fog cleared, we reached our destination and landed. I was dressed in my business suit and my fine leather shoes. I stepped from the helicopter and felt my shoes sink into the wet, muddy ground. Somehow, it was a suitable end to the journey.

Leslie himself recalls:

I didn't believe the story about fog because I was convinced they had let someone else have our helicopter. I insisted that our trip would go ahead. I rang Michael to say we would be taking off 10 minutes late. He said, "Great start!".

*I was quite pleased there was a lot of noise when we eventually got on board. We were passing notes backwards and forwards and then suddenly we hit the thickest blanket of fog I have ever seen. I said to the pilot that I didn't think it would be this bad. He shouted back, "I ****ing told you so!". We had to dodge the pylons and Michael was ashen-faced. I could imagine the headlines in the papers the following day about a crash and our bodies being found. We eventually arrived into Galway, very shaken.*

We were so relieved to have made it safely that Michael made me cancel an official dinner we had planned for that night, so the two of us could just go out together and quietly celebrate still being alive.

INVESTING IN THE FUTURE

Whilst I didn't foresee the Celtic Tiger, it could not have happened without what we did at Telecom.

I was given an early insight into the problems we faced by Tony Mullen, who was the senior engineer. Keen to learn as much as I could about the telephone system, I discovered that 'step and repeat' was the old system, which we were beginning to replace with the 'crossbar' system, which America had at the time. Tony persuaded me that there was a new, much better system coming out: digital. But the government had already spent £50 million on buildings across the country to install the crossbar exchanges. When I took over, these commitments already existed and the Taoiseach boldly said there were going to be 20,000 new phones installed. I said that there were two chances of this happening: no chance and no chance at all. The system was just unworkable.

Tony Mullen asked me to go to Sweden with him to look at developments there. I found that this new digital technology used fibre optics, where a much smaller cable could be used for many more phones. We saw that was the way for the future. Saudi Arabia was the first country to install this new system, so I went to Saudi

Arabia and saw how it worked and I was very impressed. It required only a small corner of a room to accommodate the equipment, as opposed to the whole room, so I got the Board to scrap all the orders for the crossbar technology and we jumped from first generation to third generation. Ireland was one of the first countries in the world to install digital phone technology.

Thanks to Tony Mullen's foresight and my own acceptance of technology, Ireland missed installing the second generation. This was very important because, if we had installed the second generation, we could never have afforded the third. Without the third generation technology, we could not have had Intel and Microsoft and Dell moving into Ireland, because they all required instantaneous communication. I believe that we just dodged a bullet.

Later, Tony Mullen lost out on becoming Chief Executive of Telecom. Just before I had dinner with him and the Board in Cork, I told him that sadly he was not going to get the position, because it was going to a rival candidate, Fergus McGovern, who turned out to be absolutely the right man for the job. In fact, we had three people who could all have done the job very well. Tony was unlucky to lose out but we went through a careful interview process.

At the dinner, Tony had a few drinks and he effed and blinded and cursed me in front of everybody. I didn't react to the abuse, but I did say to Tony that, if I had been in his shoes, I think I would have felt the same. The next day, he felt a bit worse for wear and I said to him, "I don't want you to leave Telecom. You know your country needs you. At least, this organisation needs you, and despite what you think of me, which is your personal opinion, I want you to stay".

Happily, that is what he did and I was very pleased. He became the number two executive in the company and did a great job.

AN UNHAPPY ENDING

Unfortunately, my time in charge of Telecom Éireann did not end on a happy note.

The company needed new headquarters and I came across what looked like the ideal place on the same day that I picked the site for the Smurfit Business School. We were driving through Ballsbridge and there it was. I said, "I didn't know the Johnston Mooney & O'Brien site was for sale". It was the perfect site in the perfect location and Telecom Éireann bought it for something like IR£8 million. This was considered a fair bit of money, but it was a unique site. It suited the company perfectly but, later, there was an accusation that I had made money from the deal, which was totally false.

The suggestion was that a company in which I had made a small investment some years before had owned the site at one time and that, in some way, I personally had benefited financially.

Because Telecom Éireann was a State body, the press took it up and made a big hullabaloo of it. It was annoying and a source of concern to me that I was getting this type of press coverage, which was totally unwarranted, but because I knew I had done nothing underhand or wrong, I was not too worried. When the story first came to my attention, I had called the Minister, Seamus Brennan, and told him that there was nothing for him to worry about as I was not involved and nothing improper had been done.

Charles Haughey was Taoiseach at the time, and I knew him well. I was a regular guest at his home in Abbeville and he was often my guest at mine. Dad had been a good friend of his father-in-law, Sean Lemass, who was Taoiseach in the early 1960s. The government appointed an inspector to investigate the claim and it appeared clear to me that neither Brennan nor Haughey were prepared to accept my word that I had done nothing inappropriate in respect of the Johnston Mooney & O'Brien site.

In 1991, coincidentally on the opening day of The K Club in Straffan, Charles Haughey was asked in a radio interview whether he thought I should step aside from my post as Chairman of Telecom Éireann. He said that he supposed I should. Haughey had not told me that he was going to say this and he hadn't thought it through. You cannot simply 'step aside' from the position of Chairman of a large institution. You cannot put the place into limbo, particularly as I knew the inspector could take anything from one to three years to complete the investigation. To have me as an absent Chairman for that length of time was neither logical nor practical – never mind fair.

And it was not just about me. Dermot Desmond, Chairman of Aer Rianta (the Irish airport authority) and Seamus Paircéir, Chairman of the Customs House Docks Development Authority, were all implicated by Haughey in the radio interview. He said that we should all step aside from our posts pending the outcome of the investigations. It was an outrageous and stupid statement for Haughey to make and I took it very badly, as I believe I had a right to do. So did Dermot Desmond, so did Seamus Paircéir.

I was very upset and went to my Board at Telecom and told them what had happened. My Board were very supportive but I told them that I had decided to resign. I knew that, sometimes, a resignation can be taken as a sign of guilt, but I thought, "To hell with it, I don't need this". All three of us – Desmond, Paircéir and myself – resigned from our positions.

I never spoke to Charles Haughey again. I make a great friend, but I don't make a good enemy. I'm not a vindictive person, I just cut people who do me a bad turn out of my life and have nothing more to do them.

However, I remember one of Haughey's sons, Ciaran, came to me and said he supposed he was going to lose my business with his company, which hired out helicopters. I asked, "Why? You're not responsible for what your father did. My relationship with you will not change in the slightest". Why would I take something out on the child, when it was the father who had been in the wrong?

Charles Haughey did a great deal for Ireland; nonetheless, he cast a stain on my name that eventually got erased on the outcome of the inquiry, but I would have preferred to have left Telecom in different circumstances.

Two years later, the inspector completed his report and I was vindicated. The investigation cost millions of pounds and the inspector finally exonerated me, and all the Telecom people, and found that we had acted totally correctly. And I never even got an apology from Haughey.

I think I did a different and, in some ways, better job in Telecom than I did in Smurfit because I built Smurfit up gradually over a long period of time, knowing exactly where I wanted to get to. In Telecom,

I came into an unadulterated mess. There were no accounts, no one knew how much we were making or losing; you couldn't even get a phone. We brought the telephone company into the modern age and brought long-term benefits for the country. Without a good telephone system, Ireland would not have been able to develop the vibrant indigenous IT sector, let alone attract the global players in that industry and to the International Financial Services Centre in Dublin, all of which are so critical to the economic growth of the country.

CHAPTER 15
RACING AHEAD

Winners count; seconds don't matter.

Although I have very happy memories of being with my father at the Grand National and other horse races when I was a boy, it was my oldest son, Tony, who got me involved in the sport in a serious way.

Norma's father, Mo, was staying with us in Dublin and, one day, just as I came home, I saw Tony going into the house. I asked him where he'd been and it turned out that he had been to the bookies … with his granddad, very much on the quiet. It turned out that Mo, who was a keen racing man, and Tony had been going to the bookies for some time but had kept their enthusiasm quiet because they thought I would not approve. Strangely, instead of disapproval, my discovery rekindled my own interest in racing.

I had always loved the atmosphere of a busy race meeting. As a boy, I had been thrilled by the hustle and bustle and energy of the race track and the larger-than-life characters the sport attracts.

As a younger man, I had enjoyed more active sports like golf and skiing, until my back was badly injured in a boating accident in the Mediterranean. I had to be flown home to Ireland and that was the start of long and painful treatment. I think I have had 12 epidurals in all and my back has been a painful problem ever since. Not being able to play golf as well as I used to before my back injury, horse-racing became a bigger attraction.

I started to sponsor races. The Smurfit St Leger became a highlight of the racing calendar, as did the Smurfit Champion Hurdle at Cheltenham.

I met the trainer Dermot Weld and got to know him well. We became good friends and we've had some success together.

MY EARLY DAYS AS AN OWNER

When I got into horse-racing as an owner, one of the very first horses I bought was called *Greasepaint*, an Irish horse that had been owned by Michael Cunningham. *Greasepaint* had been second in the Grand National in 1983 to a horse called *Corbiere*, which famously made its trainer, Jenny Pitman, the first woman to train a Grand National winner. Dermot Weld was known primarily as a trainer for racing on the flat. He had never been a trainer of jumping horses, but I persuaded him to take them up and *Greasepaint* was one of his first.

At the 1984 Grand National, *Greasepaint* was not that much fancied, as he was carrying too much weight and the ground was against him. Nevertheless, off he went and lo and behold, we couldn't believe it, coming over the second last fence he was in the lead. My horse was about to win the Grand National! But he just got caught on the line by a horse called *Hello Dandy*. *Greasepaint* came second again.

We were in the second's enclosure and, of course, all the chatter was about the winner. I said to Tony, "Son, I want you to learn a lesson. Here in the second's enclosure, we might as well be on Mars – it's all about being over there, in the winner's enclosure. Winners count; seconds don't matter". That phrase became another of our business mottos. But, to be honest, we were very happy to be second because it was our first real thrill with horse-racing. We'd won a bit of money with an each-way bet and there was money for coming second as well – but being first would have been a lot better.

FOURNOUGHTS & CLASSIC THOROUGHBREDS

Pretty soon, I decided that, if Tony was going to be backing horses, he ought to start to take a serious interest in the sport. By now, I had made a bit of money and I wanted a place in the country to breed horses. Dermot suggested some suitable land, which I purchased to build Fournoughts stud farm. I put an enormous amount of money into the stud, far more than I originally envisaged, and eventually it became one of Tony's businesses and his home when he was in Ireland. Making that purchase was a great decision.

As part of my interest in racing, I launched a venture called Classic Thoroughbreds, along with Vincent O'Brien, the legendary trainer, and that extraordinary genius, John Magnier, the owner of the now globally-successful Coolmore Stud. The theory in horse-breeding is that you pick the parents and their offspring should be even better – but 99 times out of 100, it doesn't work. You can have a horse with a useless pedigree that becomes a champion.

Classic Thoroughbreds bought and bred horses and raced them, but we didn't have much success. We won one big race when a horse called *Royal Academy* won in the Breeder's Cup. It was a $1 million race and it was a great moment but, outside that, we had no luck.

Vincent O'Brien retired as a trainer in the late 1980s and John Magnier now has the most successful studs in Ireland, Kentucky and Australia, along with other business interests.

I was instrumental in winding up Classic Thoroughbreds after a few years because it was failing, though we former partners remained firm friends.

THE MELBOURNE CUP

Nowadays, my involvement in racing is much reduced. I rely very heavily on my son Tony, my trainer Dermot and Tony's stud manager, Dermot Cantillon, when it comes to breeding and buying horses.

The best horse that I ever had was called *Vintage Crop*. He won 16 races in Ireland and England, including the Smurfit St Leger twice, but he is most famous for being the first horse from the Northern Hemisphere to win the Melbourne Cup in Australia in 1993. *Vintage Crop* was originally from Gilltown Stud, which was owned by Bert Firestone at the time and now belongs to the Aga Khan. He had no stud value and Bert had no interest in keeping geldings and jumping horses. So Dermot Weld had him gelded and I bought him to go over jumps, until later we found out as he matured that he was a better flat racing horse than a jump horse. His breeding was all about flat horses.

When Dermot told me he had the idea to take *Vintage Crop* to the Melbourne Cup in 1993, I thought he was crazy, or 'cuckoo' as I call it. But Dermot isn't a cuckoo guy, he's a very shrewd trainer indeed. He is a veterinary surgeon who had worked in Australia when he was a young man, so he knew the country well. It had always been an ambition of his to take a horse from Ireland to run in the Melbourne Cup. Conditions there are so different from Europe that it was always thought impossible for a European horse to take part, let alone win the race. Just getting the horse over there is a story in itself, but that's Dermot's story to tell.

There were considerable logistical difficulties with transport and quarantine regulations but Dermot's determination was remarkable. We got a lot of financial help from the Victoria Racing Club because the authorities in Australia wanted to involve horses from the Northern Hemisphere. Dermot and I were trailblazing, because nobody else would come down. Nowadays, a third of the runners are from the Northern Hemisphere. In the end, our chances of success came down to what weight we got: the more weight we had to carry, the less chance we had of winning. When the weights came out in the first week in September, we were quite pleased.

The Melbourne Cup is probably Australia's biggest sporting and social occasion. Held on the first Tuesday of November every year, it attracts more than 100,000 people to the Flemington course. Melbourne holds a public holiday and parliamentary proceedings are stopped so that members can tune in to it. It's watched on television throughout Australia and right round the world. There is a fantastic atmosphere and it's a race that everyone who's interested in horse-racing would want to go to, all the more so if you actually owned a horse that was running, and especially if that horse had come over from Ireland.

Unfortunately, I couldn't attend the race that year. I had to be in St Louis, at an important board meeting with Morgan Stanley that I just couldn't get out of. Even worse, I remember the meeting turned into a major argument with the Morgan Stanley executives. I more or less told them all to "shove off" and I went up to my room and listened to my horse winning the Melbourne Cup on the radio. It was still exciting, although I bitterly regretted not being at the great event. The radio commentary was confusing as well, because there was a horse called *Great Vintage* in the race and, at first, I thought it was *Great Vintage* that had won, and not *Vintage Crop*. But, ridden by Michael Kinane, my horse achieved what many observers reckoned was impossible and he flew first past the winning post at 14/1. I was very proud and particularly pleased for Dermot, but it was disappointing not to be there.

The prize was $2 million Australian. I don't believe that you race horses to make money, but that certainly helped to pay our bills for racing that year. The remarkable victory helped to make *Vintage Crop* become one of the most popular and successful Irish racehorses of all time.

I eventually retired him to the National Stud, as an attraction for visiting members of the public. Lots of Australians came to take a look, I'm told. His statue stands at the Curragh racecourse and the cocktail bar at The K Club in Straffan is named in his honour. The walls of the bar are decorated with racing trophies and memorabilia from him and from my other Melbourne Cup-winning horse, *Media Puzzle*.

Dermot and I were not content with winning the Melbourne Cup once. We decided to do it again!

This time, I was taking a short break relaxing with friends in Spain in November 2002, when *Media Puzzle* stormed down the straight to win the Melbourne Cup by two lengths. This was a race we won with mixed feelings because it was a very tough day for *Media Puzzle*'s jockey, Damien Oliver. He had lost his brother Jason in a track accident just a week before the race and he dedicated his win to his brother.

The only time I actually attended the Melbourne Cup and had a horse running in the race was when *Vintage Crop* came in third, which I believe was by far his best run ever, because he actually had the top weight and he missed the start and was last out of the gate.

WIN SOME, LOSE MORE

I first started in horse-racing as a member of syndicates, where there would be three or four of us sharing ownership of a horse, with Dermot Weld as our trainer.

We won a race called the Cartier Million, with prize money of IR£1 million, with a horse I owned along with the late Robert Sangster and Tim Mahony.

The joy of winning is always tempered by the fact that you inevitably lose far more times than you win. You've just got to accept that, with horse-racing, there is no sure thing. In fact, the only sure thing is that there isn't a sure thing. All sorts of different factors come into play: the conditions of the track, the horse getting a virus, the jockey having a problem, a rival horse that no one expected to do anything coming from the back. It's unpredictable.

Along with the successes, I've had all the disappointments you can possibly imagine in horse-racing. I can still recall the let-down of coming second in the Grand National in England with *Greasepaint*. And when we won the Irish Grand National with a horse called *Perris Valley*, I wasn't there to see it win.

Racing brings all sorts of emotions into play. We won the Irish Derby with a horse called *Zagreb*, when Dermot wasn't going to run it in the race until I insisted. There is an adrenaline rush when the race starts, which rapidly dissipates when you see that your horse is not going to do well.

But, as an owner, I believe you have to remember it's a hobby – you are not in it for the money. It's a one-way street. Every so often, you get lucky and win some money, but on average you lose money every year. Or, at least, most people who own racehorses do.

For me, the attraction is being part of the enjoyable social gatherings, full of different people from all walks of life. The atmosphere of a race-track can be electric, particularly on big days, like Derby day or Grand National day.

Different courses and different races all have different atmospheres. Cheltenham is my number one choice for atmosphere in the whole world. It's like an Irish race meeting that just happens to be held in England. Thousands of Irish people go over for the festival in March and Irish horses have a great success record there. Royal Ascot is another great meeting for atmosphere, followed by the Derby and, of course, the Galway Races, which is one of my favourite events: I love going there. One time, I had six winners there in three days.

Flat racing tends to have a more middle to upper class audience, while jumping seems to bring together more of a farming community who go to point-to-points and hunting. Flat races are over very quickly, whereas you get a decent run for your money over the jumps where a race will last three or four minutes. I much prefer watching jumping to flat racing, although I participate in both.

I don't always have a horse running when I go racing, I'll sometimes go just for the enjoyment. I try to let my trainers know in advance when I'll be able to go to certain races, in the hope that I can have a horse running on the day.

When you own a racehorse, you need a lot of patience. It's a very different world from my business life.

Dermot Weld says:

There is a side of Michael Smurfit that a lot of people don't very often see. He comes across very much as the tough, hard-nosed businessman, but there's a gentler side. He has been kind and caring to many people. He has a heart of gold, but he doesn't let many people see that. He is very loyal to his friends and I'm privileged to be one of them, and I think I'm one of the few people who know the real man. I believe you see the sort of man he is by the way he treats his old horses when they come to the end of the line.

I back my own horses from time to time but I wouldn't be considered a punter by any stretch of the imagination. I've had the odd flutter, but I wouldn't place a serious bet. I certainly don't always back my own horses. I find gambling is a mug's game. I got to know JP McManus long ago when he was my bookie and we became good friends. He's now one of Ireland's leading businessmen, which maybe tells us that it's wiser to be the person who takes the bets than the person who places them.

RUNNING THE RACING BOARD

The late 1980s and early 1990s was probably the busiest time of my life. I was running Smurfit, which was rapidly expanding. I was Chairman of Telecom Éireann. I was a director of Allied Irish Banks. I was a major stockholder in New Ireland Assurance Company. I was a very busy bee but I had lots of energy and I very much enjoyed using it.

In 1987, my achievements as Chairman of Telecom Éireann and in business, combined with being a racehorse owner and a member of the Turf Club, led to the Irish government asking me to become Chairman of the Racing Board. This was a very prestigious position. Although I hardly seemed to have much spare time, I accepted. I felt I should give something back to Ireland, because the country had been very good to me. I decided to take the job on for five years, and I insisted I wouldn't do any more than those five years. The government didn't give me a brief as to what they wanted me to do, except that they wanted the racing industry to become more profitable, because they would benefit from those increased profits. Irish racing wasn't exactly in crisis, but it was an industry that wasn't going anywhere.

Ireland was still a poor country then. We were educating our young people and then sending them abroad, exporting the cream of Ireland's brains. Some people wondered why I was wasting money on improving racing. I understood their feelings, but I said an improved racing industry would create jobs – and it did. The aim was to provide opportunities so that our best horses remained in training in Ireland, raced in Ireland, and were enjoyed by race-goers experiencing the best racing and social facilities.

At the start, I set out key tasks I was determined to complete during the tenure of my chairmanship. The first thing I planned to do was to build a new Racing Board head office, because the office that we had was grotty. It was right in the centre of Dublin, and it was an appallingly inefficient building. It was a rabbit warren of little offices, and it was grubby, inefficient and generally horrible. I just didn't want anything to do with it. The Racing Board owned its own tracks

– one of these was Leopardstown, a beautiful site. I got designers and builders in and used the money from the sale of the old building to pay for bright new offices. The staff loved the switch.

The second thing I wanted to do was to improve Leopardstown itself. In spite of what seemed its obvious potential, it wasn't doing very well financially. The golf course in the middle of the racecourse was earning only about £100,000 a year, while it should have been earning at least £500,000. We quickly turned it into a major profit centre. I used that money to make more improvements at Leopardstown. We built what we called the 'top suites' for race-goers and they proved popular. They were the best suites in Ireland with fantastic views.

An even more important innovation, which at the time was very difficult to bring about, was to introduce Sunday racing. It is now an accepted thing here in Ireland, but back then it was very difficult to get the unions to agree. People had entrenched views. I argued that Sunday was much more of a leisure day for Irish people than a Saturday. It wasn't a religious issue, though some people questioned the idea of gambling on a Sunday. I replied that this was a lot of nonsense because they did it in France and Italy, strongly Catholic countries. Eventually, we got Sunday racing through and then we computerised the Tote. That meant more difficult negotiations with the unions and took two years to resolve. But it was another important step in the right direction.

One of the jobs of the Racing Board is to give out money to race-tracks for improvements. Some of the race-tracks are proud of their history and traditions. Tracks like Fairyhouse, home of the Irish Grand National, which was modelled on Sandown racecourse in England and opened in 1888, and Punchestown, which also has a history going back over 150 years and is the home of Irish National Hunt racing, were hardly enthusiastic about change, even if they were prepared to welcome investment. Some had their own Boards and owned the courses themselves.

The Racing Board couldn't show favouritism to anyone and I was adamant that we wouldn't put our money where we didn't think the plans were viable. Loads of pie-in-the-sky ideas came across my desk that were never going to get off the ground. Too often, they just wanted too much for too little, but somehow we managed to get racing turned around in a positive way.

By the end of my five years with the Racing Board, I had achieved the aims that I had set out. When I started as Chairman, the Racing Board was losing money and, when I left five years later, it was making IR£500,000 a year. The thoroughbred industry in Ireland is now thriving and this was part and parcel of the benefits of improving our horse-racing industry. Racing in Ireland is now on a very firm footing. We laid the foundations for that.

Dermot Weld is probably best placed to recall the improvements we made:

> *The late 1980s was a tough time, when there was very little money in racing. As Chairman of the Racing Board, Michael Smurfit did a marvellous job, holding the purse strings together and keeping racing going forward, getting sponsorship, and updating the Tote. He was one of the first Chairmen to look at the whole aspect of improving race tracks and looking at ways of encouraging young people to go racing. Although there were a few run-ins with the Turf Club, who administer the rules, generally most people realised he was doing an excellent job in a difficult time.*

> *Michael Smurfit has made a huge contribution to Irish racing, both as an owner and as an administrator. He gave it a great deal of credibility by his presence and encouraged many people from all over the world to get involved in Irish racing.*

> *I was quite a successful trainer before I met Michael but he has made an enormously positive impact on my life by showing he believed in me. He is the sort of man who can instil great confidence and he has had that effect on me. I'm happy to say that, along the way, we have become very close friends.*

CHAPTER 16
A GOLFING TRIUMPH

If you have a vision, make it happen.

I don't believe my work with Telecom Éireann or the Racing Board ever affected my contribution to driving Smurfit forward in a time of considerable growth and success. I have always taken care to manage my time and I believe that my performance in business and the corporate world was stimulated greatly by my two spells of 'National Service'. But before I return to concentrate on the development of the Smurfit Group, which remained far and away my main concern, I would like to recount a third new job I took on: the development of The K Club and the battle to win the Ryder Cup for Ireland.

THE SEED OF AN IDEA

While I had been travelling the world and seeing different places, I had seen a great many different golfing establishments and I had been impressed by just how good they were, particularly in America. They all seemed to be clean, efficient and professionally run. By comparison, in Ireland back in the 1970s and early 1980s, many of the clubs seemed shoddy and second-rate to me. The idea of building a world-class country club in Ireland had been germinating quietly at the back of my mind for years, but I had no specific plans.

By this time, in the late 1980s, Smurfit had become a true multi-national, which was fine – but it also put us in a difficult situation. A large proportion of our assets were outside Ireland and, when the double taxation laws were written in the 1930s, they were written on a one-way basis so that overseas companies with operations in Ireland would not be taxed in Ireland as well as in their home country. No one in Ireland had taken an Irish company abroad, until we did it, so there had been no thought given to the reverse situation.

We found that, on every penny we brought back to Ireland, effectively we paid 80%. We paid taxes in America; we also paid taxes in The Netherlands, where we had a holding company; then, on top of that, we paid taxes on what was left to the Irish Exchequer. It did not even end there: the recipients of earnings from our shares had to pay tax on that income as well, so there were four levels of taxes payable on a dividend coming back from our overseas subsidiaries.

The net result, perhaps not surprisingly, was that we didn't repatriate much of the money. We had a huge amount of cash – at one point, we had €1.5 billion in cash – and we couldn't distribute it to the people who owned the business, the shareholders, because it would have been financially irresponsible to expose their money to such high levels of taxation.

I went to see the Minister of Finance and the Taoiseach and did what I could to bring pressure to bear. Their answer was to offer Irish businesses that created jobs a tax relief on the amount of their investment. We already had created jobs and wealth for Ireland, and we couldn't see a way to create several hundred more jobs in our own business. We already dominated most sectors of the paper packaging market in Ireland and there was little left for us to invest in. And there matters stalled – for the time being.

STRAFFAN HOUSE

One day when I was at the Curragh Races, Jacqueline O'Brien said to me, "Michael, you should buy Straffan House". I knew about Straffan House from my childhood. It was near Clongowes Wood College, where I and my brother Jeff had gone to school. I had walked through the grounds when I was a boy. But I didn't know it was for sale.

So, I went to take a look at it. I liked what I saw and, more or less on the spot, I bought Straffan House for IR£3.5 million. The sale included all the furniture, all the silverware, all the paintings on the walls, everything.

There had been a house on the site for many centuries, but the Straffan House that I bought was constructed in 1832 by Hugh

Barton, one of two members of the Barton family who farmed in County Kildare. They were not Catholics, but they supported the 1798 revolution in Ireland against British rule. When it failed, like many Irish people at the time, they fled to France, to the Bordeaux area where they became involved in wine-growing. They were very successful and, from 1798 to 1820, made so much money that they were able to send a lot of it, together with an architect, back to Ireland to re-build the family home in Straffan. The new house was a fabulous family home in the style of a grand French chateau, on the banks of the River Liffey in beautiful County Kildare.

It was originally built with nine windows across, but in the 1930s Captain Barton, the then owner, ran out of money and found the house too cold and uncomfortable to live in. Instead of simply locking up and leaving empty the rooms that he didn't want, he demolished two-thirds of it, reducing the façade to just three windows wide, thus destroying the original elegant proportions.

In the 1970s, a young entrepreneur from Dublin, Patrick Gallagher, bought the property. He employed a firm of architects who faithfully and completely seamlessly rebuilt what the Bartons had knocked down. Unfortunately, having done all this work, Gallagher had problems with his business enterprises and ended up selling the house to an English entrepreneur, Alan Ferguson, whose wife spent more than IR£7 million decorating and furnishing it. But sadly, in the stock market crash of October 1987, Ferguson ran into financial difficulties and had to sell.

Straffan House then was bought by two businessmen from Northern Ireland and I bought it from them. This was a personal deal for me, nothing to do with the Smurfit Group. It was a private house and I intended to turn it into a country club. Myself. Not the company. I was out selling 'Golden Memberships' to my friends at IR£100,000 to play for 50 years with no dues. I had sold 50 of them, more or less straight away, which is IR£5 million. I would have had all of them sold if it had not been for the stock market crash.

Then came a new development. Robert Holmes, the Smurfit Group's CFO at the time, was negotiating with the government about the tax-related job creation proposals. He came to me and said, "We think that Straffan House should be bought by the company and turned into a country club". My contract with the Group was very specific; there was nothing I could do privately that I didn't offer the Smurfit Group first. It had not appeared initially that Straffan House would be of interest to the Group but, of course, with the job creation scheme allowing the Group to bring back IR£70 or IR£80 million to shareholders, it became an attractive proposition.

THE K CLUB

In the end, the Group took over my project and I developed it as The K Club on behalf of Jefferson Smurfit Group, although I would have preferred to keep it for myself. However, much later, in 2005, I finally managed to buy it back again for myself, this time for over €100 million! But I'm getting ahead of myself.

As I went to work on the Straffan House project, my initial idea was to make it a very exclusive country club, with a very small hotel, maybe 25 or 40 rooms. The economics of that model didn't work out and it was soon rejected.

A little later, it occurred to me that we could develop the site on a much larger scale. As a result, over about 10 years, the Group spent about €150 million building The K Club. Thanks to property sales and tax benefits, on a purely economic basis The K Club was a stunning success. Effectively, it cost the Group nothing: it got its money back and tax relief on the investment. It was a home run.

When I bought Straffan House, it was set in 320 acres of land. I bought more land to make 550 acres. I took an option on the land across the way, which turned out to be a shrewd investment. I paid IR£2,000 an acre for the option to buy at IR£10,000 an acre. The Smurfit Group bought Straffan House and all the land. Today, that land is worth much more.

When we started to develop Straffan House, the village of Straffan was one of the areas of highest unemployment in Ireland. That's been totally reversed. The K Club was started initially to create 150 jobs, but it has gone on to create many more. I think the local people are proud of what we have done. We're committed to supporting the local community in different ways and we have good community relations. They have been very supportive of what we have done and we are grateful for that.

The architect I commissioned to expand Straffan House and create The K Club as a first class hotel was Brian O'Halloran, whom I have known since my late teens. But it was his ability as an architect that won him a number of projects for me, including the Jefferson Smurfit Group World Headquarters in Clonskeagh, built in the 1970s, an innovative design way ahead of its time. I wanted Straffan House to be developed in its original style, which has a flavour of the architecture of the Loire region of France. Brian didn't let me down.

The hardest thing for an architect probably is to satisfy the demands of a committee. With The K Club, Brian was dealing with a committee of one: me. His stipulation was that I would have to make myself available – and I did. No matter where I might be travelling in the world, every two weeks I would turn up for a site meeting. The routine was that we would meet on site, we would inspect what was going on, we would walk around in muddy boots, and then we would go over to Fournoughts, where I was living at the time, for dinner and do all the paperwork. Then there would be hand-to-hand combat that you just can't imagine. I wouldn't like some of the things I saw, and Brian would say I had already given my approval, and we would battle it out.

I wanted a say on everything, from the shape of the windows to the height of the ceilings, but it was impossible for me to have the time to decide on every detail. But I was involved with the important decisions, like the height of the balcony in the clubhouse, which was settled only after I commandeered a fork-lift truck and had the driver hoist Brian and myself high into the air so we could decide on the exact height I wanted. Every time I stand there now and take in the wonderful view of the course and surrounds, I am happy that I was such a stickler.

To design our golf course, I picked the great Arnold Palmer. Why Arnold Palmer? I was thinking of giving the job to Gary Player, the famous golfer from South Africa, but unfortunately South Africans were banned at that time due to the apartheid regime. I was playing golf at a tournament in Florida and Arnold Palmer personally came to see me and asked me if I wanted him to do the job. Because he took the trouble to see me, I said, "Mr Palmer, it's yours".

I told him to think big and design a great golf course that could host a tournament. He did a first class job. The land around Straffan House was rolling parkland with mature trees and the River Liffey running through it. It lent itself completely to the creation of a superb course, without having to change the landscape very much. The K Club now speaks for itself. It is the premier Irish resort by far.

GETTING THE RYDER CUP

Early on in the development of The K Club, my vision was somehow to bring the Ryder Cup to Ireland, where I knew our new facilities would meet the challenge of staging such a prestigious competition. Irish players have been instrumental in winning a number of Ryder Cup tournaments and five Irishmen – Eamon Darcy, Christy O'Connor Junior, Philip Walton, Paul McGinley and Graeme McDowell – have made the winning putts. And yet it had never come to Ireland. Irish people are fanatical about their golf. I believe we have more golfers as a percentage of the population than anywhere else in the world, except possibly Scotland. Why shouldn't we host the Ryder Cup?

There were two selling jobs to be done. First, I had to persuade the PGA that there were a number of venues in Ireland that could handle the Ryder Cup if they agreed to bring it to Ireland. The venues turned out to be The K Club, Mount Juliet, Druid's Glen and Portmarnock. Of that competition, Portmarnock was taken out of the equation because the club didn't allow female members and still doesn't.

Eventually, I persuaded the PGA that the Ryder Cup should come to Ireland and the agreed date was 2005, but because of the terrible terrorist attack of 9/11 on the twin towers of the World Trade Center in New York, it was put back until September 2006.

The second selling job was to get the Ryder Cup for The K Club. I felt that we were strong favourites because Smurfit had been sponsoring junior golf in Ireland for decades. We sponsor the local

PGA tour and we also are the main sponsor for one of the top three tournaments in Europe on the European tour. Both Mount Juliet and Druid's Glen understandably were keen to get the Ryder Cup, but I never really feared them as competition. As I saw it, we had everything, Mount Juliet had two-thirds of everything, and Druid's Glen was in a similar position.

So in the final negotiations in London, I said to Ken Schofield, the Executive Director of the PGA, "Ken, here's my proposal. Smurfit's contract to sponsor the European Open runs out in 2002. We are prepared to sponsor that for a further 10 years, if we get the Ryder Cup". That was worth a lot of money to him, maybe £20 or £30 million, but we were going to do it in any case, although he didn't know that. Ken hemmed and hawed, then he shook hands and said, "You've got the Ryder Cup".

I insisted that we announce immediately that the venue was going to be The K Club, because I didn't want any ambiguity about it. I wanted it in black and white and I wanted people to know what was going to happen. It was a great thrill for me to get it for The K Club.

I don't think there was any resentment from the other Irish courses that were competing for the event. I think they knew that we were a strong contender and that they would benefit in the longer term because we would increase the awareness of golf in Ireland. And for the Jefferson Smurfit Group, getting the Ryder Cup increased the value of The K Club significantly.

A DREAM COMES TRUE

For the 2006 Ryder Cup, Ireland really rose to the occasion to play host to what I believe is the greatest sporting contest of them all. The world's greatest golfers came together in the world's most hospitable country and, after a titanic tussle, the Europeans defeated the mighty Americans in a hard-fought competition happily marked throughout by the highest standards of sportsmanship and great comradeship. The K Club really made its mark as television coverage of this great event travelled round the globe. Afterwards, I was left feeling elated, exhausted and proud.

But I had not expected to become the owner of The K Club by the time of the great event. When Smurfit later went private (in 2002, see **Chapter 19**), Madison Dearborn Partners agreed that they would not sell The K Club until after the staging of the Ryder Cup 2006.

But, in 2005, Madison Dearborn wanted to raise some money to invest elsewhere and they were prepared to do a deal with me, which was fair to both sides, under which I would buy The K Club. We had a lot of difficult negotiations to get through and my attitude throughout was "if it happens, it happens". It was never a question of "I must have this thing". The K Club is an expensive item to own, and although I certainly thought it would be very nice to have it, I knew it wasn't going to make me any money unless and until I eventually sold it.

I approached some property developers and others. In the end, Gerry Gannon became my partner, for a number of reasons. First, he was passionately in love with the place and had been coming there for years. On the previous Christmas night, I had met him at The K Club and he had said that, if ever I was doing anything here, he would like to talk to me. I remembered that, so I talked to him and I told him what I had in mind. I told him the structure of the transaction and he went around the various properties and decided that he could make a go of it. It was an excellent deal for both of us.

I said we needed to raise money, and we did that. I went back to Madison Dearborn and said that I thought that we could do the transaction. We shook hands on it and got it done.

Just before the first ball was driven off in the Ryder Cup in September 2006, I became the proud owner of 51% of The K Club. I was living up to one of my long-held maxims: if you have a vision, make it happen.

PRE-RYDER CUP CHALLENGES

As it turned out, buying The K Club was by no means the most difficult mountain we had to climb. In the lead-up to the Ryder Cup, we had innumerable problems and obstacles. Perhaps most irritatingly, we had to endure significant criticism from a constantly-carping and largely ill-informed press.

There was a negative attitude in the press before the Ryder Cup, sneering that the competition was all about money. The first point to make is that the players don't get any money, because they play for free. It's all about playing for the team and for the honour of the game. The big money is needed for staging the event – about €70 million. All the marshals are volunteers, so you have to have over 1,000 people prepared to give up their time. Then, of course, you have to hire security and you have to pay for the Gardaí (the Irish police force), and other costs. There are many costs involved. And any money generated from the Ryder Cup is used by the PGA to help young golfers and to develop the game. This is not like an ordinary business, where someone makes a profit and the investors take their share. Golf is what profits from the Ryder Cup.

ON THE DAY

Then the elements presented us with yet more last-minute problems. The day before the tournament began, we had to weather a powerful hurricane the like of which had not been seen in Ireland for a century. We had people up all night clearing the fairways and the greens of leaves and twigs. By morning, the course was back in pristine condition. We couldn't have asked for better.

We had wild and windy autumn weather throughout and, in my view, it added to the event. But, fortunately, the opening ceremony was blessed by perfect weather, as was the closing ceremony and most of the crucial last afternoon. We just had some difficult times in between. Rain was a constant companion and we were within a quarter of an inch of rainfall of having to abandon one whole day. That's how near it got, but we just got the games played.

The crowds were fantastic. They were good-humoured throughout, in spite of the weather. They were singing as the rain was pouring down on top of them in the stands, and the course held up very well.

For me, it was a very busy time. I was walking on average 36 holes a day and I didn't use the buggy except for an hour or so on the Thursday. We had former US Presidents George Bush Senior and Bill Clinton and many, many more VIP guests whom I met in the special area that I had as President of the event. I was invited to three or four dinners a night and I would put my head into two, with one course in one place, another course at another. Then, on the Sunday night after it was all over, I went over to the Members' Room very late at night and ended up on the stage having to sing to the members and their wives with Prince Albert of Monaco. The members suggested that I do it, so I did, and I enjoyed it.

I probably slept no more than four hours a night and, on the final night, I didn't sleep at all. I was absolutely knackered by the time I'd finished, but I was on such a high that I didn't feel it and the time went so quickly. All the things that we planned for, and hoped would happen, happened just as we thought they would.

In my speech to welcome the teams on the Tuesday evening, I was careful to point out that, without the support of the Irish government, Kildare County Council, the police and other organisations, we couldn't have staged the event, one of the biggest events there has ever been in the history of the State of Ireland.

People living locally in the Straffan area had a tough time in the period leading up to and during the Ryder Cup. For months, the roads were being worked on and their lives were constantly disrupted. I understand their complaints but they have to be weighed against the improved facilities that the area has now, the upgraded roads and the better water supplies. Now the Ryder Cup is over, everyone is happy with what it has done for the area.

HIGHLIGHTS OF THE RYDER CUP 2006

For me, the Ryder Cup had five important highlights, key moments that I will remember all my life. They were nothing to do with the ceremonies or the opening or closing events or the winning or losing or the shots. They were just human events that touched me deeply.

The first one followed a letter from a very sick 11-year-old boy, Conor Sutton, who wrote to me through the Make-a-Wish Foundation saying that he would like to go to the Ryder Cup. I wrote back to say that I would be happy to make his wish come true and would like to meet him when he came.

We had to postpone Conor's visit, planned for the Wednesday, because it was pouring torrential rain. On the Thursday, he came. I met him and his parents, took him around the course in a buggy and spent about two hours with him. Tiger Woods came over, wrote in his book and autographed his cap for him. Jim Furyk did the same. So did Phil Mickelson, and all of the Americans and all of the European team too. Everybody was great to him. We joined his parents in my private area and had lunch. I think we made Conor's dream come true and it showed the human side of the Ryder Cup.

Another day, I was walking around the course when I saw a young man in a wheelchair, who couldn't see anything because of the crowd, so I said to his father, "Come with me". Security stopped us, but I brushed them aside. I brought him inside the ropes and told him to stay there as long as he wanted. Things like that are what made the Ryder Cup memorable for me.

Later, on Sunday at about 4pm, another key moment arrived. I was feeling very pleased that all the safety issues had been dealt with. I was on the 16th green and Darren Clarke from Northern Ireland was coming in, three up with three holes to play, so it was possible that his putt would win the Ryder Cup. Darren's wife, Heather, very sadly had died just weeks before the tournament at the age of 39 and he had received great warmth and encouragement from all the other players, from the crowds and from everyone involved in the event. As Darren walked past the crowd, there was clapping and emotion, people were crying. He came over the special little bridge over the river to come on to the 16th green, which is an island green, where I had my President's tent. I was waiting there. He caught me out of the corner of his eye. He left the group, came over, put his arms around me and cried on my shoulder. He just said, "Thank you".

At that moment, the crowd surged forward through the ropes right to the edge of the Liffey. I said, "Oh my God, this is terrible".

The river bank was very slippery and people could have been pushed in and somebody could have been drowned very easily. So I rushed down with my arms raised and I got people to calm down. I called across, "People at the back, don't push, stay where you are, but stop!". Everybody stopped. I nearly had a stoppage of the heart myself because, along the river bank, people were within inches of the river and the bank sloped dangerously down. Fortunately, nothing happened and marshals got control of the situation and eventually got the crowd back.

Another emotional moment I had was when Arnold Palmer said to me how wonderful it was to be the designer of the course. He stopped talking several times because he got so choked up. He was so pleased because this was the first time the Ryder Cup had been played on a golf course that he had designed, and that the course got positive remarks from everybody.

Then the final moment that stands out in my memory was about 2am, when I went into the American team's private room in the hotel after they had lost on Sunday night. The final result had been convincing: Team Europe 18.5 points, Team USA 9.5 points, but the American team were partying as if they had won. There they were, smoking cigars and drinking beer. Tiger Woods was chatting away and his wife was trying to get him to bed, without any success. I had to say to them, "I'm sorry, you can't smoke in here". But I might as well have talked to the wall.

Those are my five captured magical moments. Of course, there were dozens more great memories from a fabulous event. But, for me, those five are the human side of everything, the real side of everything, and for me it was special.

IT WAS SPECIAL!

I was very proud to be a prime mover. I got a huge ovation when I went into the clubhouse at the end of the Ryder Cup. People started clapping and, all of a sudden, there was a great big roar and for about five minutes they were clapping.

I received thousands of letters, so many that I couldn't respond to them all. But I've read all of the letters and 75% of them said something like: "Dear Dr Smurfit, first of all I don't play golf, but I wanted to say that this was a wonderful event for Ireland". There were countless women who wrote that they knew nothing about golf, but they switched on the TV and were just enthralled by the spectacle.

But it was the crowd who made it. The difference between this Ryder Cup and any other Ryder Cup, apart from the Irish setting and the Irish weather, was the people, the crowds. They were tremendous. They were just ordinary golf fans from all over the country and all over the world.

I think finally people understood what I was trying to do. Most people had never been to a Ryder Cup and didn't know how big it was and didn't know what it was like. Indeed, many of the commentators didn't have any idea until they experienced it. It's become the biggest team event in the world.

I am delighted that the 2006 Ryder Cup worked out the way we thought it would, and better. I knew it was going to be good, and even that it was going to be great, but this wasn't just good and great, this was stupendous. It was the best Ryder Cup by far. I've been to all the Ryder Cups in the past 30 years, so I know there's nothing compared to it and not just in my view, but from all the feedback I've had. It's not just me talking; it's the world talking.

My vision was that we would have a first class hotel and golf club in Ireland and that the Ryder Cup would be played there. It took over 30 years from having the original idea to achieving it, but I never gave up on my vision, and the end result was even better than I could ever have hoped.

POSTSCRIPT

The publication of this book was delayed by my long and intense negotiations to acquire the 49% of The K Club controlled by the National Asset Management Agency (NAMA), which spanned almost two years. Now that the matter has been finally resolved, with

The K Club coming 100% under my family's ownership, I can conclude my book in happiness. While undoubtedly The K Club still faces strong headwinds given the ongoing nature of Ireland's financial crisis – and, indeed, the Euro crisis, as well – affecting disposable incomes, I am confident that it will find new markets and new opportunities. Many people have been helpful in the process of concluding arrangements to acquire The K Club, including staff and members who stayed loyal during a very difficult time, and I want to take this opportunity to thank them for their support. It was truly invaluable.

My father, John Jefferson Smurfit.   My mother, Ann Magee.

Dad (back, right) on his wedding day, 10 June 1934, Belfast, with Alan
Yates (back, second left), Auntie Nellie (back, third left), Kathleen Yates
(front, second left), Mazzie Magee (front, right) and friends.

The honeymooners.

Dad (second left) on holidays with friends.

Mazzie Magee, with baby Michael and Dad.

Dad's first car.

Dad (left) and Dermot Barnes enjoying a quiet drink.

Dad (right) with Cliff Armstrong, at Ashbrooke
Rugby, Cricket & Tennis Club, Sunderland.

John Jefferson Smurfit (Dad) in his early 20s; the photo was
probably sent to his mother from St Helens.

Brothers and sisters: Dermot, Alan, Jeff, Michael, Kay and Sheila.

Clongowes Wood College, 1953, cricket team: Michael Smurfit, Captain (centre), with (standing L to R) F. Smith, J. Lappin, J. O'Kane, J. Smurfit, Vice-Captain , T. Shaw, D. Tuohy and (seated L to R) D. Dunne, B. O'Higgins, D. Acton and N. O'Sullivan.

Dad with the last horse he ever owned, *Rocking*.

Racing my E-Type Jaguar at Brooklands
(photo from *Motoring Life*, April 1962).

Jeff.

With Jeff at the Smurfit AGM, 1968.

Answering questions at the Smurfit AGM, 1992, with
Howard Kilroy on my right.

Speaking at the Smurfit AGM, 1985, with
Alan Smurfit and Howard Kilroy.

With Group COO, Paddy Wright.

With Don Hindman, chairman of Time Industries.

With Ruairí Quinn, Minister for Finance, in 1993, at the launch of the
Smurfit Job Creation Enterprise Fund.

Albert Reynolds, former Taoiseach, and Ray McSharry,
former Finance Minister, both Smurfit Board directors.

My mother, Ann.

Brothers and sons: Tony, Alan, Michael, Dermot, Michael Jnr.

Receiving the award of Knight Commander of the Most Excellent Order
of the British Empire from Her Majesty Queen Elizabeth II.

After the award ceremony with my son, Alexander, and
my daughters, Sharon and Tracy.

With Brendan Grace and Prince Albert and Prince Rainier of Monaco.

With Tiger Woods and Mark O'Meara.

My photo, printed on the last sheet of corrugated board
made at the Clonskeagh mill and signed on the reverse by
all staff present on the day the mill closed.

In full regalia for Prince Albert of Monaco's wedding.

Life's not all work!

Sometimes you win!

In conversation with Jim Malloy.

Congratulating Howard Kilroy on his retirement.

With Seve Ballesteros at the start of the Smurfit European Open.

Launching the Smurfit European Open.

With Bono and Naomi Campbell.

With Nelson Mandela at a Prince Albert of Monaco Foundation dinner.

With Warren Buffett, Bill Gates and Dermot Desmond at The K Club.
(photo: Justin Mac Innes)

With Bill and Melinda Gates at The K Club.
(photo: Justin Mac Innes)

With the then President of Ireland, Mary McAleese.

With former US President, Bill Clinton at The K Club.

Members of the European Round Table of Industrialists
meeting at The K Club.

With UCD President Dr Hugh Brady at the conferring of a
Doctorate of Laws on Dermot Desmond, 2007.

In pensive mood.

V
TO THE SUMMIT & BEYOND

CHAPTER 17
EUROPE IN OUR SIGHTS

Smurfit has a clear vision of where it wants to be, a strong balance sheet, solid earnings potential and a capable management team to sustain this vision.

It had been very difficult for me to move away from Ireland to a new country because I had no friends there, all my friends were in Ireland. But I was focused on building my new life, on moving to a new place with a new lady and starting a whole new period in my life, while continuing of course to build the business.

When I was appointed Joint Managing Director in 1966, Smurfit faced an uncertain future with the advent of the Anglo-Irish free trade agreement. It was a case of take-over or be taken over. We chose the former. Our strategy of growth through acquisition through the 1970s and 1980s served the Group well, based as it was on a clear vision. And, following Theodore Hesburgh's dictum: "It's got to be a vision you articulate clearly and forcefully on every occasion", I was never shy in articulating Smurfit's vision: our new model of doing business within the sector, basing capacity expansion on demand for our product today and not tomorrow. We were consistently profitable, we delivered our strategic and financial commitments and our track record in terms of dividends was unparalleled within the industry. The market recognised this: our capitalisation increased at an annual average rate of 24%.

TROUBLES IN SPAIN

It was in the UK, in January 1989, that we made our first investment after the Container Corporation of America (CCA) deal – the acquisition of the Cundell Group. It is particularly memorable for me because this led to our investment in INPACSA, then the largest

Spanish manufacturer of pure kraftliner, which in turn led me to appearing in court proceedings in Spain.

We acquired INPACSA from Torres Hostench, a very large company run by Javier de la Rosa, who I had met a number of times. Javier knew me because of his involvement in the paper business and I wanted to get to know him better because he had the eyes and the ears of the Kuwaiti Investment Office, which at that time was investing lots of money in Europe. I figured if they were prepared to invest with Torres in Spain, why wouldn't they invest with Smurfit, the fastest-growing paper company in the world?

In the meantime, Javier decided to sell off his corrugated box interests, which married very well with what we had taken over from CCA, because they included a Spanish operation called CartoEspaña. So we decided to buy INPACSA from de la Rosa, in three or four transactions, for £68 million. We had international financial and legal advisers advising us on the transaction. Everything we did was public and there was never any hidden agenda so far as we were concerned. It was a completely straightforward deal.

Torres had set up a structure for the sale, which they said was for tax purposes, involving a Gibraltar company and a Dutch company. It was a legal and acceptable business practice. We might have done exactly the same sort of thing. The problem was that we discovered later that not all the money went to Torres; some of our money went to other people.

The charge against us was that the Smurfit Group had aided and abetted the transaction by agreeing to pay the money to Croasis Limited, the Gibraltar company set up by Javier on behalf of Torres to take payment. Our counter-argument was that what happened to the money after we had paid it over was nothing to do with Smurfit. If you go to a supermarket, pay for a bag of groceries, and take them away, the deal is over for you. If the man you paid the money to doesn't put all the money into the till, how can you be in any way responsible? We had announced the deal publicly, so that everyone knew what we were buying and what we were paying for it. It was a completely open transaction and it was up to the shareholders in

Torres to make sure that the money that we paid for INPACSA went to the company.

In spite of our insistence that we were in no way involved, nine people were charged with financial wrongdoing – including me in my capacity as Chairman of the Group!

In the end, after a long and painful legal process, three people were found guilty, including Javier de la Rosa, and six of us were acquitted, again including myself. But I was still forced to endure three months of going to Spain every week to appear in these lengthy criminal proceedings.

Even when you know you have done nothing wrong, it is a hard situation to be taken to court. In every court case, there are two sets of lawyers: one says you are right, the other says you are wrong – and one of them always turns out to be wrong. It was a bad time in my life. It was scary sitting in the back of a court dealing with accusations of wrongdoing and often not understanding a word of what was going on.

We had an eminently defendable case. We had the top law firm in Spain, whose lawyers said it was absurd for us to be drawn into this. Nevertheless, we had to put up a bond of £46 million, in case we lost the case. The court found against Torres and fined them the same figure of £46 million. It took a long time for us to get our own £46 million back from the Spanish courts, but we did get it back in the end.

It was a chilling experience, particularly when we had done things by the book.

MEETING MURDOCH

But Smurfit was such an exciting place at this time to work in and to be part of. There was always something happening, the next deal was always coming along. We were getting bigger, our name was getting known, we were becoming more powerful, customers respected us and we were among the first people to do pan-American deals to supply packaging.

There never seemed to be a great deal of time in my life to socialise because I was always building up the business. And when I wasn't working I was looking after my family. But, even on holidays, I met some very interesting people. For instance, long before he became well-known, I met Rupert Murdoch in St Moritz and got to know him a little bit, which eventually helped a deal some years later, in December 1990.

In fact, we were instrumental in helping Rupert Murdoch get through a crisis at that time. He had come over from Australia to the UK and bought the *News of the World* newspaper, which had been controlled by the Carr family. He beat Robert Maxwell in a bitter battle to take over the *News of the World*, which was the foundation of News International and the huge empire that Rupert Murdoch built at that time. The *News of the World* owned a paper mill called Townsend Hook in the South of England. Townsend Hook then went from producing newsprint to producing packaging papers. It was making very good money and Murdoch, who was riding high, wanted £100 million for it. We offered £85 or £90 million for it and were turned down flat.

A year or so later, he contacted us. Murdoch then had run into some financial difficulty. He had to get money fast, so he went to my brother Dermot and asked how much we would now pay for Townsend Hook.

I'll let Dermot tell the story because I know it's one of his favourites:

> There was great urgency about the deal to buy this mill. Certainly, Rupert Murdoch was very keen to complete the transaction. And, certainly, we were not going to pay anything like the figure we had offered previously. After long discussions with teams of accountants going over all the figures, we reduced the price to £55 million. Time was very tight and the deadline coincided with the annual Jefferson Smurfit golf tournament in California. With lots of top professionals involved, Michael was playing with Gary Player. I was Chairman and CEO of Smurfit UK but I wasn't involved in the golf. I was busy trying to get this deal concluded in time.

Everything was pushed to the last minute and I found myself, in my suit, chasing onto the course to get Michael's signature. I had a plane booked, ready to rush the cheque to the bank. I was a little hot and bothered but Michael and Gary Player were on the first tee swishing their clubs waiting to drive off.

At last, Michael turned to me and said, "All right, do the deal … for £50 million". I said, "Look Michael, all the papers are done for £55 million. Where on earth did you get £50 million from?". He just said, "I want to feel that I've made some money today". That's Michael.

In the end, I got the mill for £38 million.

THE RISE & RISE OF SMURFIT

Throughout the 1960s, 1970s and 1980s, the rise and rise of the Smurfit Group was remarkable, even though I say so myself. By the middle of the 1990s, we had become one of the largest print and packaging companies in the world and, along the way, we had seen a fantastic increase in our profitability. From a single box factory in Dublin, we had grown to be a thriving and dynamic organisation with plants and interests all over the world. It was quite a journey.

We produced packaging to protect fresh flowers and fine glassware and to transport heavy machinery around the world. We invested in trees to grow in our own forests to provide prime raw material for paper and we recycled paper and board on a huge scale. Growing environmental concerns led us to produce paper-based, recyclable packaging as an alternative to plastics, polystyrene, wood and metal. We had established dedicated research centres in the USA and Europe. Each of our companies undertook its own R&D in order to improve our technology and systems and to develop materials and styles of packaging to meet our customers' needs. We had systems in place that enabled our operations worldwide to share knowledge and experience quickly. If we developed the wheel once, then every operation had immediate access to that wheel.

I believe we were one of the first companies in the world to see the value of recycling. It has been a boon to society. All these bin-liners you see nowadays are made from recycled plastic, that's why they're black.

We were one of the first people to produce plastic paper, which you see everywhere today. The invention came from Tommy Hutt in Pretoria, South Africa. I obtained the license for Europe and Marks & Spencer became our first big customer.

We were the first company into many product areas. We attached a huge importance to innovation and always placed great emphasis on the environment. These were essential components for our medium and long-term success.

But it was all done with great care. Simply spending money is the easiest thing in the world to do. Spending it wisely is the hardest thing in the world to do. I always looked upon the company's money as if it were my own. And I watched every penny. I turned down thousands of projects because they were too expensive with no chance of an adequate return.

OPPORTUNITIES DOWN UNDER

All the time we were developing our operations, our processes, our systems, our people and our products, but try as I might, as the 1990s went on, I found it hard to see opportunities for further large-scale development of our business. All I could see were in-fills, sections where we were not doing business and where we should be doing business.

Australia was one area that I had looked at for expansion. In fact, I tipped my toe in the water Down Under, but then decided to withdraw. We invested in Island Cooler, a drink with wine and lemonade, and then sold it for a nice sum of money. We also printed T-shirts. These were exploratory bridgeheads that took us into the market to see if we wanted to do more.

My original idea for Australia was to set up a similar concept to our plant at Clonskeagh: a milligator – effectively, a totally integrated production facility, with waste paper arriving in one door, and corrugated paper leaving from the other door. Nothing like it existed in Australia then. Indeed, the Australian market at that time was fragmented between a number of competing companies. Australian Paper Mills was the prime producer of paper and there were a number of box plants. I knew that we would succeed if we went into Australia, because we had the key to the door: we were already well-established in the waste paper market, with a paper mill and a box plant. That was the level of our integration.

The Australian experience was interesting, but ultimately frustrating. We met some nice people and made some good friends in our area of operations, including Richard Pratt. The Pratt family ran a company called Visy Board and Richard, who sadly is now dead, had inherited the business from his father in 1969 and was keen to develop it into a substantial size. He quickly saw that, if I came into Australia in a big way, I would be his competitor – and would beat him.

The more I studied it, the more I realised that, while it would probably be a success, Australia would be a pretty long haul. It is a very hard place to get to, so the management issue became an important factor. Who was going to manage it? In the end, we decided to withdraw from that market.

Unfortunately, soon after, Richard Pratt's major Australian competitor, Amcor, came into the UK. They employed Charlie Mustard, a former Smurfit employee, and proceeded to build three new corrugated box plants, for which there was absolutely no need in the marketplace. They said they were going to be a low-cost producer, which I thought was total nonsense. In my view, LCP, the paper industry's acronym for 'low-cost producer', should stand for 'less company profit', because that's what happened to many companies that went down this route. I travelled to Australia a couple of times to try to explain to them how wrong they were but, perhaps not surprisingly, they wouldn't listen to me. As a result, Amcor lost a fortune on box production in the UK and ruined the English market. This is now only just beginning to recover, following the recent acquisition by Smurfit Kappa of the three box plants started by Amcor all those years ago, turning the industry around remarkably.

THE WORSE IT IS, THE BETTER IT GETS

Yet now that we had developed a substantial global business, I was still looking very hard at how we could expand it further. Europe was certainly somewhere we needed a bigger presence. In the UK and Ireland we were fine, but not on the European continent. I was on the hunt in Europe and I was also looking at Asia for the first time. I was trying to figure how to get in there so I also started to travel to Hong Kong, China, Indonesia and Malaya. I was hunting around.

Smurfit never won an open bid in its history. By open bid, I mean a situation when a company goes to a merchant bank and puts itself up for sale. In those cases, typically the bank finds a few prospective buyers and, generally, the highest bidder gets the prize. We never won one of those, not one. We were always the lowest bidder. The only time we won bids was when we went to the person one-on-one and got them to sell the business to us direct.

For instance, in June 1995, I bought a Swedish company called Munksjö, in the Hotel de Paris one night. It produced bleached pulp, speciality paper and board. The man from Munksjö came down from Sweden to meet me, and it was not a long negotiation. I said, "I'm interested in buying the company". He said, "That's the price," and named a figure. I said, "OK," shook his hand and the deal was done. Back he went to Sweden and we closed it in a few days.

I reckoned he'd got the price wrong and I was proved to be right, because we made £200 million on that deal. Afterwards, I didn't feel remotely guilty that he'd badly undervalued the company because, in my opinion, we made the money. It wasn't what he sold us, it was what we made of it. His earnings were on one level and we took them up to a much higher level. I could see that potential when I did the deal. He couldn't.

When we went into a company, we knew how to strip out costs, we knew how to refocus things, get rid of low margin business and improve the output. The man from Munksjö had got into a crisis and he needed the money and I was able to provide the money and do it quickly. That's happened a number of times in my life. I've made a lot of money because I was able to deliver very quickly.

Smurfit was in a difficult industry, but I was able to buck the trends for three decades because I could grow against the trends. I was a 'contrarian', as Gary McGann put it. I coined the phrase, "The worse it is, the better it gets", because nobody ever came to the front door and offered me a very good business at a low price. They always came because they had a problem and what they wanted was a very high price. I wasn't ever going to pay a high price. So, often, I had to wait until someone made a serious mistake or a company got itself into real trouble.

I rarely had to wait long. The paper and board industry is hugely capital-intensive. Company managements simply did not understand the basics of 'Economics 101'. The industry focus was on production, not profitability; there were too many engineers looking for the biggest, fastest, cleanest, best machines. They increased capacity where none was warranted, basing their capital allocation decisions on the prevailing price. But, as soon as you put new tonnage into the market, your revenue declines – since the price reduction required for the market to absorb the new capacity contaminates existing production also. The result is that the real cost of bringing on new capacity is often two to three times the cost of the machinery installed. A lot of companies did the same thing at the same time, ramping up production and swamping the market to their own detriment as well as that of others. And when their home market was well and truly over-supplied, they turned to brokers and agents to ship their surplus overseas – China, Europe, you name it – damaging the competition there too. As a result, the industry as a whole suffered sub-market performance and dismal returns for years – which we were able to turn to our advantage.

This happened in 1994 with an Austrian company called Nettingsdorfer, which produced kraftliner in central Europe. When we acquired them, they had just spent £135 million on developing their paper machine, but the market turned against them and they were in huge debt. This family firm was then in difficulty. So I went in through the front door. I bought just under 30% of the company initially, later increased our holding above 50%, and eventually bought the whole lot out.

We turned Nettingsdorfer around in no time, partly because we bought a lot of material from them and used it ourselves, so the whole thing made sense.

Although we got the first tranche of Nettingsdorfer cheap, we agreed in advance a fair valuation basis for the later share purchases. In a way, we worked against ourselves because the more we improved the business, the more we paid for it in the end – but we were fair.

It was an opportunity for us and, at the same time, it was an opportunity for the family who owned Nettingsdorfer to solve their problems. There is no room in the marketplace for a small business like that because the supermarkets dictate to the food manufacturers, demanding lower cost packaging, and you can't meet their price demands if you have a high overhead. You have to be able to produce large volumes at low cost.

Another reason we were able to buy into companies cheaply was because we could move fast – important if the buyer is selling because of their own financial difficulties. We were able to do a number of deals because, even though our offer may not have been the highest, it was comparatively more attractive as the deal was never subject to financing.

I insisted that the Smurfit Group keep a cash 'war chest'. I was prepared to pay the loan/deposit premium to ensure that if a target acquisition became available at a bargain price, then we would have cash on hand immediately to allow us to move quickly. I knew that the banks would not be able to give an approval fast enough should a bargain target become available and they would never be happy with the absence of full due diligence that we sometimes had to accept. So even though this meant paying interest on bank loans that we had cash available to repay, I accepted this 'unnecessary' cost for the strategic flexibility it gave us.

CELLULOSE DU PIN

There has always been cross-border trading in corrugated board to some extent, particularly in places like The Netherlands. There is no natural impediment to business, The Netherlands being a very open country, so you have German, Danish and Belgian companies competing in the Dutch market. I foresaw the day when that competition would expand to cover Poland and the Eastern European countries, which it does now, and my dream European target acquisition was always the French paper and packaging company, Cellulose du Pin, which was a part of France's huge Compagnie de Saint-Gobain.

Cellulose du Pin owned a company called SOCAR and a very famous kraftliner mill in Facture in France. I knew the company and I knew their factories very well, but I never thought it would come up for sale. However, I met the Chairman of the Board of Compagnie de Saint-Gobain, Jean-Louis Beffa, as a fellow member of the European Round Table of Industrialists on which I represented Ireland for many years. The meeting was an opportunity I could not resist. I said, "Mr Beffa, if you are ever interested in selling Cellulose du Pin, I would be keen to buy it". He looked at me carefully and invited me to Paris for a meeting in his apartment.

When I went to see him in Paris, he said, "We are looking at doing a major acquisition in America and we have too many assets in France, and I think we would be able to do a deal with you. We're not going to put it on the open market. We want it to be done with a company like yours, which is family-orientated. Importantly, you are Irish, which is very acceptable to the French government. I've checked you out". It just shows how intangibles, things you might never even think about as being important in a deal, can be key.

We started to negotiate with Cellulose du Pin, and we had to pay a heavy price. It cost Smurfit more than $1 billion and was one of the most expensive deals we ever did. But I figured we could get a lot of cost savings out of it, which turned out to be true. I also reckoned that many of its management were turned off because they were part of a big conglomerate, a vast company. Saint-Gobain originally had belonged to the French state. Cellulose du Pin had done a good job of maintaining itself, but the executives in charge wanted to get rid of it and, fortunately for us, it wasn't in bad shape when we took it on.

We got Cellulose du Pin for two main reasons: we were Irish and we managed to move quickly. We had 200 people working in Paris night and day to get the transaction done and there was not one leak of the planned take-over. The dealers couldn't believe it. It was a complex transaction, because Saint-Gobain had bought companies all over France and there were many different companies and many different legal entities, but we got the job done in the end. When we announced it, I was delighted that it came as a complete surprise to the rest of the world. Overnight, we became the biggest packaging manufacturer in Europe.

It was one of the best deals I ever did because, in buying this company, we acquired the 'Bag in Box' business. It was very small when we first took it on, but we built it from nothing to become one of our stars. The Bag in Box is a flexible bag in a cardboard box, developed to hold liquid. We developed it further, and we marketed it, and nowadays it is used to hold everything from fine wine to motor oil. We sell not just the packs but also the filling, closing and packing lines. Smurfit built it up from nothing into a multi-million pound business.

In many ways, soon after the end of the 1980s, we had arrived at the top of the mountain and the 1990s was not a great time. Once we got to the top of the mountain, we had nowhere else to go. At one time, Smurfit accounted for 25% of the Irish stock market and was bigger than the two Irish banks combined. We had battled to become a presence in the world packaging business. We had become by far the biggest in the industry. But there were only some small acquisitions we could make. I felt that we had gone past the days when we could double the size of the company with a single business deal – I was proved wrong later.

So, in the absence of acquisition opportunities, in the early 1990s, I was heavily involved in rationalising our French and Italian operations. There were 50, 60 or 70 factories to visit. I didn't get around all the sheet plants, but I visited all the corrugated box plants. There were lots of dinners and meeting executives, getting to know them and getting them to know and accept our style. Slowly but surely, they warmed to us. It took time but today we have a number of French executives in senior positions in the Group, along with executives from many other countries.

A KEY APPOINTMENT

Paddy Wright, one of our directors, said to me one day that I should meet Gary McGann with a view to him joining the Smurfit Group. Although Gary is an accountant and I had a negative opinion of accountants' ability to run large companies, he quickly impressed me with his intellect and determination. He joined the company as Chief Financial Officer in 1988 and the rest, as they say, is history.

Gary later took over from me on the European Round Table of Industrialists, on which I represented Ireland for about 15 years. You had to be recommended to membership by an existing member. I was recommended by Tony Ryan, who was retiring from it.

I enjoyed it very much and met a lot of key people across the 50 or so top industries in Europe. We met twice a year. Generally, Sunday night was dinner together; on Monday morning, we had a meeting; and we disbanded on Monday afternoon, all very efficient.

As an industry, I felt we were right to be represented and I had no hesitation in putting Gary forward and he was accepted.

CHAPTER 18
CREATING A DEFINING MOMENT

The Smurfit Group grew from a country with no developed forest product industry, to become a global leader in our chosen markets. Our aim always was to be the best. Along the way, we also became the biggest.

The packaging business, by its nature, is cyclical. It goes through good times and bad times, and experience taught me this is something we always needed to take into account. Understanding the industry cycle – and taking advantage of it to time our acquisitions – was critical to the success of the Smurfit Group.

We would never judge one of our own companies by a single accounting period. We would look at what it had achieved over several years. Often 25% or 30% of a factory's production would be going to one customer and the contract with that customer might be for, say, three years. If we lost that contract, we would have to support that factory either until we won the customer back, or until we replaced the customer with other business.

It was a difficult and continuing problem. If a company becomes dependent on a single customer for production and profit, then it is not always easy, or even possible, to increase business from other customers and reduce the dependency on that main client. But if that key customer leaves, then our company might instantly become highly unprofitable and there could be no alternative but to close the factory. This is the nature of most businesses. That is why, in an ideal situation, you should never have all your eggs in one basket, even though in the real world it happens. My strategy to counteract this dangerous vulnerability was a rule that no customer would ever be allowed to become more than 3% of our total business worldwide.

CREATING SMURFIT-STONE

The Cellulose de Pin deal had made us the largest packaging company in Europe and, throughout the 1990s, we continued to invest and grow in all the countries where we had interests. Through Jefferson Smurfit Corporation, our US publicly-held company quoted on the NASDAQ market, we moved into China for the first time and started to build our business there.

One day, one of our executives, Ray Curran, came up with a very clever idea. He said, "We need a defining moment in our US operations". This led to me setting up a meeting in Bermuda with Roger Stone, a man I once told bluntly that he and I would never be able to work together.

It was important that news of any possible merger with Stone Container was kept quiet and confidential. Unfortunately, word of my meeting with Roger got out to the financial world because there are companies in America that track the movements of company aeroplanes. Roger had a jet and I had a jet so, when someone tracked the two of them together, it didn't take a rocket scientist to work out that one and one made three. When that piece of information got out into the financial world, stock prices started to move.

In the first stage of talks, we couldn't agree on a transaction, but things started to deteriorate in the US pretty dramatically for Roger. He was heavily leveraged and then, in October 1998, the US stock market crashed.

In the end, we agreed to merge and to create a really great, giant company. It became clear that this was a defining moment in the industry. A lot of fees were paid, a lot of money changed hands with the banks and Smurfit-Stone Container Corporation was born. Jefferson Smurfit Group ended up owning 38% of Smurfit-Stone instead of the 68% that it had in Jefferson Smurfit Corporation, plus it was an associate company and non-dividend paying, and we had a lot of money locked in there. But, structurally, this was the only way to galvanise the industry, because the plan was to close two million tonnes of capacity almost immediately. Overnight, this would create a proper balance between supply and demand. We had to act decisively because prices had gone down dramatically. And, in the end, we needed to force through the merger between Smurfit and Stone because Stone was in trouble.

MANAGING SMURFIT–STONE

After the merger, Roger Stone was appointed Chief Executive and I was made Chairman of the Board. Ray Curran's position was Chief Operating Officer.

After we merged, we discovered that Stone Container had a lot of problems, and it quickly became apparent to me that Roger's style of business was utterly different from ours. In effect, Roger was a one-man band. Obviously, he had done very well in building his business up to the size it was, but in the process he had taken on too much debt and had done many deals that later created a lot of trouble. We decided to set about making the thing work, but only after some serious second thoughts.

We started by selling off the assets that we had planned to dispose off. Ray organised the sale of our newsprint operations in California and our forest lands – all at a very good price. We got rid of this plant, got rid of that factory, exchanged the contracts, and got on with the job.

But my prediction, made years earlier, that Roger Stone and I could never work together proved all too true. That dated back to a time when I was much younger and Stone Container Corporation was much larger than we were. Then I had nothing to offer, but now what we pulled off was in effect a take-over, even though it was treated as a merger. It didn't last very long with Roger Stone. It soon became clear to me that the situation was completely unworkable.

Ray Curran became particularly frustrated. He learned that Roger had invested in a Venezuelan paper company that competed with Smurfit Group operations in the same country. This investment was in serious financial difficulty. Even though Smurfit-Stone was only a minority shareholder, Roger decided he wanted to support the operation by sending $10 million to it. Ray took Roger down to the street level of the head office in Chicago and said, "Roger, let's get the

$10 million now and put it into this bin and then either you or I can set fire to it, because that is what you would be doing in sending the money".

Roger was undeniably a gifted businessman but he was poor at communicating in the manner that I felt a sizeable company should be communicating. He was used to doing everything himself and taking his own decisions. This soon caused massive problems. For example, I happened to hear on the grapevine that he was considering selling off our Canadian division to a partner of ours in Canada, MacMillan Bloedel. But we had a pre-emptive right that he had not taken into account. I wanted us to buy MacMillan Bloedel. This was the type of quite absurd conflict that began between us. And it escalated as the months went on.

It became very clear to both of us that we just couldn't work effectively together. We had totally different ways of running a business and we each felt that we were the dominant partner in the business. The upshot was that he decided to resign.

It happened quickly. Within a year of the merger, Roger was gone. Off he went with a severance package of $15 million. I think he was probably bitterly disappointed at the time, but soon afterwards he started another business and did very well. It wasn't one of the better leavings but I never regretted the deal. It was what made us the world's biggest packaging producer, with 20% of the US market. The next company was half our size and we were the major player in the white-top market and the semi-chemical market. Overall, we were in a tremendous market position.

Immediately, I put Ray Curran in to replace Roger. Ray was an excellent financial man and I said to him, "Ray, I want you to go in and clean this company up financially for a couple of years and then come back to Ireland".

It took a lot of time and a lot of business dinners and executive meetings to change the Stone management culture to conform to the Smurfit culture. We had to 'Smurfitise' them and that process still wasn't complete by the time I left.

At the time of the deal, Ray was kind enough to say:

Michael's a visionary and he has great long-term perspective. He's an excellent corporate strategist. He knows how to get the right combination between business and finance. He has been way ahead of his time in this industry in that sense.

ENTERING CHINA

My last major strategic objective, after we had achieved a critical mass in America, Latin America and Europe, was to get into China.

I realised that the only way for us to establish ourselves successfully in China was through a local partnership. I found that with a wonderful gentleman who owned a company called Leefung-Asco in Hong Kong. They had factories in China and were in the printing business. They weren't in the packaging business but they were in cartons and they also had a big outlet for graphic board. It made sense for us to buy them. That's exactly what we did. They provided our base in China where there were about 4,000 people in seven factories. We suddenly became the biggest commercial printer in China. This was going to be our foundation for moving into the country. We then started a corrugated box plant in one of the factories with a brand new corrugator and box plant.

When we merged with Stone Container, they already had a number of packaging interests in China, including three box plants in a joint venture with a Taiwanese family who lived in Hong Kong. So now Smurfit-Stone had four box plants and we were beginning to make a bit of noise.

Stone also owned the Packaging Solutions Centre in Hong Kong, which I visited. It was very impressive. I thought it was one of the most innovative things I had ever seen in the packaging industry. They had put together a very creative group of people who were designing packaging for the likes of Walmart, Nike and Sears, Roebuck. They designed the packages in Hong Kong to have them made in China to their specifications, then shipped them to the US. Not surprisingly, the business was building very well.

Mirroring other cultures came naturally to me, I didn't find it difficult at all. For example, in Asia, it was all about losing face. If you went to the factory with the factory manager, you could never talk to the junior manager first. You had to go and talk to the factory manager initially, or he would get very offended. And the junior manager would get offended if you talked to a worker without talking to him first. So it was all about doing the right thing and behaving in the right way. When they served Chinese tea, which I hated, I had to pretend to sip it instead of saying, "I don't want it".

I remember the mayor of a town in China once gave me a luncheon that started at 12 noon and, at 3pm, the meal was still going on. Three hours and there were more courses coming and there were more pretty girls dancing. I don't really eat lunch, but he meant well because he was doing his best to show off his town and to thank us for the investment and the creation of jobs and so on, so the lunch went with the territory. But I tried to avoid that kind of invitation again. Somehow, I always managed to find an excuse to be leaving just before lunchtime.

DISAGREEMENT ON DIRECTION

But in business, as in life, not everyone sees things the same way. When Ray Curran was put in charge of Smurfit-Stone, one of his first actions was to take a look at the Hong Kong operation and say to me, "I want to shut it down". I was astonished and said, "Ray, you are off your head. This is one of our great businesses".

We didn't close it and it remained a very profitable operation. I used to go over to Hong Kong and the China mainland every eight weeks and we had a first class team in place managing the operations.

In spite of that disagreement, Ray did an outstanding job and fulfilled the challenging brief I had given him for Smurfit-Stone.

Ray was a very good finance guy and he thought he also had the operational skills. Ray had grown to like Chicago and the life that he had in America. Perhaps it was understandable. He had a very powerful job there running a big company, with his own aeroplane, and there were a lot of nice things about running Smurfit-Stone.

But I had made it clear from the outset that his role in the US would not be long-term. So when I wanted him to change from being Chief Executive of Smurfit-Stone and to come back to the Group, because I believed Smurfit-Stone needed an operating expert as Chief Executive, I was surprised at his negative response. I went to the Board and said that, in my opinion, Ray was fully qualified to do the job that he had done, but he wasn't qualified to do the job that we needed doing to take the company forward. I received the Board's unanimous agreement that the change was necessary. I had dinner with Ray and said to him, "Ray, I'm afraid I'm going to have to ask you to leave the company". He was upset of course, but when I told him that the Board supported my position, he resigned and left the company with a good financial package.

I saw him from time to time afterwards and there was no animosity between us. I don't believe you can dodge difficult decisions and, once you have made your mind up, it is your job to carry out whatever changes are necessary, however uncomfortable they might be. But Ray was a good man (sadly, he died last year) and he did some great work at Smurfit-Stone.

SMURFIT-STONE & ASIA

Smurfit-Stone was firmly established now as the major force in the US packaging industry. Smurfit Group was strong in Latin America and in Europe. My strategy then was to expand further into Asia and develop it as a significant part of the business.

We were already in Indonesia, we were going into Thailand, and we were making inroads into China. The attraction of the Asian markets was that they were fast-growing and it was a new area in which we could use our well-established and unique connections. We knew the Coca-Cola and Procter & Gamble people and I knew we could get involved in bigger and better deals with them. We were the only people who could give these global businesses a deal in Latin America, in America, Canada, Europe, Eastern Europe and now a deal in Asia. Who else could do that and guarantee quality and continuity of supply?

INDUSTRY RECOGNITION

Although I never sought recognition or awards for myself, I always was delighted to accept them on behalf of the Group and its employees. One of the most prestigious awards I received was the inaugural Global CEO of the Year, chosen by 200 security analysts, investment officers and portfolio managers in the paper/forest products industry.

This was in 1999, just a year after the Smurfit-Stone merger. A press release announcing the award hailed the merger as "the model for efficient capacity management in the US, creating the dynamic for the restructuring and recovery of the industry ... it has changed the way the industry looks at business, from one focused on selling as much linerboard as possible to one where optimum profitability is what counts". According to one analyst, the award was for:

> ... *bold leadership of the containerboard industry, and the rapid reversal of market conditions which he engineered. ... no other industry CEO has had such dramatic impact on the outlook for his or her business as Dr Smurfit. The deal to merge Jefferson Smurfit Corp. with Stone Container was difficult, and at times analysts expected it to fail. The deal succeeded because Smurfit was willing to pay what seemed like a high price in the short run, in exchange for substantial medium to long-term gains. ... Smurfit-Stone's actions have served as an example for investors, and other industry managers, of the potential impact industry leaders can have if they get serious about addressing industry, rather than company, problems.*

In accepting the award, I noted:

> *To be honoured by an industry association is always tremendous, by peers and competitors, better again, but to be recognised by those who determine where equity, that most valuable commodity, is best deployed – this is perhaps the best tribute of them all.*
>
> *In honouring me for this, you also are paying tribute to everyone in Jefferson Smurfit Group. In particular, to my Board and Executive Committee for their shared vision and wise counsel and to all of the other Group executives and support staff; to the shareholders of*

Smurfit Group for stepping up to the plate on this deal, one which was unprecedented in scale for our Group and which represented a daring and courageous new departure for the company; and to the employees of Smurfit-Stone Container Corporation and its management team.

The merger this time last year represented a first step in a process. The subsequent shutdown of 1.1 million tons of high-cost inefficient capacity proved beyond doubt our commitment in what has been called a classic case of thinking long-term and acting short-term. They didn't have to be our mills – we could have waited for someone else to take the pain. But that is not our style. We operate on a simple theory – that action has more potential for value creation than inaction. This time, not only did the shareholders of JSG and SSCC benefit but, industry-wide, investors saw the value of their shareholdings increase as, overnight, the outlook for containerboard improved.

The theory was simple, as good theories always are. Consolidate and rationalise our position in the US market, which in turn drives the world market, and JSG, as the largest global producer, would stand to benefit the most. Beyond theory and compelling strategic imperative, however, the merger is a case study in concept, strategy and execution.

As for the merger itself – what a compelling partnership it has turned out to be. Strategic fit is superb. The operations are balanced in terms of integration and fibre base. The combined logistics system is by far the largest and will be one of the most efficient of its kind in North America. Culturally, JSC's disciplined approach to financial management complements Stone's outstanding marketing expertise. Synergies of $210m a year to date have been achieved and a run rate of $300m looks achievable by the year-end. Over $1.8 billion has been applied to debt reduction ...

From Smurfit Group's perspective, it has afforded us the opportunity to increase our scale, perspective and exposure to the US. And in terms of scale, together with our associates, Jefferson Smurfit Group now has operations in over 30 countries and commands an 11% share of world sales. Not bad progress from the days when the full complement of our facilities consisted of one small box plant in downtown Dublin, housing a couple of corrugated machines designed by my Dad, a tailor by profession.

PRELUDE TO A SALE

When we originally did the Smurfit-Stone deal, the plan was for Smurfit Group to take over the rest of Smurfit-Stone at some time in the future, but markets had gone very much against us in the meantime. We were stagnating in Europe, the Stone debt load was very heavy and it wasn't coming down fast enough. In the Smurfit Europe balance sheet, we had €1.5 billion in the bank, €2.5 million of equity and strong dividends growing every year. Smurfit-Stone had hardly any equity, it had huge debts and we had to give up our dividend. We had gone from a financially totally secure company into one that would have been, in my view, a little bit shaky.

So we didn't merge Smurfit-Stone and Smurfit Group together, because financially it didn't make any sense for the Group shareholders and also because, even though Smurfit-Stone was heavily indebted, its PE (price to earnings) ratio was considerably higher on average than Smurfit Group's in Europe, where we were very lowly-rated.

Following the Smurfit-Stone deal, we had so much of our assets in associate companies, it was proving very difficult for the analysts to follow us. We were a little bit like an investment bank, with Smurfit Group and its interests in Europe and Latin America, and Smurfit-Stone with investments in the USA and China. We had Munksjö in Sweden, which was another deal I'd done and was an associate company, as well as other associate companies with no cash flow, so the valuation of the Group started to slip in the marketplace as a result of these moves – something that I had not anticipated.

I thought we would get a premium rating because of the risk-mitigating structure of the Group but, with new accounting rules coming in as a result of the bankruptcies and the frauds that had happened in Enron and elsewhere, everything was to do with clear lines of communication. So we started to clear that up by going for full control of our associate companies, until we were left with our biggest associate, Smurfit-Stone.

The stock market was not giving us the rating we deserved, so I started to look at the alternatives. One of these was to distribute all the Smurfit-Stone stock to Smurfit Group shareholders as a one-off dividend, to buy back in our own stock with all the cash that we had and leverage the company. The other was an outright deal with somebody else. At that time, I wasn't thinking that we would one day go private.

One by one, we went through all the options. For several reasons, I decided that buying back our own stock was not a great idea. It would increase the family's percentage, which might be perceived as an attempt to take complete control. In any case, it would have taken forever to get back to 51% and I had enough control with the equity that I had. So I discounted that, as I didn't want to use up the cash.

Distribution to shareholders became an option, but we decided against this, because all in all it didn't make financial sense to me.

That left the last alternative, which was to sell the whole business.

CHAPTER 19
TAKING SMURFIT PRIVATE

We became the world's biggest packaging producer, with 20% of the US market. We were in a tremendous market position.

Misinformed public criticism is no help to any business and it made the Smurfit Group annual general meeting of 2001 difficult. Prior to this, the company had been subjected to sustained criticism from sections of the media. An environmental group even came from Colombia to criticise our policies on trees! That was a load of BS because we had enormously increased the numbers of trees, but we had to deal with it.

FACING CRITICISM

A lot of the questions revolved around my pay. That was always a contentious issue that journalists, who had bought one or two shares to get into the meeting, liked to write about. I took the view that it was nothing to do with them. I created a great deal of money for the shareholders – around €5 billion. That is what I was paid to do. When people asked questions about my pay, I just said, "I believe I have created a huge amount of value for the Smurfit Group shareholders. The remuneration committee decides my pay". End of conversation. Of course, that didn't satisfy the newspapers. It became a frenzy, as journalists constantly built it up into a huge issue. I never let it bother me personally. I felt quite justified in what I earned. I gave up an awful lot for it. I worked hard for very long hours, but it was an exciting job. And part of the excitement was getting well paid for it.

We were unfairly criticised when we had to shut down a plant. I knew all about the human impact of closing down a factory. It was terrible, and I felt it. When you're a family business and you close down a plant, in a place where you know there is very little alternative employment, particularly in a rural area where the factory just cannot be fixed, it's very hard to take. The truth is that we certainly kept more factories open for social reasons than we ever shut. So many times, we kept factories open for another year just to help a village or small town.

A company is not just an instrument for stockholders or even for its employees. It is a thing that has a level of social responsibility to the community as well. That is why Colombia has its own foundation, as does Venezuela, so we can give back money and help people improve their lot.

When we have to close a factory down, our first question always is, "What about the workers?". When you have a factory in which you have spent a fortune developing a huge amount of skill and knowledge, it is sad and frustrating if it becomes uneconomic. Closure is always the last resort and, in those cases, we would do everything we could to help our workers. Our executives knew what they were doing. It's stupid to throw anything away unless there is no alternative.

LOGICAL OPPORTUNISM

Growing the Smurfit family firm was a fantastic experience, which took me all over the world. First to the United States, then all over Europe, North and South America and even Australia and China and many parts of the Far East. Eventually, we came to have companies in Ireland, the United Kingdom, North and South America, in many countries of Europe, as well as in Nigeria, Australia, China and Indonesia. I spent most of my time travelling the world and it was always great to see three flags flying at each of our operations: the national flag of Ireland, the national flag of the country we were in, and the Smurfit flag.

Here was a little Irish company that, in the lifetime of one man, had become the biggest packaging company in the world. How could that happen? Because of risk-taking, because of measured steps, and because we knew the business better than the people we were taking over from.

I think it was Mark Kenny who coined the phrase 'logical opportunism' to describe what we did – it captures excellently the balance in how we grew. Our acquisition strategy might not have been that obviously strategic – we didn't spend time sitting around 'strategising' – but it was always logical and it was opportunistic. Put the two together and it becomes strategic.

From the beginning, the value we created was real – not based on some ludicrously-bloated multiple of earnings, but grounded in excellent products, great technical knowledge, asset-rich operations, strong fundamentals and a clear commitment to change for the better. We provided shareholders with strong returns by aggressively acquiring, expanding, and investing in very good assets at fair prices and then running them well.

We grew fast. Many of the deals we did doubled our size overnight: Temple Press in 1968. the Hely Group in 1970, Tremletts in the UK in 1973, and the CCA deal all doubled our US operations. These deals not only transformed the business, but they happened every three years or so. The pace never let up, because there were plenty of opportunities to apply our formula of identifying, acquiring and integrating undervalued assets at the optimal point in the industry cycle. The Smurfit Group never set out to be the largest of anything and it was never our goal. Rather, our goal always was to be the best at what we do. As a result, we became the largest, but that was an outcome, never a target.

Having arrived at the peak, we found ourselves in what was perceived as a low-growth, boring though cash-generative business. From our position as the industry's number one, I looked around and saw the way our rivals could raid us. I saw the way the whole issue of an unsatisfactory structure was going to hit us, because we had Smurfit-Stone as an associate company with a huge chunk of non-cash-generative assets stuck in it, which was causing the market to discount our stock. I had to find a solution.

We talked *ad nauseam* about possible mergers, but we couldn't reach an agreement with anyone. For the first time, I began to think that we should cease to be a public company.

ENTER MADISON DEARBORN

Then an interesting thing happened. When we were looking to expand in the USA, one of the companies that had attracted our attention was Packaging Corporation of America. Its majority stockholder was Madison Dearborn Partners, one of the largest and most experienced private equity investment firms in the USA, whose offices were in Chicago, where the headquarters of Smurfit-Stone were based.

We were interested in acquiring Packaging Corporation of America, but hadn't made up our minds. Through mutual banking contacts, we sent out some exploratory feelers to Madison Dearborn. You never want to appear to be too eager, so you do it very low key in the initial stages. I didn't get any real response for a couple of years.

For some time, I had known of the fine reputation of John Canning, the Chairman and Chief Executive Officer and co-founder of Madison Dearborn. One day, I got a call from a friend of mine, Don Keough, an ex-president of the Coca-Cola Company and Chairman of Allen & Company, a famous boutique investment bank in New York. Don said that he would like to introduce me to John Canning and he arranged to put us in touch.

Soon afterwards, I received a call from John Canning himself who said that he would like to come over and meet me. I arranged for him to stay overnight so we could have dinner together. I always prefer to dine with people because, during the day, I have limited time, but in the evening I can give my undivided attention, until three in the morning if need be. John Canning came over and, happily, we instantly clicked.

During the course of the evening, he totally took me aback. He was not there to talk about the Packaging Corporation of America, he was there to talk about the Smurfit Group. "Have you ever thought about taking the company private?", he asked. I said that, from time to time, I had thought about it, but I had not seriously considered it. He said, "I feel that with the earnings structure that you have and with the market positions that you have, it could be a very attractive deal for your shareholders".

The thought of selling the business hadn't seriously dawned on me until this moment. My gut instinct was that we might have no alternative but to do it, because my job was to act in the interests of the shareholders, not to act in the interests of myself and the family. The family were shareholders, but we weren't all the shareholders. I had to determine quickly how serious this approach was.

I replied very clearly, "John, I am very flattered by what you have said because it's not every company that gets an approach like this, but our share price is around 210 pence and, if you want to buy the company, it's going to have to be at 310 pence per share. That's the valuation, it's the highest price we've achieved and that's what we're worth. You need to think about that number, and if you can get your head around it, we can talk further. If you can't, there is no point in talking".

I was not trying to negotiate. The figure of 310 pence was my price and I stuck by my guns the whole way through, despite every attempt they made to bring it down. I said, "That's the number. That's the number I would be prepared to recommend to my shareholders. It's the highest number it's ever been and I can justify it". I didn't think they actually would go for it.

John and I stayed up till three or four in the morning and I got to like the man very much. Personal chemistry is very important in very large deals, particularly in one where effectively you are going to become partners, because it was clear to me that I was going to be staying on in some role.

Of course, in accordance with my responsibility, I reported our conversation to the Smurfit Group Board. John Canning returned to the US, and a couple of weeks later, I had a call to say that Madison Dearborn wanted to talk further. I knew they would want to negotiate on the price, but I said, "It's very simple. I don't know how these structures work, you can explain all that to us in due course, but I've got to have the feeling that you are prepared to pay the price. If I get the feeling that you are not prepared to pay the price, then I'm not going to take it any further, but once I know that you are going to pay the price, then we will move the process forward, because there are many hurdles to be examined".

I came to the view that it could be a very good deal, for the shareholders, for the family and for Madison Dearborn. I was reaching a certain age, as were my brothers. It was very clear that family-type companies were finished in the marketplace.

Madison Dearborn swiftly became serious about the project and I went to the Board and said that potentially this was looking like a transaction that they might want to do. I kept using the word "might" because the minute we got to the stage where we were going to do something, we would have to announce it. I didn't want to announce anything until I knew exactly what was going to be done.

GOING PRIVATE

Going private is a process that slowly sucks you in. Madison Dearborn sent a team of people over to us in Dublin, and we put a team of people together who would give them the documents that they wanted. They wanted to know where we paid taxes, how our American operations worked, what our relationship was with Smurfit-Stone, and so on. Some information was in the public domain, but the bulk of it was not. This operation alone cost them a great deal of money, because they had to send people over, put them up in hotels, go out and talk to banks about raising money, so for them it was obviously a very important proposition.

There was a long series of crunch meetings throughout the whole process. At one of these meetings, it was determined that, instead of paying cash for the Smurfit-Stone stockholding, we would issue it as a tax-free dividend to shareholders. That's how we became separated from Smurfit-Stone. Every Smurfit stockholder ended up getting shares in Smurfit-Stone, which most of them sold, including myself.

The decision to issue the stock in Smurfit-Stone was a wrenching decision for me to take, because I had formed Smurfit-Stone. It was originally Jefferson Smurfit Corporation, which I had laid the foundation for in the early 1970s. The whole thing was an emotional experience because here I was parting with a business that I had built into a world-renowned company in a very difficult industry.

But we had not had the performance we wanted in the late 1990s and early part of the 21st century. It was no longer what it had been in the decades before, due to a seismic change in the industry.

And that seismic change was definitely not for the better. Growth rates had levelled out in Europe, where there was the rise of independent containerboard producers who installed vast machines with tax incentives from the European Community, effectively destroying the industry. In the US, growth rates were minimal, because of manufacturing companies transferring work to China. Suddenly, all the boxes were being made in China, close to the manufacturers, rather than in America. But we foresaw all these enormous changes.

Smurfit was attractive to Madison Dearborn because of the cash flow of the company. We were now rated on an EBITDA (earnings before interest, taxes, depreciation and amortisation) basis rather than a PE (price to earnings) basis. We were paying a large dividend, which would stop. We were paying a large amount of corporation tax, which under the new structures would be reduced, and we had a very high level of depreciation. You don't get value in the stock market for EBITDA, you get value for PE ratios, whereas in the private equity market, it's all about EBITDA. And in a low-growth industry, debt, properly used, can provide a better platform for returns. At the end of the day, my job was straightforward: to create shareholder value. The reason Madison Dearborn eventually paid millions for Smurfit was because I created shareholder value. The market decided not to recognise it, but Madison Dearborn did.

The structure of the transaction was very interesting to me personally. I believed in it and invested £65 million back into the private company, which was a large proportion of the money that I was getting out of it.

It was an absolute requirement of the deal that the existing Smurfit management would stay in place and they were given very strong incentives to do so, because Madison Dearborn couldn't run the business from Chicago. Although they had a good knowledge of business, their interest and their expertise was financial and they had no interest in the day-to-day running of the business. They buy railways, cable companies, TV companies, paper companies, wood companies, any type of companies and they employ people who know those businesses to run them. Madison Dearborn are financiers, they are only interested in one thing: money. I don't think that the industry that they are in interests them in the slightest. They have keen brains, and they are very practical and pragmatic business people. They want to get a result and they judge the people managing the businesses on performance. They knew how we worked and they were attracted by that but, at the end of the day, it was a very simple equation: they were here, using our balance sheet for whatever period of time they were to be involved with us, with the sole objective of making money.

That is a crucial function in the world. Businesses that make money create jobs, create opportunities for suppliers, provide customers with good service and good products at competitive prices. Businesses that make money create a lot of wealth that spreads way beyond the people who own the businesses. If you are running a business, never forget that you are doing it to make money.

We finally came to an agreement with Madison Dearborn. Although they tried many times to come in with a lower price, the price we got was the original price that I set, partly achieved by issuing the Smurfit-Stone shares to shareholders. My concern was to get the best for the shareholders, and the shareholders had just one interest – cash. They were not concerned about whether I would stay on as Chairman, or what role our key executives Gary McGann or Tony Smurfit would have. They were going to take cash out and be happy. Clinching the deal was my job and I delivered on it because I was not going to undervalue the business. I knew that was what the business was worth. It wasn't worth a penny more, but I wasn't going to take a penny less.

There were no objections from the Board or the shareholders to the deal going ahead. Once you start down the road, it becomes difficult to halt if everything goes to plan. You might meet a roadblock but, whenever we did, we found a way around it and solved it.

The right price for the shareholders was my focus and I had total tunnel vision on this. You only sell your business once. I had been buying businesses all my life, so I knew very well what it was like to be at the other end. I had learned from experience that you name a price and you stick with it. The people I'd bought from didn't always do this. Once I had them hooked with the pound signs and they had smelled the money, they might want £10 million, but I'd offer them £8 million, and they would think that was great. They'd rather have £8 million in the bank than nothing. But because I knew both sides of the coin, I was prepared to name the price and stick with it. If they hadn't agreed to the price, I would have walked.

Madison Dearborn brought a number of positive things to the company. They got rid of some underperforming assets, which you can do when you are a private company, but which you can't when you are a public company, because it would hurt earnings too much. You tend to live with your problems as a public company. If you have a subsidiary losing £1 million a year, and it costs you £10 million to close it down, that would reduce your profits or increase your losses by £10 million in one year. So, rather than losing the £10 million that year, you live with it and keep losing £1 million a year. But when you are a private company, you just shut it down.

This was all factored into Madison Dearborn's calculations. They factored in that they would sell profitable parts of the business to reduce debt, which in a public company structure I would not have sold, because they were giving us a profit. Madison Dearborn raised cash by selling the Smurfit Group World Headquarters building in Clonskeagh, Dublin and the whole site that we owned there. They sold anything that was surplus to requirements, pieces of land, everything. We would never have done that, because we would have kept it for 'rainy days'. I wouldn't have sold the Group Headquarters because the money would not have made a great difference to us, while to a leveraged company it meant a lot. It's a different financial game, and it solved a lot of problems for us, and I started to see th̶ my legacy was being protected. I knew that it wasn't the e̶ story, there were more chapters to come, and one d̶ public company again.

From the Madison Dearborn viewpoint, we were a company that was both cash-rich and asset-rich, with strong earnings power and a very talented management team. We were an attractive company with the potential to get their investment back and make money.

The negotiations with Madison Dearborn were quick and harmonious. We liked them as people and they liked us too. I understand that they had never found a cleaner company in their lives, and they have bought many companies. Everything we said turned out to be true. We had not performed financially as well as we would have liked, but only because the market had turned against us. We had done what we said we would do: we had achieved that and more. I believe they considered us to be outstanding managers of a business in a very difficult climate.

BUSINESS AS USUAL

The day they finally bought us and we ceased to be a public company, it was business as usual, but business in a different way. We still had to sell our boxes, we still had to settle our debts, we still had to manage our company. We just didn't have the same Board, although I and several others still served.

But the culture of the Smurfit business remained the same. It was agreed that we would keep the Chairman's Dinner in Dublin every year, an important event. I had started this many years before because I thought Ireland needed an event, not just to bring senior Smurf le together, but to bring us together with executives fr inesses. The annual Innovation & Environmental which I had introduced in order to encourage ation in all parts of our business as well as ss across the Group. The Company of the e Year Awards continued, to recognise the plants and the people. It was very e running the same business, but in a

CHAPTER 20
THE FINAL DEAL

**Smurfit has been involved in the two biggest deals in
the history of corporate Ireland.**

Madison Dearborn's belief in our management team led to them
giving us their backing for the biggest financial deal that Smurfit had
ever done.

A NECESSARY MERGER

When I first met John Canning, I had mentioned Kappa Packaging to
him and the potential of a deal involving them, but I thought it
would be extremely difficult for all sorts of reasons. Kappa Packaging
BV was a Dutch company and one of Europe's largest producers of
containerboard, as well as solid board, corrugated and solid board
packaging, graphic and speciality board.

Then Gary McGann and my son Tony began to push the idea that
we should look seriously at Kappa.

I coined a phrase many years ago that: "The worse it is, the better
it gets". You can never buy a company that's doing very well,
because you've got to pay top price for it and they don't want to sell
to you. But by 2005, Kappa, Smurfit and the industry in general had
had a very tough couple of years. Prices had gone down and costs
had been increasing dramatically because of energy costs. So Kappa
was in a situation, as we saw it, that they had no alternative but to
merge with us.

What this deal offered was an opportunity to share synergies. By
bringing the two companies together, we expected to save something
in excess of €150 million – at six times EBITDA, that's worth €900
million and €900 million shared between us is a lot of cabbage.

The deal also would cost money because plants would have to be closed and jobs would be lost. But the truth of the matter was that Smurfit would have to close these places any way, as we had done earlier with Dublin, irrespective of the merger. Increased energy costs had made many small paper mills totally unviable. Energy is now the number two cost in our industry, when once it was number three.

Kappa suited us because we were much better sellers of corrugated boxes and they were better producers of paper. They had bigger mills and were more cost-effective, so this was an ideal marriage for both parts of the business. They were the largest producers of white top liner paper in Europe and also the third largest producer of recycled paper. I saw this as a unique, special opportunity. We had to get it through the EU Commission and we had to sell some parts of the business because of monopoly concerns.

Because we were competitors right up until the last minute of the deal; we didn't know all the details of their customers and they didn't know ours. If, for some reason, we had not been able to merge, then we would have continued to compete against each other, so there was certain information that was withheld by us to them and by them to us, by law. That is the difficulty with mergers: you don't get to do due diligence completely.

But because we knew the industry, we had a strong idea about Kappa's affairs. I don't think anyone has the market information that we have. We have always kept an eye on our competitors worldwide. From my earliest days, I bought a small number of shares in each of our competitors, just so I could get their annual reports and gain access to information about them.

Smurfit approached Kappa and we got the usual response we got when we knocked on someone's door with an offer, which was "Go away". It took them about six months to come around to seeing our point of view, because they were trying to find alternative courses of action. Meanwhile, the industry continued to get worse. Oil prices shot up dramatically and costs were increasing, while prices for finished goods were going down, so the squeeze on both Smurfit and Kappa was at both ends. It was clear that there was no solution except the one that we offered. Kappa's management finally saw that.

In September 2005, the proposed merger between Jefferson Smurfit Group and Kappa Packaging was announced. The aim was to create a business employing over 40,000 people in 23 European countries and nine Latin American countries, with capacity to produce over six million tonnes of containerboard and over five million tonnes of corrugated a year. The merged company would become a world leader in corrugated, a European leader in containerboard and would retain market-leading positions in both paper grades in Latin America.

Hundreds of people worked on putting this deal together, working long hours, seven days a week, as we got closer to finalising the deal. The transaction cost €100 million to put together. We didn't start spending serious money until we had the agreement with Kappa, but the real issue was whether the EU Commission would say 'yes' or 'no' to the merger.

I wasn't very involved in the detail of the Smurfit Kappa deal. This was probably the first major deal that I wasn't closely involved with on a day-to-day basis, but I was kept up-to-date with events. I saw the other side wobbling from time to time, and advised our team to keep a straight course. We came to the conclusion that they had nowhere else to go. This was the only deal available to them.

SMURFIT KAPPA

By January 2006, Smurfit Kappa had been formed. I was appointed Chairman of the Board, with Frits Beurskens, who had been Chief Executive Officer of Kappa, as Deputy Chairman. Gary McGann was Group Chief Executive Officer (the first non-Smurfit family member to run the company), Tony Smurfit became President and Group Chief Operations Officer and Ian Curley was Group Chief Financial Officer.

Neither Gary nor Tony had done a transaction of this scale before so they did not have the direct experience of what needed to be done afterwards. I knew what to do because I had done it a dozen times. I knew how to motivate people, 'Smurfitise' people as we called it. This put me back on the treadmill of travelling from place to place again, visiting the Kappa people and operations, but it was something I enjoyed.

I guess when I did the Madison Dearborn deal, I expected that I would play less of an active role in visiting operations. But I enjoy going around the factories, giving presentations, getting a feel for the business, because how can you be Chairman of a company if you are talking about a paper mill you want to do something with, and you haven't seen it? But most Chairmen that I've met wouldn't know their individual operations. Most of them would look at the paperwork and approve it, but I want to know what it's really about.

Following any merger, people employed within the companies are worried about their jobs. For instance, Smurfit and Kappa each had a head office, and we didn't need two head offices, so a number of people left. In terms of the closure of factories, to some extent people are reasonably aware of which companies will close, because in Europe by law you have to approach the Works Council to get their approval. So we had notified them that the merger was planned and they were aware that some operations would be sold and some would be closed.

The Smurfit paper mill in Clonskeagh, Dublin, where I started my career, sadly had to be shut down because of energy costs. It went from making €1.5 million a year to losing €2 million a year, just like that. The last sheet of paper made on the site was signed by everyone who worked there and was presented to me. It is impossible for me to express how I felt about the closure.

Energy costs will continue to be a problem but Smurfit Kappa is addressing that by taking high-cost tonnes out of the system. We have the lowest cost system in Europe, in part because the merger geographically rebalanced the business to give almost complete coverage across Europe. Because our mills are located from southern Spain to northern Sweden, our ability to put our tonnes where we want at very effective transport costs is fantastic. If somebody builds a paper mill in the middle of Germany and exports to Spain, the transport costs will be €40 to €60 a tonne, compared with our transport costs of €10. So no matter how effective he is in his German mill, the further he goes out to sell, the more it costs him. And he will be selling to independent buyers who are always looking to buy cheaper paper. So even though he might have lower production costs, he has higher transportation costs and lower sales, while we have a serious cost and price advantage. Smurfit Kappa is totally integrated and we buy from ourselves. When we buy from our competitors, which we do from time to time, we find some of the prices are ridiculous.

When I handed the reins over to the new management team comprising Gary McGann and my son Tony, I told them, "You can do an awful lot with cost-cutting and fine-tuning the company. But you will be a bigger hero with a €50 a tonne increase in price – and you will be in the doghouse if you let the price drop €50 a tonne". As Smurfit produces around six million tonnes of board a year, plus or minus €50 a tonne has a significant impact. Both Gary and Tony have remarked to me over the years how right I was about that particular aspect of the business.

"THIS IS FOR DAD"

At the start of the Madison Dearborn transaction, I made a commitment to John Canning and his team that I would see it through to its success. The Kappa deal was what made it a success. We effectively doubled the size of our company – yet again. In any merger, you lose some market share, because you have overlapping customers and they won't give you 100% of their business, but overall we now have the largest share of an extremely competitive packaging market in Europe and Smurfit has been involved in the two biggest deals in the history of corporate Ireland.

Once the deal was done, I thought of just one man. In a quiet family moment on my yacht soon afterwards, I said to my sister Barbara, "This is for Dad".

CHAPTER 21
THE SMURFIT CULTURE

Tremendous vision, with an uncanny knack in terms of choice of acquisitions and their timing and, in particular, choice of senior executives.

The time of the Hely rationalisation was one of the most exhilarating periods of my life, because it was then that I really learned about business. I knew the packaging world, but all of a sudden I was thrust into understanding finance companies, retailing, distribution, television production and electronics. They were areas that I knew nothing about, but I had to learn fast. They were diverse and challenging businesses but, in the end, they all came down to finance and the control of finance.

The Hely Group gave me the financial people who helped to found the modern Smurfit approach. Gerry Cashin, Ned Grace and Robert Holmes were the three key financial people who came from the Hely Group to become the nucleus of the Smurfit finance department, which had its own ethos and its own systems of reporting. So I always had my own checks and balances against myself in my own company, because I recognised there is always a danger that you can get carried away and begin to think that you are infallible.

VISION & LEADERSHIP

Howard Kilroy once said about me:

Michael is a man of both strong leadership and vision.

He could pick good people but he couldn't always manage them well. I was the guy who nursed them and talked them out of resigning and all that sort of stuff. Or equally, despite his very hard-nosed approach, he was hopeless at firing people and that always got delegated to me.

He was a lot of contradictions, but the leadership qualities he had, which inspired people ultimately to go through fire for him, were exceptional. He is not remotely interested in small talk. But in his genes is an ability to inspire the fiercest loyalty in people.

Great leaders are not always likeable yet they have a presence and stature. They know their business or their campaign or whatever situation they're in. They are sufficiently strong and well-versed that you believe them and follow them, out of the trenches if necessary. That's a unique quality, which is indefinable.

And Martin Rafferty, who I had known since the 1960s, when he acted for me in the merger of my business with my father's, said on another occasion:

Michael is a man of tremendous vision, and has an uncanny knack in terms of his choice of acquisitions and their timing and, in particular, his choice of senior executives.

Vision was always important to me. I was always looking ahead, spotting changes in one industry and making connections to their consequences in others. Again Howard's words stick in my mind:

There are people who can see around corners and people who can only see in a straight line. Michael can see around corners, and that is the kind of quality you need to spot opportunities and a way forward.

For example, as I mentioned earlier, I realised the potential of the Internet, and the effect it was going to have both on newsprint and on deliveries of products, by an accidental visit in Chicago to an 'Internet Café'.

Again with Straffan House, I saw the potential for a world-class country club – and the potential of the adjoining land, which turned out to be a shrewd investment.

It was always about strategically seeing what the problem was – and then applying the formula: Problem, solution, result.

THE RIGHT PEOPLE

All my life, touch wood, I've had a habit of picking the right people. I've always surrounded myself with extraordinarily able people. It's a sort of intuition or instinct. I think I have an ability to read people very quickly and see what they needed from me. Everyone was different.

One of my key tasks was to get the best out of people. I wasn't doing the work myself. I wasn't down running the machines, I wasn't down doing the accounts, I wasn't doing the actual day-to-day stuff. The work was being done by a whole host of other people. I was the one pulling the company together at the top. So I was in the motivational business; I was both strategist and motivationalist.

How do you get the best out of people? By a combination of them being aware that you know the business, the accounts and the product quality as well as they do, if not better. I had a great command of detail.

During the years when I was growing the business, I had an aggressive personality and I was considered extremely tough. I used to lose my temper. "Did you really make grown men cry?", I am sometimes asked. I might have upset a few people but I don't remember actually seeing anyone cry. If I did, it is not something I would boast about. And I never bear grudges against people: when the fight is over, we move on.

I always tried to stretch people. Sometimes people fly when they get promoted; they have a new, bigger job to do and they rise to it. Other times, it's quickly clear that they have been over-promoted. I would stretch everyone to the extent a rubber band would go but not break. I would look to get the most out of them, stretch them but not break them. I did break a few people in my life and it was always to my regret. But you learn from those mistakes. If you don't make mistakes, you make nothing.

I have treated my brothers and sons harder than anyone else in the company. I try to treat everybody more or less the same but I am probably a little bit harder on family.

Dermot reminds me:

It was not easy for Tony at the start. He called me and said that he was having real trouble with his father calling him all the time and telling him to rush off to meet him in New York or Cape Town. He complained that he had no regular job. I offered him one and made him Managing Director of a company called Swains Packaging, whose headquarters was in Epsom. It was only a small business but it was a great stepping-stone. I told Tony, "The first time your dad calls, tell him to call me".

Michael called and said he wanted Tony in New York on Wednesday. I said, "He can't do Wednesday. He's got a union meeting". Again, after another call, I made excuses. Tony couldn't bat him away, but I could. I managed to show Michael he was preventing Tony from learning how to run a business.

Tony learned quickly at Swains and, in time, he went on to become CEO of Smurfit France and Deputy CEO of Smurfit Europe and then eventually took over as COO of the Group. Tony Smurfit is smarter than any of us and he has great heart. He inspires great loyalty from his people. He is a credit to his father and the whole family.

We had a multicultural senior executive team, but we maintained the Smurfit culture and you didn't get into a senior position unless you had fully absorbed that culture. Everybody must have the same focus on what we are trying to achieve and we have fun as well as work: work hard and play hard.

I've always wanted people to enjoy their jobs. It's never been just about take-home pay; it's about job satisfaction, and it's also about having fun and enjoying your working life. I would take some of the executives skiing with me and on trips to different places, or they would come over to Monaco and have dinner.

From the early days of the Jefferson Smurfit Group, we had an annual dinner for executives. At the first dinner, there were only six of us, but it expanded quickly as an event to involve up to 50 people each year. When I became Chairman in 1977, I renamed it the Chairman's Dinner and expanded it further – on one occasion, we had 800 people present.

Executives from Smurfit companies all over the world attended in the hope that their organisation would receive the Company of the Year Award or that they themselves would be nominated Employee of the Year. Although these awards were necessarily subjective, there was a significant vetting process and the whole thing was highly motivational. Not everyone who had contributed to the Group's success over the previous year could be recognised for the top award, so I also presented Chairman's Gold Pin and Chairman's Silver Pin awards. These pins were much sought-after and those who had them wore them proudly, particularly at company gatherings.

And while the primary aim of the dinner was to motivate Smurfit executives, we also invited politicians and other people of note in different fields. Our guest speakers over the years included John Major and Chris Patton, as well as Terry Wogan and Ronnie Corbett.

I always stayed close to the key people in the company because I recognised that by doing that I built loyalty and ensured that they would not suddenly walk through the door and say, "Michael, I'm leaving". I am happy to say that never happened to me.

My brother Alan says:

At the end of Michael's career, a lot of the people around him were the people who were around him 25 or 30 years earlier. Most of his friends today are the same friends he had 30 or 40 years ago. He's a very loyal guy. He pushed a lot of people to the limit but he wasn't as ruthless as his reputation indicates. 'Ruthless' would not be a good word to describe Michael, but 'impatient' would be absolutely bang on.

In one of my last Smurfit Group *Annual Reports*, I said: "Jefferson Smurfit has a clear vision of where it wants to be, a strong balance sheet, solid earnings potential and a capable management team to sustain this vision". Building that team – finding and motivating the right people – was one of my key tasks.

INTEGRITY & ETHICS

One of the 'shop window' maxims that my father taught me was: "There are only three things a man has in this world: his good name, his integrity and his word. While other things are also important, there is nothing so important as these".

There have been a couple of times when people have come to me with underhand offers that could have made me a lot of money, or maybe extracted me from a difficult situation. I've had executives suggest a way in which we could twist our figures. But I've always told them that I, and the company, won't even consider things like that. I can understand why people sometimes take the wrong path; but we just don't have that in our family's psyche. It's in our character to work hard and do things the right way. It doesn't occur to us to do otherwise. It is a very 'Protestant'-type culture. I don't know whether that gives us a good reputation or not – it's up to other people to make up their own minds.

We've always paid our bills on time, we've always looked after our people, we have very strict rules for what we can and cannot do within the company. If you join the Smurfit Group, you join up to the code of conduct. If people don't accept this and don't abide by it, they get fired, straight away. For example, if you're caught talking to competitors, that is immediate dismissal. With a company of our size, you're going to have some problem employees, you just have to have a system to deal with them.

We never took any high moral stances, because I thought they were none of our business. We don't have any issues about whether people drink alcohol, smoke cigarettes, eat fatty foods or take too much salt in their diet. It is not our job to decide; it is up to the consumer. As long as something is legal, then in my view it is not up to us to address ethical issues associated with the product. Our job is to help the manufacturer to get the product to the marketplace in the best possible condition.

However, if I were on the board of a major corporation that produced foods going to the consumer, I most certainly would be asking the executives of that company to examine the effects of our foods and their nutritional values. In that case, whether we were targeting young people with fatty foods and contributing towards obesity would be an ethical issue. We should be trying to find ways to replace that fatty food with something less fattening. So I do see ethical issues as a topic for the Board of directors. But when you are supplying only the packaging, it is not an issue for the packaging suppliers.

And I am proud to say that our integrity was second to none. In countries where backhanders and corruption were rife, we always did things professionally, legally and above board. We never got involved in anything underhand – sometimes, we lost business because of it, but that's the way we have always been.

John Canning of Madison Dearborn paid me a great compliment when he said:

> We have invested over $8bn in over 100 companies and I can say unequivocally that I have never had a better partner. Michael is a man of honour and uncompromising integrity.

CORPORATE GOVERNANCE

Smurfit has always had a unique management style with firm financial controls and strong reporting systems. We were a family company that grew into a large multinational company, yet we kept the family feel. You hear a lot about the importance of corporate governance these days but, at Smurfit, good corporate governance was always second nature. I'd sometimes say that good governance is nothing more – or less – than doing the right thing, even when no one is looking.

We didn't know how to act any way other than decently, honestly and transparently. We had a structure that meant that no one could ever do anything that was not in the interests of the company. If they tried, they were shown the door.

It would really make me mad if anything ever appeared in the press suggesting that there was any impropriety in our business or that Smurfit wasn't being run on strict ethical lines. That is one thing that would really get up my nose because I know that exactly the opposite is the case. Way before corporate governance came in, we had it in spades.

As the Chairman and Chief Executive, I had to put all proposals to the Board before any substantial action could be taken and we never tolerated any yes-men on the Board. I had to be able to justify fully any new course of action I placed before the directors. We had a strong internal audit department and always insisted on the highest level of corporate responsibility and corporate governance beyond any regulations at the time.

Corporate law is changing dramatically, particularly in America. Now when the Chief Financial Officer and the Chief Executive Officer of a company sign the accounts to say that they are a true and fair record, it carries a great responsibility. Senior executives are finding themselves in jail and there is a big culture change taking place, making people more accountable and more careful. I have never had to worry about that in Smurfit because, when we took over the Hely Group, the great things about the company were the financial controls and the computer systems that they had, which became the basis of Smurfit's controls. Thanks to the Hely Group, we ended up with a great financial division, which we still have today. We have always had good financial controls.

When you are Chief Executive Officer of a company, particularly in the US, if an executive does something wrong that damages the company, you can be exposed to a negligence claim for employing him. That goes with the territory, but what can you do? For me, it has never been an option to hide away and do nothing. But I have always been careful. The best lawyer in Ireland, James O'Dwyer, is my personal lawyer and we had Houghton Fry as one of the best company lawyers. We have always had top class legal advice and, on the Board, we had three lawyers. I've always had people minding my back.

As we grew, our size never stopped us doing our regular reviews and keeping a close eye on every area of the business. The size was academic, it just meant more meetings. As the organisation got bigger, it didn't get sloppier. We still ran a tight ship, but this is a danger that people need to be aware of when they develop and expand a business. There is a danger in any growing organisation that you will lose momentum and control.

OUR *RAISON D'ÊTRE*

One of the things the Board would question me on from time to time was why I wanted to keep on expanding. I would answer by explaining that increasing in size simply for the sake of getting bigger would be stupid.

Nevertheless, I found there was a need to get bigger because there were always valuable unseen synergies. We could sell more paper and buy more paper and improve our overall profitability. We could take costs out. We could close two or three factories if there were too many factories duplicating things. There would always be a strategic, as well as an immediate, reason.

Sometimes, we would be concerned that we had financed a deal correctly and not taken on too much debt. I would have to go back and rethink – not the deal itself but the way we structured it. I never minded because I understood that the Board had a responsibility to the shareholders. I also liked to show that this was not just a Michael Smurfit idea and that I had the support of a team.

In a big acquisition, the night before the deal went to the Board formally, I often would have all the executives come in to meet with the Board and we would go over exactly what we were planning to achieve the next day.

There are lots of deals I should have done that I didn't. I missed out on my share of great opportunities, but it's a little like horse-racing. You can't win them all. I never looked back.

Being the biggest is not – and never was – the goal. Being the best always was. The cream always comes to the top and if you're the best producer, you get the best customers. That's still the *raison d'être* of the company.

CHAPTER 22
THE SMURFIT SYSTEM

**We did so many deals that we virtually developed
a system for executing them.**

At one stage, Harvard Business School did a case-study of us, which showed that our associate, Jefferson Smurfit Corporation, was the fastest-growing company in North America for two years running. This study clearly showed what our techniques were, so our competitors started to wake up and ask, "Why is Smurfit's working capital 8% and ours 15%? Why do we have 500 people in head office and they have only 50?".

There was a gradual understanding among our competitors that we were always one step ahead of them. I was always amazed how inept our competitors were, to such an extent that I was always looking over my shoulder to see who the new Michael Smurfit was because we came from nowhere, out of left field. We had been just that Irish firm, which suddenly became that large North American firm, and then that large European firm and our competitors woke up to the unpleasant reality that we were twice their size.

They wanted to know how it happened. They had their analysts try and figure out how it happened and they saw that we had built the business step by step by step and we weren't shouting about it. We weren't going around saying, "We are the best and the biggest"; we had just said to ourselves, "We are going to be the best and the biggest, but nobody's going to know about it until we have arrived".

I was seen as a huge risk-taker but I calculated my risks very carefully. I always managed for the downside; the upside looks after itself. Applying that rule really protected me at times. We came in beneath the radar and our competitors didn't see us coming. I often shake my head and wonder how they let Smurfit get established in England and America the way we did.

CONTROL SYSTEMS

The way I controlled the Smurfit business was with quarterly reviews and those reviews were extremely detailed. I went through every company – cash flow, new customers, complaints, the whole lot – and if somebody hadn't done their homework, they would hear about it.

Maurice Buckley recalls:

> *Michael was always very disciplined and very demanding of himself. He did not tolerate fools lightly, and he had a financial ability that even accountants or financiers didn't have. It is one of his God-given talents. He could take a balance sheet and dissect it quicker than anyone I know. He got to the heart of the real problem at the speed of light, without spending days talking about it.*
>
> *He was always ingrained with financial conservatism, and yet he was very gregarious with his life. Today, Michael Smurfit might appear to be rich and flamboyant but he is the sort of man who would turn lights off in a hotel; he would be furious if someone left lights on. He is very clean and tidy, very controlled. A lot of the great people in life have a huge attention to detail and making sure everything gets done: Michael is like that.*
>
> *Michael is a genius in many ways. He is a visionary because he can see past what everyone else sees.*

We have always had very strict controls. Our 'moat system' meant that every company in the group was responsible for its own debt: it was a new idea at the time – simple, yet very effective.

Basically, you buy a company, surround it with its own debts, an internal leveraged buyout, a control mechanism and have quarterly reviews and a tight control of working capital with cash reporting daily. Businesses we acquired were expected to return the cash paid for them and the attributed cost of capital within seven years – effectively, an implied IRR of about 20%. This was an industry first – no one did this or took it so seriously.

We were the first company in our industry to worry about working capital. Companies we took over had 15% of their money tied up in working capital and stocks. We operated on 7% or 8%, so we were able to release a lot of money straight away. We got cash back very quickly. We found companies stuffed with overheads that we could take out fast. All of the companies we took over were overmanned, some of them terribly – they didn't think they were, but I did.

Alan says it well:

Dad had a great expression: 'Anybody can be a busy fool'. You have to make a profit for your efforts. Waste factors must be very low and your quality must be high. That was the secret of our success. It was very competitive.

We were probably the first major company in the world to have weekly profit and loss accounts. It took months and months of work to set up the process right so that, on a Tuesday morning, I knew how much money we had made the previous week.

We started that in the 1960s. It happened because my father one day found out that, instead of making a profit as he had expected, he was nearly bankrupt. He found that an accountant he had at the time was producing figures which did not reflect the true position and that the company wasn't doing as well as he thought. From then on, I decided we were never going to have that shock again.

We became a much more efficient company, because we knew what our waste was each week, instead of waiting until the end of the month to find out we had a 15% waste level, which is far too high. Then, even if you tackled it immediately, six weeks would be gone before you had it back to normal. But within seven days, we were onto the problem. For example, the amount of starch you use when you produce paper or corrugated board is critical. If you put too much on, you wouldn't know until you totted up your costs. Worse, all of a sudden, you would find out that the excess starch had worn out the rolls that make the corrugation, which can destroy a huge amount of paper, which is further waste. Getting all these things right adds up to a smoothly-running corrugated plant. And it's not just about control, there's also a motivational element too.

Everything was benchmarked internally. We knew where our best mills were and we knew where our best plants were – week by week.

At one time, we worked out that we could have trebled our profits if all of our operations were operating at the same level as the best in class that we had. That was the internal opportunity. It still exists today – in Smurfit and in every other business too.

It is about using accounting information the way it should be used, to look forward rather than backwards. Someone once said that "managing using annual accounts is like trying to steer a boat by looking at the wake". Twelve or more months later, it's too late – too much time has gone by. But if you're doing it on a timely basis, not only do you have that information but you can use it to motivate because now you know there's a problem and you can go fix it. That's why the weekly figures were very important.

We also had a bonus system, which was very important. I think money motivates people. Why do people work? First of all, they work because they need money to feed their families. So I always set out to achieve a family atmosphere, with good conditions, good food from the canteen, etc.

One of my rules was that head office staff should never exceed 50 people and, even in the mills, we kept a tight control on headcount. Mark Kenny remembers:

> To get a new member of staff, you had to go through a process that involved Michael and you didn't want to go there until you really had to. At one point, I wanted to hire an assistant. My boss at the time told Michael that the person I had in mind was related to one of the Smurfit Board directors.
>
> Michael's memo in reply said, "Everyone in Ireland is related to someone somewhere down the line and if Mark needs an assistant, why not an assistant to the assistant and an assistant to the assistant and so on – where does it end?". That was that.

We kept our costs low, but we paid our people well. Again, Mark Kenny recalls:

> If you made money for the Smurfit Group, Michael paid you. If you put the Group into a deal and it made money, without question, Michael would pay you for it. No discussion, no messing, no nothing.

I recognised that people are motivated by money, but they are motivated by many other things as well. We created a good atmosphere and that is why we've had so few people leave Smurfit.

We were creating something special. That is why I used to visit as many companies as possible. And as the business grew bigger and bigger and I couldn't get round everywhere, I regretted it. Although I hadn't especially enjoyed my own time on the factory floor, I loved being in touch with production areas. I understood that an office just produces paperwork while, in a factory, you see something real being produced. It makes you proud.

Also I never wasted time – my own or anyone else's. There was never a meeting for meeting's sake. There always was a purpose to the meeting and an outcome and there was work to be done after the meeting. Too many people in corporate life waste an inordinate amount of time, just to give themselves a sense of importance.

These were the disciplines that I brought to a business. Though not rocket science, they didn't exist in those days. In the years since, everyone in the industry, and in other industries, has copied the Smurfit formula.

MAKING DEALS WORK

We found out over time that we had the unique ability to make deals work. Most deals fail: research shows that about two-thirds of deals fail to deliver a proper return to shareholders. This is why most people think that deals are bad. We created, in effect, a blueprint for the way mergers should work.

How a deal works first depends on whether it is friendly or hostile. All our large deals were friendly ones, in which we were able to determine through due diligence what we intended to do after we had acquired the company. In a hostile deal environment, you must navigate many unknowns and imponderables and the risks rise commensurately. But, even in hostile deals, like the Hely Group acquisition, our first big deal, it is important to have a clear vision of what you want to achieve and how you are going to achieve it.

We never bought a company just for the sake of doing so. In every case, we had identified excellent synergies and substantial cost savings – sometimes from our due diligence, in other cases from observation and knowledge of our competitors' businesses. Always, we looked to the strategic fit. As Richard Hooper, former Investment Bank of Ireland director, puts it:

Smurfit's success has been largely due to the very successful acquisitions Michael made. In all of these, he displayed energy, acumen and a strategic view of the potential target.

The next step is the money. The obvious question is "Do you have, or can you get, the money?". Generally, a comfort letter from an investment bank provides assurance that you can obtain the funds. We received many comfort letters over the years and all of them came to fruition.

The second and third questions, less obvious and less often asked, are "Can you pay the interest on the money that you are going to borrow to acquire the target company?" and "Can you pay down the total amount of the purchase price over a realistic period of time?". Unless the answer to both questions is a categorical "Yes", you should never, never buy the company. I believe our average payback period was between four and five years although, in some cases, it was much longer and, in a few cases, shorter.

I learnt early on to take our own advice. Of course, in every deal, we had investment bankers and advisors coming out of our ears, and we were besieged with all sorts of propositions from companies hustling for business, but I generally took my own counsel and that of my financial team, headed by Howard Kilroy. We didn't always get it right, but we were right more often than we were wrong.

We always had to present our Board, not just with the acquisition details, but also with a plan on how we would run the company afterwards. And, of course, the Board would monitor the results closely. Therefore, in our presentations, we generally took a conservative view. For example, in the 1987 Container Corporation of America (CCA) deal, our biggest deal to date at that stage, we estimated savings of $150 million – I believe we achieved over $250 million in the end.

We often took over a loss-making company and made a fortune the following year because its overheads had been too high, the selling price was too cheap, or they were in the wrong markets. We could go into a newly-acquired company and revolutionise it – making money for the Group in the process.

Sometimes, it just needed a little commonsense. Mobil Oil – CCA's owner – decided to sell CCA because they couldn't make a go of it. Mobil spent $300 million in Fernandina Beach, Florida, on the biggest paper mill in the CCA system, making 1,000,000 tonnes of kraftliner a year, but it wasn't making any money for them. It wasn't their business; Mobil was a huge company and didn't need to focus on the paper division. In fact, they couldn't wait to get rid of it.

When we got control, we found that the biggest machine in the mill was being run at speeds well below design capacity. When questioned about this, the plant manager explained how the engineers at the CCA head office in Chicago had designed the paper mill drives and that, above a certain speed, they would fluctuate, which in turn would break the paper. Since head office said there was nothing wrong with the drives, the workers at the plant simply ran the machine slowly to prevent paper breaks.

As soon as we closed the head office, we gave the manager $5 million to replace the drives. When the new ones were installed, production jumped by 600 tonnes a day, which led to a huge jump in profits. Commonsense.

Smurfit never built any significant greenfield capacity; we mostly acquired it and expanded it, as it was far cheaper to do this. It's often been said that Smurfit never built a mill, that we always were buyers not builders. That's not entirely true: we did build paper mills – but more often we bought, usually at 30% to 50% of the capital cost of building from new. The hallmark of our acquisition strategy over the years was buying well-invested assets at bargain basement prices from those for whom paper and packaging were non-core. Payback was swift and the return on investment high. By limiting our investments to clearly value-creating projects, based on real, not anticipated demand and then prudently pruning and developing those assets as the market required, we were able to create superior value for our shareholders. Again and again, we found opportunities to apply our formula of identifying, acquiring and integrating undervalued assets at the optimal point in the industry cycle.

Instead, by building unnecessary and expensive machines, often part-financed by government subsidies or tax incentives, some of our competitors distorted the market, destroying the price in the process – for themselves as well as everyone else. I would single out German and Spanish producers as the biggest culprits in this.

In every deal, we always looked to manage the downside risk. Very often, we would buy a significant minority stake in a business initially. Then, after we had an opportunity to see what worked in the business and what didn't, we would increase our stake to control (50%+) and sometimes later to full ownership. This associate structure served us very well when we were growing. When we didn't have a lot of money but wanted to gain access to new markets and new businesses, we used that structure to minimise risk in a way that wasn't capital-intensive. And, in using this structure, we learnt that markets often are very different from the inside looking out than they might appear when you are on the outside looking in.

THE ANATOMY OF A DEAL

We did so many deals that we virtually developed a system for executing them. It worked like this.

In any large deal, I would arrive at the acquired company as soon as the deal was concluded with a team of executives and we would start to work on the balance sheet. We would tackle working capital first, by reducing stocks, offering shorter but better credit terms to customers and having fewer suppliers and extracting from them longer payment terms, often as much as 120 days. This process often released enormous sums: in the CCA deal, I think we were able to earn back over 20% of the total purchase price out of working capital alone within the first year.

Next, we would work down through each item in the company's cost structure – transportation costs, overheads, salaries, etc. – and, in nearly every instance, we were able to make good savings in almost every area of the business.

In the third step, I would take another team of operational executives to visit all the factories, determining how much waste they had, getting the managers to come forward with quick payback capital items. I would ask, "If you had the capital, what could you do that would give me a payback in six months, 12 months or two years?". In many instances, we found that good projects had not been done in the past because of lack of capital. This was no constraint as far as I was concerned if the payback was quick. There were always numerous opportunities in the business once the managers opened up and could see that they had access to the top guy in the company, myself. And to my surprise, again and again, we found that previous chief executives or directors had never even once visited the factory.

Step four would be to determine what the acquired company did better than we did at Smurfit. Hely Group, for example, had a superb computer system and a much better financial control system because their company was much more complex than Smurfit back then. As a result, we built our systems around theirs. In nearly every acquisition we made, we found some things were done better than we were doing them and, accordingly, we incorporated these things into our systems. Often, this was helpful from a motivational point of view for the acquired executives to see that some of their systems were being used and that Smurfit was not always right about everything. It helped to get them into the Smurfit culture and our way of doing business.

Then I would have a 'welcome dinner', at which we laid out our plans and our expectations of each executive. These often focused on getting them to improve margins, reduce the number of outside suppliers, increase credit from suppliers and a whole range of other ideas and programmes. We would show the executives what the ideal corrugated factory looked like, corrugated being our largest business, and where their factory stood in comparison. We called it 'best in class'.

Next, I would set about interviewing all the key executives in the company and determining who was going to fit into our way of thinking and whether they were up to the job. In most instances, I am pleased to say we kept on the acquired management but, where a person was over-promoted, totally unsuited to the job or downright useless, not having a clue about the business that he was theoretically responsible for, my job and that of my team was to assess these people quickly. Just as one bad apple destroys a whole barrel, the same applies in a company,

Another part of the deal process very early on was to take the senior managers back to Ireland where they could get to know the Smurfit people in a wider sense and see the company's origins and how we had built it up from modest beginnings. Again, we found this was very motivational. People in companies that have been taken over, be it a hostile or friendly deal, tend to be nervous, sometimes even defensive or hostile. You have to get through that barrier by a combination of charm, them finding out that you know the business as well as they do, and them being aware of your determination to take no prisoners if they do not come on board.

On these factory visits, I would always have with me my PA, a position that I used to train numerous executives in the company. Paddy Wright was my first PA; he went on to be top dog in Smurfit. Another of my PAs was Mark Kenny, whose father wrote the *Foreword* to this book; Mark went on to set up his own company, which he later sold at the top of the market. Roberto Villaquiran from Colombia, who today runs the corrugated division, and Smurfit Kappa's Group Chief Financial Officer Ian Curley also held this role, which allowed them to learn the business and the Smurfit systems very thoroughly.

Ian Curley remembers:

One of the things I really appreciated coming through the organisation was Michael's faith in young people. We were allowed to do many things – acquisitions, for example – that we would never have had the chance to do in another company. I also appreciated Michael's decisiveness. You never got a "may be", always a "yes" or "no", and that decisiveness made working for Michael quite easy.

As a self-discipline, I reported to the Board on a regular basis on the performance of our acquisitions against the targets we had agreed with the Board at the time of the acquisition. Most times, we would beat target but there were occasions when market sentiment changed and, when the markets do turn against you, it is very hard to swim against the tide.

Simply put, success in deal-making is more about the price and the execution, not about doing the deal. We always looked to buy undervalued assets at the optimal point in the industry cycle: it became our formula. We executed extremely well primarily because of the due diligence we did, not just on the financial or environmental side, but on the production and potential production increases in paper mills or box plants as the case might be.

LOOKING BACK

Many, many times in my later years, I have looked back at the growth of the Smurfit Group and wondered how it all happened. I think that the one key thing – overriding everything else – was the lack of understanding of our industry on the part of our competitors. Very few people in the industry had the grounding that I had acquired by my father's insistence that I learn the workings of a paper mill or corrugated box plant, as well as the customer's needs, from the shopfloor. Many of them had little knowledge of the intricacies of the way in which packaging companies worked worldwide. As a result, we were able to step into that breach, take advantage of their weaknesses and overtake them. When eventually they woke up to what we were doing, we were ahead of the game.

One exception was Richard Pratt in Australia, who early on saw very clearly where I was going and understood exactly what I was doing. Richard and I were firm friends before he passed away some years ago.

In the end, Smurfit became the biggest paper packaging company in the world. The Smurfit team kept a low profile, operating with deadly precision and superb execution – and the outcome was fabulous results.

CHAPTER 23
REFLECTIONS IN RETIREMENT

Well done. You have done a very good job.

A few years ago, I had a meeting with Gary McGann and my son, Tony. They said they believed we should think about taking the company public again. Without thinking, I borrowed a phrase that I had heard from Dad many years before and said, "It's a good idea, fellows, but I don't think you will be able to do it".

On 13 March 2007, Smurfit Kappa Group was refloated, and the shares were oversubscribed by five times. Echoing another of Dad's phrases, I said to Gary and Tony, "Well done. You have done a very good job".

That day was probably one of the most emotional of my life. Our flotation was a huge success. My daughter had given birth to my 12th grandchild, Julia, just a few days before and it was exactly 30 years and one day after my father John Jefferson died.

As I said at the 'Celebration of a Legend' evening that was so generously staged for me, it marked the end to 54 years of work. It has been a wonderful journey – one that I wouldn't have missed for the world.

During this time, I have received many honours and decorations. These are listed in the Biography section at the end of this book. I am deeply grateful to all those institutions and people who considered me worthy of such recognition.

MY WONDERFUL FAMILY

Looking back, it was extremely difficult for me to be the sort of father I would like to have been.

I spent two-thirds of my life travelling; work was a seven-day week. I had up to 200 business dinners a year, generally arriving home late and leaving early in the morning – especially when we were still building the company. Six hours' sleep was a great luxury.

Norma comments:

Michael is very kind-hearted and he means to do the best by everyone. I don't think he was ever going to be the sort of father who came home from work and sat and put his feet up. He saw a road – a road less travelled, as they say – and took it. He sacrificed something for that.

However, as a family group, we came together every year for a couple of weeks in Majorca, where Dad had bought an apartment, and two weeks at Christmas, skiing in Switzerland. From time to time, we had other trips but these were my main bonding times with my children.

All my children became excellent skiers, including my two youngest sons, Alexander and Christopher, although most of their skiing was done with their mother in Courchevel where I own a hotel.

I made sure all my children got a good education. Tony and Michael went to St Gerard's, Sharon and Tracy attended Mount Anville and Alexander and Christopher attended Le Rosey in Switzerland. All my sons have university degrees. Michael Junior has a Master's degree from the Michael Smurfit Graduate School of Business, where he met and subsequently married Kathy Muldowney, who gave me my first grandchild, Conor. This alone made my involvement in the school worthwhile.

I still remain close to my children and we meet for dinner and catch-ups regularly.

We also have a family week once a year when we all get together. This is a wonderful event as we get to know our wider family, which includes my brother Dermot and his seven children, Alan and his two, Barbara's three and Ann's three – plus spouses and now 13 grandchildren. It makes for quite a gathering.

From an early age, I taught my children values that they still have but basically the upbringing of my family was in the hands of their respective mothers. Both my wives did an excellent job in this – I am very proud of them all.

But one deep sadness in our family was the tragic and untimely death of my nephew, Jason, in Hounslow in England in 2006, not far from where the 1972 Staines aircrash claimed the lives of a dozen Irish businessmen *en route* to Brussels. Although Jason was engaging and attractive, he was also a very troubled young man. *Ar dheis Dé go raibh a anam.*

PERSONAL IMPROVEMENT

As the Smurfit Group grew larger, we introduced a Profit Improvement Programme to the business. It was a carefully thought-out attempt to improve performance in all areas, reduce expenditure, reduce wastage, increase sales, improve performance and find every possible way we could to improve our profits. It was a sound procedure that gave me an idea.

I thought, "We've got Profit Improvement Plans every year, what is my Personal Improvement Plan?". So I started around Christmas time and would say to myself, "What would I like to be this time next year, different from what I am this year? What are my failings?".

One year, I decided to dress better. I had all sorts of shirts and I decided to standardise everything. I got a standard shirt with two pockets, which is what I always wanted.

I don't do personal improvement so much now that I am older, because the sort of things that irritated me about myself have been sorted out, more or less. The one thing left that I would like to do now would be to reduce my cigar consumption.

But every time I enjoy a cigar, I think of my brother Jeff.

After Jeff died, I was entrusted to handle his estate and was shocked by how many people came out of the woodwork and said that Jeff owed them money. When I investigated, I found that he didn't. So, about a year later, I was in London at the Ritz Hotel when I got a fax from my office in Dublin from Dunhill's, just up the road, asking what did I want to do with Jeff's cigars and when was I going to pay the bill. I thought, "Another bloody bill", but off I went down to Dunhill's, where I was shown into a room that was absolutely full of cigars. I said, "How many of them are my brother's?". The assistant replied, "All of them".

There were about 2,000 of the finest quality Cuban cigars. I thought this was going to cost a fortune, but when I asked how much was owing, the answer was £45. The vast majority of the cigars were paid for. I thought the assistant was joking, but when I realised he wasn't, I gave him a cheque and put two or three cigars in my pocket. And that was when I started smoking cigars. Every time I light up one up, I remember my brother.

I AM WHO I AM

I know I am self-aware and self-critical, but I don't judge other people in the same way. They have their own mountains to conquer and they have their own individual personalities. I try not to change people's characters. I try to help them improve, if that's what they want, but I wouldn't try to change them.

I had to force myself to be more outgoing: it was totally against my nature. I can clearly remember the first speech I made. I thought I was going to die, but I knew that I had to do it. I had to become somebody I wasn't.

I think I would still be considered a bit of a loner. I don't mix easily at cocktail parties and that's why I don't go to many. I'm often alone and I am very comfortable with my own company. I don't like crowds. Even though I have to be in crowds a lot, I'm much more comfortable with my own small group of friends.

In the early years, I was absolutely a ball-breaker. I was probably as much feared as I was liked for the first 20 years that I was building the business. I had a volatile temper back then and I took no prisoners because I really knew what I was doing. I was a bit of an angry young man because of my upbringing. Early on, in my reading, I came across George Bernard Shaw's comment: "All progress depends on the unreasonable man" and I suppose I took it to heart.

There was a time when I was tough and demanding. I would set up meetings five or six days in a row, and from 9am until 6pm I would go through line by line the details of the results of the companies. In those circumstances, the guy opposite me had better know his stuff, because I knew it, and he was the one running the business. It annoyed me intensely if a person didn't do his homework. Here I am doing my homework and coming prepared to the meeting, and if I meet the guy who runs the business and he doesn't know what's going on, doesn't know his pounds, shillings and pence, then I used to be unhappy. I just could never accept that.

But Lawrence Crowley sees it a little differently:

I recall being invited to Michael's office in Clonskeagh to give an account of my stewardship. He asked searching questions – some of which I would have preferred he would not have asked – but he was always supportive, encouraging and highly motivating.

And my brother Alan says:

When he was younger, Michael was a very demanding manager but his bark was always worse than his bite. Now, in his later life, he has obviously mellowed.

Sometimes, people felt intimidated by me and they would be nervous, but that didn't explain why they hadn't done their homework. If I felt that someone was made anxious simply because of me, I'd give them a chance to get over that. It wouldn't make the person good or bad at their job, it was just a factor that had to be taken out of the equation before you could determine how good he was. Gary McGann once told me that I was "a tough man, but a fair man".

I am self-reliant. I like to be in charge and I am a totally self-taught person. I have never been worried about making a fool of myself, because I never knew I was making a fool of myself until I had actually done it. Then I would be embarrassed. I would go bright red, feel like an idiot and wonder what people would think of me. But if I got anything wrong, I'd go back and get it right. As my Dad told me many times, "The man who never made a mistake, made nothing". In life, you have to make mistakes; you have to learn from your mistakes and not be shy about them. I've said to my brothers and I've said to my kids, "I don't care what mistakes you make in life, but don't make the same ones that I've made, because we've already learned from them".

UNDERSTANDING & RESPECTING THE CAPITAL MARKETS

One of the questions I get asked by people is about the advantages and disadvantages of taking a company public. I suppose I have unique experience in that I started my own private company, merged it with my father's company which went public not long afterwards (and against my advice at the time), ran the Smurfit Group as a public company from 1967 to 2002 in Ireland and the US, took it private, and was its Chairman from 2002 to 2005 and Chairman of Smurfit Kappa Group from then until its flotation in 2007.

Denis O'Brien says:

> *The first time I went to New York, everybody was asking "Do you know Michael Smurfit?". Such was his reputation on Wall Street for the success he created.*

Going public is a very serious step for any company. The main reason to do it is for access to the capital markets, where you can raise money. However, I have advised numerous people in the past not to go public because there's a huge burden in terms of responsibility and accountability that doesn't exist or exists to a lesser extent when you're running a private company. A private company only has a small group of shareholders to deal with and everything remains behind closed doors; in a public company, you are subject to rules and regulations that are much more onerous. I don't know what it costs Smurfit today to be a public company but it must be in the millions. When you make the transition, which we've done a couple of times, you can see the burden factor. And you can see the reason for the regulation but there's no doubt that it's an additional cost on a public company.

The other disadvantage of being a public company is that your success is dependent, in part, on market sentiment. For example, the markets currently don't favour debt but it's an essential part of any business. That's been a huge change of sentiment in the last few years since the crisis. Before that, if you weren't geared, you were an idiot. Now if you're geared, you are an idiot. That's a total swing. Both are wrong, there's a sensible balance in between. You need to be able to combine being expansionist with financial discipline. Smurfit could; a lot of businesses can't or don't.

Again, up to privatisation, we used the associate structure to grow, while minimising risk. And the markets loved us for it. But then the markets started to see this as 'trapped cash' and penalised our share price.

So that exposure to sentiment is another side of going public. Sentiment tends to feed on itself; negativity tends to feed on itself, just as a positive thing going up feeds on itself. The market is all bulls or all bears.

And last, you have peer pressure, having to perform against your competitors: are your numbers better than their numbers, is your efficiency better than theirs? Analysts don't follow private companies, only public companies. Some analysts are very good but I have never found any analyst who read the future. No one can.

ADAPTING TO RETIREMENT

It was with some anxiety – and, I must admit, a little fear – that I faced my retirement. I knew from my experience of enforced retirement from Telecom Éireann that one day you appear to be all-powerful in a company and the next, nothing. No more early morning risings, no scheduled board meetings, no country or factory visits, no company annual dinners. Everything just stops, so literally overnight, that I was deeply concerned about how I would be able to handle it.

But, as I look back seven years later, I am quite amazed at just how easy the transition has been for me. After 54 years of stress and mostly working under intense pressure that I never really learned how to turn off, I could now relax, totally and completely.

Since retiring, I have enjoyed immeasurably the amount of free time that I have. It allows me to read books rather than business reports, to watch sports on TV or to go to a football match now and again, or to travel for pleasure to places that I longed to visit, like Egypt and Dubai, but never had the time for. I have taken boat trips on the *Queen Mary 2* and the *QE2* to the US, the *Sea Goddess* and the *Seabourn Legend* around the Mediterranean and, best of all, I can sleep eight or nine hours at night.

A few years back, Prince Albert asked me to take charge of raising funds for his Foundation and this has been successful. I am also on the Board of the Princess Grace Foundation, and have a host of other light duties that I enjoy. I turned down many offers of directorships, except Sean Mulryan's offer to join the Ballymore Group Board.

Simply put, I am enjoying my retirement and the freedom it has given me. I celebrated my 75th birthday with close friends and family at The K Club in 2011.

MY RUSSIAN CONNECTION

My retirement has been made so much easier by an entirely new development in my life: what I term my 'Russian connection'. Although I had dreaded the thought of it, I have been surprised by how much I have enjoyed retirement. In part, this is due to meeting so many new friends within the Russian Federation.

During Soviet times, I had been to Russia on a number of occasions to visit paper mills and to buy paper to import into the UK, although then Russian paper was of a very poor quality. I started to go back to Russia in the late 1990s to see what opportunities might exist for our company there and, indeed, in all of the former communist countries.

On one of my visits, I got to know Burak Oymen, a Turkish gentleman, who among other things built the Ritz-Carlton Hotel in central Moscow. I also met a successful property developer called Preston Haskell. It was very unusual at the time to find an American doing so well in Russia. Preston had a Russian chap, Gocha Arevadze, who was doing some work for him. For reasons I cannot now recall I gave Gocha my telephone number and sometime later, following a row that he had with Preston, he called me in the middle of the night. I arranged for him to come to Monaco and thus began a friendship that endures to this day.

Gocha started to develop his own interests here in Monaco and is now a successful businessman in his own right. Along the way, he became a close friend of Prince Albert and has accompanied the Prince on his numerous trips to Russia, both as his interpreter and *confidant*.

When Prince Albert made his famous arctic trip to the North Pole, he invited Gocha and me to the island of Svalbard, owned jointly by Norway and Russia, to meet him as he finished. I was the first person to speak to Prince Albert when he arrived at the North Pole. Gocha and I stayed the night before in the only town, Longyearbyden, a desolate place very far north. Although we arrived at about 9pm, it was still bright outside due to the almost 24-hour sun at that time of year, so I decided to go down to the lake for my daily one-hour fast walk. On the way down, I noticed a lady pushing a pram up the hill – with a gun across her shoulder. When I asked her why she had the gun, she replied (in perfect English), "In case the bears come. One of my friends was killed by a bear near here last year". I found out later that this was quite true. Needless to say, I turned around and started to push the pram for her back up the hill as fast as I could. I did not fancy grappling with a polar bear, as I understand they are extremely dangerous.

That night, we went to a restaurant and I could not believe my luck when I asked for a wine list. The waiter said that, because people there drank mostly beer and schnapps, they had wine in the cellar stored for many, many years. They had a Chateau Haut Brion for €80 a bottle and a very good vintage Cheval Blanc for €90, so I asked how much they had and bought the whole lot to welcome Prince Albert back. It was extraordinarily good wine at an exceptionally low price relative to the market price – and they were as delighted to get rid it as I was to buy it.

From Svalbard, we flew the next day to have dinner and attend a concert with President Putin in the Kremlin. Due to a mix-up, however, when I arrived at the President's private quarters in the Kremlin, there were just the four of us: Putin, Prince Albert, Gocha and myself. Putin is a man who looks you very straight in the eye and quickly makes up his mind about you – one of my own traits – so we eyed each other up and quickly determined our assessment. I consider him to be an extraordinarily astute and clever person, who struck me as not being afraid of anything.

During my many trips to Russia, I helped to found the Moscow Life Check Center in the Ritz-Carlton Hotel, developed horse stables outside of Moscow and met some very interesting and flamboyant oligarchs along the way as well. I got to enjoy the country very much. I have been to St Petersburg a number of times, including with my own yacht. In short, I have come to love Russia.

PEOPLE IN MY LIFE

I have had the pleasure of meeting and getting to know many famous and interesting people during my long career. For example, my good friend Don Keough, of Coca-Cola fame, brought the Warren Buffett group to The K Club for their annual conference one year. I met Bill Gates and his then new wife, Melinda, and many other very famous Americans like Katherine Graham, owner of *The Washington Post*, Larry Tisch of Loews Corporation and Bob Murphy, Chairman & CEO of ABC. In my welcome speech to them on the first night, I said I thought it was the first time in my life that I was the poorest man in the room (which I probably was).

I also met former US President Bill Clinton, who asked me to help him raise money for his Foundation. We had a successful €1 million fundraising dinner at The K Club, at which he was present and made an inspired speech. Bill Clinton and George Bush Senior were both guests of mine at the 2006 Ryder Cup at The K Club.

As Ireland's Honorary Consul in Monaco, I became a close friend of Prince Albert. I am on the board of his Foundation and have helped him raise tens of millions of euros for it. At one of Prince Albert's dinners, I had the pleasure of being seated next to Nelson Mandela, who I believe is the second most important person during my life-time – the first being Winston Churchill and the third probably Mahatma Gandhi: three people who really changed their respective worlds.

I met Arnold Palmer in Florida and was very impressed by him. As a result, I had him design both golf courses at The K Club. The reason I had him do both was because I did not want anybody comparing the courses, saying that one designer was better than the other. Although the two courses he designed are very different, they were both laid out by the same wonderful man whom I came to like a great deal for his honesty, straightforwardness and utter integrity. He is without doubt golf's greatest ambassador – the people's golfer.

I got to know Tiger Woods quite well on his many trips to The K Club. He first was brought to The K Club by his good friend Mark O'Meara, also a Master's champion in his own right. Tiger caught his first fish at The K Club's stretch of the River Liffey.

Through Nick Diaco in Los Angeles, I got to know Sylvester Stallone, a fun guy to hang out with. And I had the pleasure of meeting Arnold Schwarzenegger, as we shared the same manager of our aircraft based in Burbank, California.

Because our company was headquartered in Ireland, I saw it as one of my jobs to get to know the political ruling classes on both sides of the island. I knew every Taoiseach and many senior ministers during my lifetime reasonably well. Indeed, two former Taoisigh – Jack Lynch and Albert Reynolds – joined the Jefferson Smurfit Group Board. I probably would have recommended Charlie Haughey for appointment to the Board, if he had not made that infamous "Step aside" speech at the time of the Telecom affair. It still irks me to think of that time.

Some decades ago I got to know Claude Marret, the Director General of the Byblos Hotel in St. Tropez, where incidentally I met my wife Birgitta. Having discovered Courchevel 1850, I remarked to Claude that I thought there was an opportunity for another hotel. He visited a number of times and decided to build the Byblos de Neige Hotel. Sadly, in 1984, Claude and four others flying to Courchevel crashed in Chambéry; all were killed except the chef from the Byblos Hotel, one Alain Ducasse who has gone on to become one of the most famous chefs in the world and who I meet from time to time at the Louis XV restaurant in the Hotel de Paris, Monaco.

IRELAND'S FUTURE

It goes without saying that the timing of my retirement was fortuitous, as the financial and property calamity that has engulfed Ireland happened after I left office. Nonetheless, I am quite confident of Ireland's ability to recover its poise and get back into growth mode again. With our people and our educational system, we will develop the entrepreneurs we need and, one day, we will look back on this terrible nightmare and put it all behind us.

If I were asked to advise a young person starting out in life, I'd make three points. First, I think this is an information technology world, which means it's very important that a person is computer-literate and IT-literate. And I think that formal education is far more important today than it was in my time, so that means getting a degree. Hence the importance I attached to all my children getting the best education possible.

Second, try to find something – in Henry J. Kaiser's famous words, "find a niche and fill it". My young son Alexander recently got the idea of renting out shishas. A shisha is a waterpipe, through which you smoke tobacco – they are common in Turkey and the Middle East. The Russians are mad about them here in Monaco, so he has organised the hotels to rent them from him for their guests. No one had thought of doing that before. He also has a bakery store in Moscow, where he's going to make American cupcakes. Find a niche and fill it.

Third, never give up. If you fail, try again, try again. I can't count the number of times I nearly gave up on my own business, especially when I started first. I would get disheartened: machines didn't work or we had labour problems. It was very tough for the first few years – but I never gave up. I kept at it and at it and slowly but surely momentum held and it got better and we took off. But, looking back, those early years were scary.

As a country, we have got to stay the course and there's no alternative to fixing the banks. If you don't have a banking system, you don't have a country. The banks will have to get back to lending sooner or later but I don't see that happening for the foreseeable future. For the next year or two, they will be shrinking their balance sheets – money in, not money out – and yet banks only make money by lending money. You don't make money by hoarding money.

Ireland was terribly unlucky. We always were going to have a property crash but a property crash combined with an international financial collapse was a perfect storm. One thing led to another and the banks stopped lending to each other because of that perfect storm, so Irish banks got strung out. We would have had a much more orderly run-down on the property scenario had it not happened. I always said it was going to be one hell of a hangover, but I never realised it was going to be so bad.

To dig ourselves out of this problem, the first thing is to get public spending and the debt under control which is what we're doing. It's austerity and taxes for the next three, four or even five more years. I cannot see any alternative to that. But we have an educated workforce, the youngest workforce in Europe, which I think is very positive, and we're very lucky to have an export sector – despite all our problems, we're one of the few EU countries with a trade surplus. All these things are positive.

The wealth we built in Smurfit is enduring wealth. Brick by brick, we did it the hard way. But in the boom, I think that whole mindset changed. A lot of the property stuff was easy money and people got very lazy. But we can change back again and build it all again.

THE CHALLENGE OF A LEGACY

Alan said recently:

Michael is, and always has been, a man of vision. He had the ability to see opportunities where others only saw danger. He was able to turn his vision into reality. When you think about the enormous wealth he created from the £500 Dad started the company with, it is just mind-

boggling. Many times, I have wanted to pinch myself and find out it's not true.

But all of this didn't just happen. It was made to happen by my brother. A lot of hard work and a lot of agonising days but it worked for us. It will go down in business history.

Kind words indeed. It is up to others to judge how well I have done in life, but I believe that I grasped with both hands the challenge I was given as a young man and, in so doing, I honoured to the best of my ability the legacy that was left to me by my father.

All in all, I can honestly say that it's been **a life worth living**.

BIOGRAPHY

Born   7 August 1936.

Father   John Jefferson Smurfit.
Founder, Jeff Smurfit Limited, tailor, St Helens, Lancashire.
Acquired interest in James Magee & Sons Limited in Dublin
in 1938; changed its name to Jefferson Smurfit & Sons
Limited in 1942; floated on Irish Stock Exchange in 1964,
forming foundation for the Jefferson Smurfit Group plc.
Born 1910, Sunderland; died 12 March 1977, Dublin.
Married Ann Magee, 10 June 1934; eight children, eldest of
whom was Michael.

Mother   Ann Veronica Magee.
Born, Belfast; died 30 May 1983, Dublin.

Siblings   Jefferson Junior (Jeff), Ann, Kathleen (Kay), Alan, Dermot,
Sheila, Barbara.

Education   Presentation College, Dun Laoghaire.
St Michael's College, Rathmines.
Clongowes Wood College, Co. Kildare.

Married (1)   Norma Triesman, 21 March 1963, London.
Divorced, 5 November 1985.

Children   Anthony (Tony), 19 December 1963.
Michael, 8 January 1965.
Sharon, 14 March 1968.
Tracy, 13 August 1972.

Married (2)   Birgitta Beimark, 20 June 1988.
Divorced, 9 April 1998.

Children   Michael Alexander, 22 March 1985.
Jonathan Christopher, 31 March 1989.

Grandchildren Conor, 13 December 1998.
Anthony (Tony) Junior, 27 April 1999.
Charlotte, 28 July 2000.

Mark, 10 December 2000.
Michael Junior, 6 March 2001.
Tom, 12 October 2001.
Anna, 12 October 2001.
Francesca, 6 June 2002.
Matthew, 18 October 2002.
Joseph, 31 October 2003.
Aurelia Ann, 29 June 2005.
Julia, 10 March 2007.
Angelina, 17 March 2012.

Career

1952-1962, Jefferson Smurfit & Sons Limited, Dublin.
1958, Continental Can Corporation, USA.
1962, founder and Managing Director, Jefferson Smurfit (Packaging) Limited, Wigan.
1966, Joint Managing Director, Jefferson Smurfit & Sons Limited, Dublin.
1969, Deputy Chairman, Jefferson Smurfit & Sons Limited, Dublin.
1977-2002, Chairman & Chief Executive Officer, Jefferson Smurfit Group plc.
2002-2005, Chairman, Jefferson Smurfit Group plc.
2005-2007, Chairman, Smurfit Kappa Group plc.

Orders and Decorations

Compánach de chuid na Craoibhe Ríoga (Companion of the Royal House of O'Connor) (Ireland).
Confraternity of the Knights of the Most Holy Trinity (Ukranian Orthodox Church).
Knight Commander of the Most Excellent Order of the British Empire (United Kingdom).
Knight Commander of the Order of the Eagle (Georgia).
Legion d'Honneur (France).
Military and Hospitaller Order of Saint Lazarus of Jerusalem.
National Order of Merit (Colombia).
Order of Francisco de Miranda (Venezuela).
Order of Grimaldi (Monaco).
Order of Merit of the Equestrian Order of the Holy Sepulchre of Jerusalem.
Order of Merit of the Italian Republic (Italy).
Order of Merit of the Republic of Poland (Poland).
Order of Our Lady of the Conception of Villa Viçosa (Portugal).
Order of *Pro Merito Melitense* of the Sovereign Military

Hospitaller Order of Saint John of Jerusalem and Malta.
Order of Saint Charles (Monaco).
Order of The Holy Cross of Jerusalem (Greek Melkite Catholic Church).
Royal Médaille pour Oeuvres Mérite (Egypt).
Royal Order of Francis the First (Bourbon Two Sicilies).
Royal Order of Isabella the Catholic (Spain).

Public Sector Boards   1979-1991, Chairman, Telecom Éireann.
1987-1992, Chairman, Racing Board.

JEFFERSON SMURFIT GROUP HISTORY

1934 James Magee & Sons Limited incorporated as general box makers in Rathmines, Dublin.

1938 Founder and late Chairman, JJ Smurfit Senior purchased majority stake in James Magee & Sons Limited.

1942 Name of company changed to Jefferson Smurfit & Sons Limited.

1950 Two paper machines built.

1964 **June:** Irish Stock Exchange quotation obtained.
October: Land in Walkinstown purchased.

1966 **May:** JJ Smurfit Senior resigned as Managing Director of Jefferson Smurfit & Sons Limited, remaining as Chairman and Chief Executive.
MWJ Smurfit and JJ Smurfit Junior appointed Joint Managing Directors.
December: Production at Walkinstown commenced.

1967 **March:** Capitalisation issue 1 for 5 (240,000 shares).
October: 51% of E Pak Cartons Limited acquired.

1968 **February:** Wood Rozelaar & Wilkes (Ireland) Limited acquired.
March: Pakrite Limited established and Irish Paper Sacks Limited acquired.
April: Stapling Limited acquired.
May: New corrugator installed in Walkinstown.
June: New paper machine put into operation. Temple Press Limited acquired.

1969 **January:** Rights issue of 1 for 4 (374,160 shares).
August: Temple Press Limited acquired Doherty Associates (1962) Limited and Wilson Packaging Limited.
October: London Stock Exchange quotation obtained.
December: Michael Smurfit appointed Deputy Chairman.

1970 **January:** Browne & Nolan Limited acquired.
February: 25% of Paclene purchased; name of company changed to Jefferson Smurfit Group plc (JSG). The Hely Group Limited acquired.
Cork corrugated plant start-up.
August: Capitalisation issue 1 for 1 (3,174,680 shares).

1971 **January:** Merger of Educational Company of Ireland Limited with Longman, Browne & Nolan Limited.
June: Holding in Paclene increased.
December: 18% of WJ Noble & Son Limited, UK, acquired. Talbot Press revived.

1972 **February:** Jefferson Smurfit (Packaging) Limited, UK, acquired.
April to November: 50% of Capital Spicers acquired.
June: 100% of Henry Jackson Limited acquired.
July: Holding in WJ Noble & Son Limited increased to 100%.
September: US-based Continental Can Company Inc increased its equity stake to 20%. Corrugated factory opened in Cork. Alan Smurfit co-opted to the Board of Directors. New subsidiary Smurfit Property & Investments Limited formed and acquired 10% of Finlay Packaging Limited.

1973 **January:** Holding in Paclene increased above 50%.
March to July: Print and packaging division of Tremletts Limited, UK, acquired, including associated Nigerian companies.
October: 1 for 3 rights at IR160p (3,227,736 shares). TransPack Cases Limited acquired. Limerick Waste Paper Company Limited acquired. Murphy Rentals Limited acquired.

1974 **March:** 40% of Coates of Ireland Limited acquired.
July: Capitalisation issue 1 for 1 (10,496,077 shares). Holding in Finlay Packaging Limited increased to 13.7%.
September: 40% of Time Industries Inc, Chicago, USA, acquired.

1975 Dermot Smurfit co-opted to the Board of Directors.

1976 **February:** Holding in Time Industries, USA, increased to 51%.
April: Alliance Alders Box Company Limited, UK, acquired.
July: Capitalisation issue 1 for 3 (7,861,083 shares). Joint venture company formed with Thomas De La Rue & Company Limited, UK.

1977 **February:** Remaining 49% shareholding in Time Industries, USA, acquired; renamed Smurfit Industries Inc.
March: Founder and Chairman JJ Smurfit Senior died.
July: Capitalisation issue 1 for 3 (11,847,838 shares). Goulding Industries Limited, Waterford, acquired; renamed Smurfit Plastics Limited. 50% of Eagle Printing Company Limited, Cork, acquired.
December: Remaining 51% shareholding in Irish Paper Sacks Limited acquired. Smurfit Cartons (Witham), UK, acquired.

1978 **March:** 51% of Mistral Plastics Pty Limited, Australia, acquired.
April: Svenska Cellulosa Aktiebolaget (SCA) purchased 49% of the Group's Irish and UK corrugated interests.

July: Continental Can Company Inc disposed of its holding. 45% of Tele-Rents Limited acquired.

September: Fixed assets and stock of Centralia Container Corporation, USA, acquired.

December: Nigerian indigenisation decree requiring the divestiture of shareholdings to local Nigerians resulted in Nigerian subsidiaries becoming 40% associates.

1979　**March:** 27% of Alton Box Board Company, USA, acquired.

August: Rights issue of 1 for 6 (7,920,740 shares). Further 22% of Alton acquired; Michael Smurfit appointed CEO of Alton.

1980　**January:** 26% of Woodfab Limited acquired.

June: 51% of Gemini Publishing Company, UK acquired. Holding in Alton Box Board Co, USA, increased to 80%; renamed Alton Packaging Corporation.

1981　**May:** 49% of Petroleum Royalties of Ireland Limited acquired.

July: 1 for 6 rights issue at IR170p.

August: Capitalisation issue 1 for 1 (64,719,293 shares).

October: 70% of Clearprint Limited, Australia, acquired. Holding in Alton Box Board Company, USA, increased to 100%. Canadian papertube facility established.

December: US$80m loan raised; part-used to finance US$55m modernisation programme at Jacksonville mill.

1982　**June:** 50% of Quality Packaging Materials Inc, New Jersey, USA, acquired through Alton Packaging Corporation.

July: Central Bank of Ireland granted banking licence to joint venture with French bank, Paribas, to be known as Smurfit Paribas Bank.

September: Paper and packaging interests of Diamond International Corporation acquired in joint venture with Clarke Holdings; renamed Smurfit Diamond Packaging Corporation.

1983　**March:** Smurfit Paribas Bank commenced operations. Holding in Smurfit Diamond Packaging Corporation increased to 100%.

April: 50% of Diamond Match Company acquired from Diamond International Corporation.

September: Exeter Graphics Inc, California, USA, sold; 34% of purchaser acquired.

US operations of the Group reorganised, with majority becoming subsidiaries of Jefferson Smurfit Corporation (JSC).

October: JSG's UK corrugated interests merged with MacMillan Bloedel Limited, forming MacMillan Smurfit SCA Limited trading as UK Corrugated.

November: 22% of JSC floated on the New York OTC market.

1984   Record profits of IR£50m achieved in the Company's jubilee year.
January: JJ Smurfit Junior resigned as Assistant Chief Executive and Deputy Chairman; Alan Smurfit and Dermot Smurfit appointed Joint Deputy Chairmen.
May: 9% of Southwest Forest Industries Inc., USA, acquired. Remaining 50% of Diamond Match Company acquired. Holding in Woodfab Limited increased to 51%.
December: 76% stake in Executive Travel acquired. Swains Packaging, UK, acquired.

1985   **January:** *Forbes* magazine placed JSC #1 in survey of 1,000 top US corporations ranked by earnings growth over five years.
February: JSG re-registered as a plc.
April: TMG Group acquired.
July: Capitalisation issue 1 for 2 (65,930,522 shares). New joint venture with Sonoco UK. Holding in Groveton Paper Board, New Hampshire, USA, increased to 31%. Holding in Southwest Forest Industries Inc, USA, disposed of.

1986   **February:** 80% of Publishers Paper Company, USA, acquired by JSC; renamed Smurfit Newsprint Corporation (SNC). 50% of Container Corporation of America (CCA), USA, acquired from Mobil Oil in joint venture with Morgan Stanley Leveraged Equity Fund; JSG effective interest 39%.

1987   **January:** Option to acquire CCA's European interests exercised; companies acquired: Italy, VosaCec SpA; The Netherlands, Mercurius Verpakking BV; Spain, CartoEspaña SA.
August: JJ Smurfit Junior died.
October: CCA's Venezuelan and Puerto Rican operations acquired.
November: Cartindustria Mantovana SpA, Italy, acquired. New corrugated container plant opened at Juarez, Mexico.

1988   **January:** Industrial Cartonera SA, Spain, acquired. 30% of Papelera Navarra, Spain, acquired. Mistral Plastics, Australia, sold.
December: 30% of PCL Industries, Canada, acquired by Smurfit Papertube, a 70% subsidiary of JSG. Marpack, UK, acquired. Business of Sonofit Containers Limited acquired; renamed Smurfit Fibreboard Converters.

1989   **January:** Cundell Group, UK, acquired. 35% of Industrias del Papel y del Celulosa SA (INPACSA), Spain, acquired; Cundell later sold to INPACSA.
March: IR£115m 9¾% Convertible Unsecured Loan Notes issued. Rolex Paper, UK, acquired.

April: Corrugator Ondulato Imolese, Italy, acquired.
May: Tri-Pack Corporation, Chicago and New Jersey, USA, acquired by JSC.
June: Options over CCA's Colombian and Mexican interests exercised.
July: Cartonera Nacional, Puerto Rico, USA, acquired by JSC. Joint venture with Flairline Fashions to develop the Riverview Racquet & Fitness Club, Dublin. Irish Paper Products sold to EPPIC (formerly INPACSA).
September: Plan to invest IR£10 million in Irish forestry over five years announced.
October: Plan to build new state-of-the-art corrugated container plant in Montgomery, Alabama announced by JSC.
December: Major restructuring of the Group's US interests completed, including CCA purchasing the 50% of its shares not owned by JSC, the purchase of the 22% minority stake in JSC and a new joint venture company with Morgan Stanley, SIBV/MS Holdings, acquiring JSC/CCA from the Group thus releasing cash to the Group. Holding in Woodfab increased to 74%.

1990   **January:** JSC in partnership with Temboard & Co, Canada, to build and operate a bleached paperboard mill. CD Haupt, Germany, acquired.
March: Euronda, Italy, acquired.
April: Golden State Newsprint and Pacific Recycling, California, USA, acquired.
May: Keystone Container Corporation, St Louis, USA, acquired by JSC.
June: Compagnie Générale des Cartons Ondules (CGCO), France, acquired. Texboard, UK, acquired. SCA's 49% stake in Smurfit Corrugated Ireland and its 24.5% stake in UK Corrugated acquired.
December: Townsend Hook group of companies, UK, acquired.

1991   **January:** Lestrem group of companies, France, acquired. Hollandia Verpakking, The Netherlands, acquired. Two corrugated container facilities acquired from Boise Cascade Corporation, USA, by JSC.
February: Atlas group of companies, Mexico, acquired.
March: 50% interest in Smurfit Panasonic Ireland Limited disposed of.
April: Centre de Dechets Industriels, France, acquired. Remaining 50% of Phillips Packaging Group Limited, UK, acquired by a JSG subsidiary.
July: The Kildare Hotel & Country Club (The K Club) opened. Holding in Monroe Paper Company, USA, increased to 100% by JSC.
September: 10% of De Halm, The Netherlands, acquired. US$600m syndicated loan arranged through Chemical Bank.

1992   **January:** Finlay Packaging plc, Northern Ireland, acquired by JSG subsidiary.

Interest in Temboard sold by JSC.

May: Holding in De Halm, The Netherlands, increased to 100%.

June: Holding in Woodfab Limited increased to 100%.

July: 25% of Winera, St Lucia, acquired. All IR£115,103,226 9¾% Convertible Unsecured Loan Notes converted into 32,886,636 Ordinary Shares and all 10,000,000 Preference currency units were redeemed.

August: Restructuring of the US interests completed, with US$400m equity investment by the existing stockholders in SIBV/MS Holdings. As part of this restructuring, JSG agreed to convert its Preference Stock at the end of 1993. Pending this conversion, JSG's stake in JSC/CCA fell from 50% to 36.8%.

September: 1 for 1 capitalisation issue took effect; dealing in 243,031,687 new shares began.

October: JSC's holding in Groveton Paperboard, USA, increased from 48% to 58%.

November: Holding in Venezuelan operations increased to 86%.

December: EPPIC's non-Spanish operations, Irish Paper Products and Cundell Group, UK, acquired. 67% of Corfab, California, USA, acquired by JSC/CCA.

1993   **February:** Agropecuaria Tacamajaca SA, Venezuela, acquired.

April: Public offering of US$500m 9¾% unsecured notes by CCA.

June: 20% of Forestal Orinoco CA, Venezuela, acquired.

August: 50% interest in Nokia Smurfit Limited disposed of.

At year-end: JSG's holding in JSC/CCA restored to 50% following conversion of Preference Stock. JSG completed the issue of US$640m guaranteed loan notes through two wholly-owned subsidiaries.

1994   **February:** Holding in Telepages Directories Limited increased to 95%. All IR£4,396,965 10.5% unsecured loan stock redeemed.

May: JSC/CCA IPO of 19.25m shares at US$13 per share. Effective reduction in JSG's holding offset by purchase of a further 11.54m shares in JSC/CCA to give 46.5% holding. Irish Forest Products Limited sold.

June: Solid board division business of McLaren, Scotland, acquired.

August to November: Paper and paper packaging operations of Compagnie de Saint-Gobain, France, acquired.

November: 1 for 10 rights issue to raise approx. IR£156.4m (48,932,668 shares). 27.5% of Nettingsdorfer Beteilgungs AG, Austria, acquired by JSG wholly-owned subsidiary.

1995   **April to June:** Les Papeteries du Limousin, France, acquired by Smurfit International BV.

May: Joint venture with company in the People's Republic of China to purchase a controlling interest in a linerboard mill near Shanghai.

June: 29% of Munksjö AB, Sweden, acquired from Trelleborg AB by JSG subsidiary. 1 for 1 capitalisation issue; dealing in 538,518,197 new shares began.

July: ADR listing on the New York Stock Exchange for JSG.

August: JSG subsidiary purchased 25m Ordinary Shares of JSG at IR£2.00 per share under authority given by the shareholders at June AGM.

November: Joint venture with Singapore-based New Toyo Group. Smurfit Capital Funding plc, wholly-owned financing subsidiary, issued to US investors US$250m 6.75% Guaranteed Notes due 2005 and US$350m 7.50% Guaranteed Debentures due 2025.

1996   **April:** JSG reported record pre-tax profits of IR£420m (US$630m) for 1995.

May: Patrick J Wright appointed President and COO.

August: Swains Packaging and Smurfit Packaging Products sold to British Polythene Industries, UK.

October: Tony Smurfit appointed CEO, Smurfit France.

1997   **June:** Majority holding in Celulosa de Coronel Suarez SA and Asindus SA, Argentina acquired by Smurfit Latin America.

July: Dermot Smurfit appointed as World Vice-President, Marketing & Sales.

August: Wellit GmbH Wellpapenfabrik and Schneverdinger Wellpappenwerk GmbH & Co KG, Germany, acquired by Smurfit Germany.

October: US$120m expansion project for Mexican operations announced.

November: Smurfit Packaging Corporation's US plastic drum division sold to Russell Stanley Holdings Inc, USA.

December: JSG's Mexican Plastics division sold to Owens Illinois Group, USA, for US$8.4m.

1998   **April:** Confirmation of merger talks between JSC and Stone Container Corporation; agreement signed in May.

June: CDI group of companies, France, sold to Interseroh Group, Germany.

July: Holding in Nettingsdorfer, Austria, increased to 75%.

September: 50% of MacMillan Bathurst acquired from a Stone subsidiary. Tony Smurfit appointed Deputy CEO of Smurfit Europe.

November: Stockholders of JSC and Stone Container Corporation approved merger to form Smurfit-Stone Container Corporation (SSCC). Condat mill sold to CVC Capital Partners. 15.3% holding in Lecta SA confirmed. Major restructuring in SSCC, including shutdown of approx. 17% of US containerboard mill capacity and approx. 400,000 tons of market pulp capacity.

1999   **January:** The K Club selected as venue for the 2005 Ryder Cup (later

postponed to 2006). JSG and Banque Paribas agreed to sell Smurfit
Paribas Bank to Anglo Irish Bank Corporation plc. 7.8m shares of Abitibi-
Consolidated Inc, USA, sold by SSCC to an institutional investor.
July: South-eastern US timberlands sold by SSCC to Rayonier for $275m.
September: Smurfit Europe (except Smurfit UK) restructured on product
basis: Corrugated, Paper and Specialities.
December: Smurfit-Stone and JSG co-ordinate European managements,
headed by Tony Smurfit, CEO Smurfit Europe.

2000 **January:** Gary McGann appointed as President and COO of JSG; Ian
Curley appointed Group CFO.
February: Norcor Holdings plc, UK, acquired. St Laurent Paperboard Inc,
Canada, acquired by SSCC.
July: Neopac A/S, Denmark, acquired. Fabrica Argentina de Carton
Corrugado (FACCA), Argentina, acquired by Smurfit Argentina.
December: Remaining 25% of Nettingsdorfer, Austria, acquired.

2001 **February:** 25% of Leefung-Asco Printers Holdings Limited, Hong Kong
and China, acquired.

2002 **February:** MWJ Smurfit announced his retirement as CEO effective in
November 2002; Gary McGann appointed as CEO and Tony Smurfit as
President and COO.
April: Holding in Munksjö AB, Sweden increased to 99.6%.
May: Confirmation of an approach from a US equity firm, Madison
Dearborn Partners (MDP), in connection with a possible offer for JSG.
July: Cash offer of €2.15 per share made by MDP for the entire issued
share capital of JSG. In the event of the take-over offer being successful,
JSG announced intention to spin-off its 29% stake in SSCC to shareholders
in the ratio of one SSCC share for every 16 JSG shares.
September: MDP offer and the associated spin-off of SSCC accepted by
shareholders, and became effective on 3 September.

2003 **March:** Acquisition of SSCC's European packaging assets completed in
exchange for its 50% ownership in the Canadian operation, Smurfit-MBI,
plus cash.
June: Holding in Leefung-Asco Printers Holdings Limited, Hong Kong
and China, sold to SNP Corporation Limited, Singapore.

2005 **March:** Munksjö specialty paper business sold to EQT III Fund.
May: The K Club and the site of the former Clonskeagh paper mill sold to
investors, including MWJ Smurfit, for €115m.
September: Announcement by JSG and Kappa Packaging to merge
operations.
December: Merger between JSG and Kappa completed, forming Smurfit
Kappa Group.

JEFFERSON SMURFIT GROUP / SMRUFIT KAPPA GROUP REVENUE (1964 TO 2012)

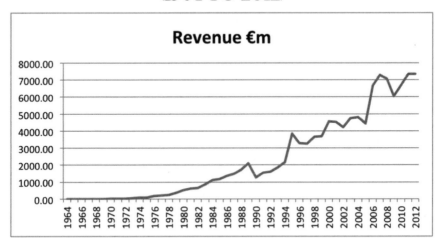

INDEX

ABOUT OAK TREE PRESS

Oak Tree Press develops and delivers information, advice and resources for entrepreneurs and managers. It is Ireland's leading business book publisher, with an unrivalled reputation for quality titles across business, management, HR, law, marketing and enterprise topics.

NuBooks is its digital imprint, publishing short, focused ebooks for busy entrepreneurs and managers.

Oak Tree Press is comfortable across a range of communication media – print, web and training – focusing always on the effective communication of business information.

Oak Tree Press, 19 Rutland Street, Cork, Ireland.

T: + 353 21 4313855 F: + 353 21 4313496.

E: info@oaktreepress.com W: www.oaktreepress.com.